The Business School of the Future

Facing questions about the status and legitimacy of business schools, many of the world's leading institutions are now experimenting with new business models. In *The Business School of the Future*, former president of International Institute for Management Development (IMD), Peter Lorange reveals how the era of virtual technology, and the shift away from conservatism in classical academic institutions, heralds the arrival of a new kind of accessible and scalable business school. Drawing on his expansive and expert experience as a professor, leader and founder of academic institutions across the US and Europe, Lorange discusses the pedagogical and bureaucratic aspects of education and includes five case studies of institutes practicing the cutting-edge approaches discussed in the book (CEIBS, IMD, Singapore Management University, IE Madrid and Hult). This guide to designing the business school of the future, incorporating industry innovations, will appeal to business school deans, educators, policymakers and commentators.

Peter Lorange is founder, Chairman and CEO of the Lorange Network. Previously he was the President of the International Institute for Management Development (IMD), Lausanne, as well as Professor of Strategy and the Kristian Gerhard Jebsen Chair of International Shipping. Lorange has written or edited over twenty books and more than 120 articles.

The Business School
of the Future

Peter Lorange

President Emeritus, IMD
Chairman, The Lorange Network

CAMBRIDGE
UNIVERSITY PRESS

CAMBRIDGE
UNIVERSITY PRESS

University Printing House, Cambridge CB2 8BS, United Kingdom

One Liberty Plaza, 20th Floor, New York, NY 10006, USA

477 Williamstown Road, Port Melbourne, VIC 3207, Australia

314–321, 3rd Floor, Plot 3, Splendor Forum, Jasola District Centre, New Delhi – 110025, India

79 Anson Road, #06–04/06, Singapore 079906

Cambridge University Press is part of the University of Cambridge.

It furthers the University's mission by disseminating knowledge in the pursuit of education, learning, and research at the highest international levels of excellence.

www.cambridge.org
Information on this title: www.cambridge.org/9781108429719
DOI: 10.1017/9781108555111

© Cambridge University Press 2019

First published 2019

Printed in the United Kingdom by TJ International Ltd. Padstow Cornwall

A catalogue record for this publication is available from the British Library.

Library of Congress Cataloging-in-Publication Data
Names: Lorange, Peter, author.
Title: The business school of the future / Dr. Dr. h.c. (mult.) Peter Lorange, President Emeritus, IMBD.
Description: New York : Cambridge University Press, [2019] | Includes bibliographical references and index.
Identifiers: LCCN 2019027748 (print) | LCCN 2019027749 (ebook) | ISBN 9781108429719 (hardback) | ISBN 9781108555111 (epub)
Subjects: LCSH: Business schools. | Business education.
Classification: LCC HF1111 .L669 2019 (print) | LCC HF1111 (ebook) | DDC 650.071/1–dc23
LC record available at https://lccn.loc.gov/2019027748
LC ebook record available at https://lccn.loc.gov/2019027749

ISBN 978-1-108-42971-9 Hardback

Contents

Contents

Preface

Most of the nonconventional approaches reported in this book have been tried out at the Lorange Institute of Business Zurich, located in Horgen, Switzerland, or at other academic institutions where I have been active. I purchased the Graduate School of Business Administration in September 2009, and this gradually evolved into the Lorange Institute of Business. Before that, I had been president of IMD, Lausanne, Switzerland, for fifteen years, from July 2003. Before that, I was president of BI (the Norwegian Business School) in Oslo for four years and, even before that, an endowed professor at the Wharton School, University of Pennsylvania, from 1979, where I also, at various times during my Wharton years, was head of the Management Department, president of the Lauder Institute, and director of the Institute of International Business. Before that, I started out as an assistant professor, then was an associate professor, at the Sloan School of Management, Massachusetts Institute of Technology. I have also spent time as a visiting professor at Stockholm School of Economics, at the St. Gallen Business School, and at IMEDE, Lausanne (IMD's predecessor). Each of these institutions gave me experience that I was able to draw on later at the Lorange Institute and that is also reflected in this book.

The Lorange Institute of Business Zurich was sold to the China–Europe International Business School in November 2015, at which time the Lorange Network was launched – an institution built largely on the web, and without any permanent faculty or campus. Perhaps this is an example of what we might expect to find in business schools of the future. So, I have been on a very long voyage to gain some level of understanding of what might become evolutionary trends in business schools, as well as perhaps in academic institutions more generally. The premise of this book is that future business schools will be largely built around a so-called network-based strategy, with entirely new roles for faculty and campus. The author's own career evolution can be viewed as consistent with this projection.

There is, of course, the question of originality when it comes to the key arguments raised in this book. Is it all new, or has it been discussed before? While, in general, the gist of the arguments raised and the "solutions" provided are indeed original, I would highlight two important works that raise many similar issues to those found in this book, one dealing mainly with the pedagogical side and the other with what future business schools might become more generally. Let us briefly discuss each one in turn.

Bowen's seminal 2012 study on how modern ICT-based technology might impact the way we teach, and therefore also improve student learning, is key.[1] In this connection, he asks, "How can ICT technology more effectively bring people together?" We shall see that the answer is "quite often" when it comes to students and professors, the topic of our present book. He suggests that so-called flipped-classroom teaching might become the norm in the future. And, above all, he discusses how the role of the professor will have to change, with more listening, more active participation in debates with students in class, and more of a readiness to "teach naked." The pedagogy has changed significantly, with the new focus being on better preparation at home, followed by cutting-edge discussions in class. The high cost of higher education is a driver in this regard, as are key advances in ICT itself. According to Bowen, students will simply demand better results through more effective pedagogy! It is perhaps paradoxical that the research that has led to these innovative thoughts comes from a different field than the business school, namely, the music department in a school of arts and sciences. Professor Brown is an accomplished musical pedagogue, jazz musician, and composer.

The other major innovative contribution comes from several accomplished academicians (Davidson, Peters, Smith, and Thomas). In 2018, they critically examined "the business of business schools" and concluded that the conventional academic value-creation model may no longer work – it is too expensive and too restrictive and, above all, too slow in its ability to adapt. They point out that a critical part of a change agenda would be to embrace a way of managing business schools in a more business-like, professional manner. The rules for how to manage a business school successfully have so far largely been set by institutions that attempt to rank business schools according to their quality (e.g., the Association to Advance Collegiate Schools of Business, the European

---

[1] Stan Shi, founder of the computer company Acer, Taiwan, pointed out that the most appropriate term to use these days might be *information and communications technology* (ICT) rather than the more conventional *information technology* (IT). Accordingly, I use ICT in this book.

Foundation for Management Development, the Association of MBAs, the *Financial Times*). The authors believe that this has, perhaps, led to an overemphasis on "abstract academia" rather than a focus on a more managerial approach when it comes to setting a strategic direction in business schools.

There are many people who have contributed to the development of this book. These include my right-hand colleague during many of my years at the Lorange Institute, Dr. Philipp Boksberger, who is the current president of its successor, the Zurich Institute of Business. At IMD, I gained a lot of valuable insights from colleagues but, above all, from working closely with Dr. Jim Ellert, IMD's associate dean, as well as with the late Philip Kohli, head of finance and administration. Dr. Knut Haanaes, previously with Boston Consulting Group, then a professor at IMD and now at the World Economic Forum, has offered invaluable support. At Wharton, Dr. Jerry Wind, in particular, gave me a lot of inspiration. He preceded me as the president of the Lauder Institute and also at the Institute of International Studies. Dr. Tom Colbjornen, retired president of BI, made numerous valuable suggestions, as did Ms. Birgitte Holter, with her invaluable practical experience from Norsk Hydro, Bene Agere, and now Yara. During my doctoral studies at Harvard Business School, I was strongly influenced by Dr. Richard Vancil, and this has lasted until this day! Ms. Leda Nishino did the bulk of the typing, and Ms. Patricia Bähr also gave valuable support. Ms. Paula Parish did a great job with the editing. Ms. Valerie Appleby of Cambridge University Press gave a great deal of support.

My thanks to all of you. It goes without saying, however, that the final responsibility for the content of this book is mine alone.

1 Why Are Business Schools Generally So Static, and Why Is New Knowledge Needed?

> Adapt or perish, now as ever, is nature's inexorable imperative.
>
> H. G. Wells

> The illiterate of the 21st century will not be those who cannot read and write, but those who cannot learn, unlearn and relearn.
>
> Alvin Toffer

Business schools are increasingly seen as being of key importance for the dynamic development of nations' economies. Educating new generations of strong leaders is key! Still, many business schools are relatively slow when it comes to embracing the necessary changes to deliver the types of qualities required today. It is, of course, far from easy to be effective when it comes to pulling off innovation. And, perhaps surprisingly for many business schools, it is particularly difficult to achieve. Why is this? This book is intended to shed light on this dilemma. My postulate is that the business school of the future must be particularly effective when it comes to self-transformation. In the course of the book, I will suggest a number of ways in which this ability to innovate might be strengthened in the majority of business schools.

A recent article in the *Economist* highlights some of the typical dilemmas experienced by those seeking a university education these days (*Economist*, 2018). While taking a university degree is more important than ever (social prestige; "sorting" requirement for getting jobs, in the private as well as public sector), the actual returns diminish (economic returns; oversupply of degree-holding candidates). This lends credence to one of the main propositions set forward in this book, namely, that the way in which students approach higher education might be changing, suggesting that they will be prepared for the emerging new technology-driven reality. Advances in web-based technology allow students to internalize many of the materials that were traditionally taught in institutions of higher education, either remotely or from home. Thus, studying at home, combined with, say, shorter, intensive workshops at school, might increasingly be the way to study, to synthetize, to focus on cutting-edge dilemmas, and to get the perspectives of other students.

This transformation in education is reinforced by the fact that labor markets are getting tighter, meaning that few individuals will be prepared to give up their professional careers to go back to full-time study. So, in sum, we may see a growth in shorter courses of study that might lead to diplomas of proficiency of various sorts, rather than the more traditional degree studies. Certainly, institutions of higher education might not only adopt distance learning technology but also have to make their curricula more flexible, to allow for the practicalities of distance learning. The governmental sector, which has traditionally funded much of the higher education sector, might also have more of its allocated resources earmarked for this purpose.

It is critical, then, that there should be a relatively high degree of consistency when it comes to the various types of learning being offered in the business school of the future, so that it might be better able to fulfill its mission.

Institutional changes are typically relatively incremental and almost always insignificant when seen in isolation. But, taken together, and if coordinated, these might then indeed have a similar effect to so-called disruptive innovations (Christensen, 2008). I feel that this is perhaps what we achieved at the Lorange Institute using a model that included small classes; no permanent faculty; a modularized, flexible curriculum; and short, intensive workshops with an emphasis on interaction. It may be seen as a sign of success that during my six and a half years as owner, not only were we able to attract high-quality students and client companies but we also managed to run the Institute with a small financial surplus, even producing a small profit at the end!

When setting out to consider what a strong business school of the future might look like, it is important to recognize that there are no absolute "rights" or "wrongs," but rather we should see this as a series of cutting-edge dilemmas. There is clearly not one particular set of prescriptions for what might constitute a good business school or academic institution, but several. There are many roads to Rome, as one might say! Accordingly, we will, in all likelihood, continue to see some of today's leading business schools retaining their prominent positions in the future, based on a well-developed campus, with dynamic faculty members, and distinguished research capabilities. However, many other business schools may have to undergo significant change to survive. Also, as previously noted, while the primary focus of this book is business schools, there are clear implications for other types of academic institutions too, not only for other types of professional schools but probably also for many modern universities.

It should be noted that there is an ongoing and intense debate about how to bring more innovation into higher education. A key starting point was perhaps Henry Eyring's book *The Innovative University*, which was published in 2011 (Eyring and Christensen, 2011). Eyring used to work at Monitor, a consulting firm cofounded by Michael Porter of Harvard Business School, and also worked with Clayton Christensen, another prominent Harvard professor. A key argument in his work is that it may now be time for a more blended pedagogical approach, consisting of a mix of actual in-residence university lectures, together with online individual learning at home. This combination is labeled "blended learning." Christensen and Horn, in their 2008 book, argue that universities and business schools run on more classical lines may also need to cope with such disruptive innovations (Horn and Staker, 2015). This view, however, has been challenged by a Harvard history professor, Jill Lepore, who argued that classical institutions of higher learning were generally not under threat (Lepore, 2014).

This book clearly sides with Christensen et al. It is clear to me that blended learning is here to stay. We will, however, discuss in detail how other key innovations might take place to enhance new pedagogy. This development has been labeled the "Campus Tsunami" by David Brooks of *Time* magazine (Brooks, 2012). Things are moving fast, and that disruption is taking place is beyond doubt. For instance, in 2012, MIT and Harvard opened up their lectures to distance learning through so-called massive online open courses (MOOCs) (Bisoux, 2017). By far the largest college in the US today is the University of Phoenix, three times bigger than Penn State (the present number two), for instance. The University of Phoenix is a big exponent of MOOCs, and of computer-based learning in general.

We cannot, of course, afford to ignore developments in China and India, which might provide us with a good example of where the future expansion of higher education might be expected primarily to occur. With their large and young populations, China and India, rather than the more traditional geographies of Europe or the Americas, might increasingly be expected to lead the way. According to Van der Zwaan, "[China] faces the mammoth task of expanding [its] number of universities and colleges of professional education by what may be a factor of 100, to meet the demand" (Van der Zwaan, 2017, p. 27).

Economic Growth and the Tightness of Labor Markets

Throughout this book, we will consider how the successful business school of the future is likely to be shaped by innovation. A primary focus will, therefore, be on an individual schools' willingness and ability to innovate, which will most often depend upon having a person at the top who treats this as their top priority, as well as being a function of the overall culture of a given school. Should we expect leading schools to be inherently innovative and open? We will discuss this in more detail later in the book, most especially in Chapters 6 and 10.

There are, of course, several more fundamental macropremises when it comes to business schools pursuing innovation. Let's look at two of these, namely the degree of basic economic growth in the particular national context of the school, and the degree of tightness of the labor market facing graduates from any given business school.

When it comes to the impact of the relatively high level of growth in an economy, as in the case of the US (Gordon, 2016; North, 1961), we find a generally high correlation with innovations in the business school sector. Examples of these include MOOCs (Wilson, 2013), "teaching naked" (Bowen, 2012), as well as a large number of new business entrepreneurial incubation centers. In China, on the other hand, where there has been a formidable macroeconomic rate of growth, there are relatively fewer innovations up to now, perhaps with the exception of the pioneering development of a multicontinental business school campus structure, such as the one implemented by Shanghai-based CEIBS (China, Africa, Europe). There have, however, been several notable innovations in many of the rapidly growing parts of Asia, such as, for instance, the SMU-X innovation incubator in Singapore.

While macroeconomic growth has been weak in Europe for a long time period, thus dampening the rate of innovation in schools there, another factor may be playing a role, namely a very tight labor market. This implies that students may hold on to jobs they already have, rather than going back to school to further their studies. Thus, they may be looking for ways to combine their full-time careers with future studies. This has given rise to innovative modular curriculum development, the adaptation of self-study based on modern technology combined with shorter cutting-edge workshops, i.e., blended learning, and an array of innovative EMBA programs.

In this chapter, we will make some preliminary observations regarding the success of innovative business schools, or the lack of it. Arguably, there are at least four sets of factors that might slow down a business school's ability to change and innovate fast:

1. Regulations. There is often a whole swathe of rules and regulations, set by several entities, such as the government or the leaders of a university of which a business school might be part, and/or by the business school itself. Rules of any sort tend to specify what might or might not be permissible, and which thus might have a potentially negative effect on a business school's ability to innovate. "Free space" is restricted. Experimentation may thus be harder or perhaps not allowed at all.

Free-standing business schools – those not controlled by a parent university, or by governmental entities, or by, say, chambers of commerce, as in France – will typically have more freedom to make changes and to innovate. But even within the relatively few business schools that fall into this category, there will, of course, be governance control processes in place, which might easily slow down change processes.

2. The status quo. The staff who work in most business schools, faculty as well as administrators, are typically rather conservative and quite content with maintaining the status quo. Why is this? Partly, since many faculty members may have been trained in certain axiomatic fields, they might not see much need for change to the curriculum. Partly also, many alumni-structures may be custodians of existing routines, which may be seen as "good enough." All in all, they may see little requirement for change.

How might the business school's customers act as a force to accelerate innovation? Regrettably, most students and executives do not tend to have much interest in this either. A major reason is the relatively short time period during which a typical customer interacts with faculty at any given business school, when they are actually enrolled in a program or course. At other times, most candidates would not bother to involve themselves with questions relating to the workings of their course of study. Typically, therefore, pressures from customers (students, participants) to innovate will be relatively light, or nonexistent! Unsurprisingly, therefore, many business schools are relatively slow to embrace student-led change.

There are two groups of stakeholders who might play particularly important roles in ameliorating this: progressive alumni organizations and advisory boards. Let us consider dynamic alumni organizations first. At best, they represent links between a school's graduates, who may now be executives in business, and the business school itself. Emerging educational needs may be funneled from leading alumni and back to the business school. Unfortunately, however, this link may often be weak or even nonexistent. At the business school, there will typically be an alumni office that would be the custodian of much of the interaction with the alumni. Useful feedback can end up here, and go no further! To make matters even more difficult, many alumni offices tend to embrace a more social/activist/political/gender role rather than a professional one.

Advisory boards may have some impact on the business schools that they serve, particularly when the bulk of their members come from the business sector, which is sometimes the case. Here too, however, the various inputs might end up with "intermediaries," such as the dean/

president, and not necessarily "reach" the faculty members. Professors typically do not attend advisory board meetings!

3. Complexity. A third factor that could weaken a school's ability to realistically pull off innovation would be a relatively complex operating context. This may partly relate to the fact that many business schools develop excessively complex formal structures, sometimes with multiple campuses, cooperation with other schools and/or jointly owned centers. The international dimension is often a main driver for this. Cultural differences and challenges caused by large distances between sites may add to the complexity. The management of all of this can easily require a lot of additional attention from a school's leadership team and there might simply not be sufficient energy left to pursue changes and innovations. But it should be kept in mind that major innovations typically require work today, with a payoff that will only take place sometime in the future. The overall managerial principle, when it comes to spending organizational energy on change and innovation, should be : "Today for today, and today for tomorrow"! But, in the case of an excessively complex and formal context, the short-term coordinating processes of a school's top management can become too intense. As noted, there might simply not be sufficient energy and time left to pursue essential changes and innovations (Lorange, 2019b).

A similar set of issues can arise when a business school faces some sort of a crisis. Such crises tend to be largely internally generated, and typically manifest themselves in excessive internal debates. This might lead to a de-emphasis on change and innovation – there would simply be insufficient time and energy left for this – as the focus shifts to clearing up current problems. Externally generated crises, say, from a loss of program income, may similarly lead to a heavy short-term bias. Innovation may suffer!

Naturally, it is always important to focus squarely on these types of short-term issues, when they occur. It may not be realistic for us to expect such business schools, having had to spend so much of their managerial energy and attention on ameliorating these issues, to be able to pursue effective change and innovation. Preserving managerial energy to be able to innovate would thus become a key leadership issue. Excessive fire-fighting will generally not lead to effective innovation!

4. Lack of vision. A fourth impediment to change and innovation concerns lack of vision at the top. The dean/president may simply not see the need for change! They may indeed find themselves very busy, but typically with relatively less important tasks. It is key for the person at the top to be able to resist being dragged into too much firefighting, and to avoid dealing with too many operational issues.

The dean/president may also not have much of a clear vision regarding the direction in which to steer a school. They might simply not possess a strategic outlook. It should be borne in mind that the dean/president is elected by the faculty at many business schools. The staff and even the students might be involved in this election process. For many of those voting, it may not necessarily be a high priority to elect someone who will introduce a lot of change and innovation. This might actually be seen as too risky, and just too uncomfortable, by many. So, electing someone who might not have much of a change vision might generally be seen as acceptable.

It is also true to say that many business school leaders have so far failed to predict the significant consequences arising from fundamental advances in the ICT sector. While most business schools have their own ICT departments, very few have incorporated key changes in curricula as well as in learning pedagogy. There may be failure at the top here! We will look at this extensively later in the book. The new generation of students is, however, here today! They typically prefer to make use of ICT-based learning to the full, by studying the basics on their own PCs at home, only coming to the business school for group discussions of key dilemmas. These so-called Generation Y (or even Generation Z) students tend to prefer a different pedagogical mode from that followed by traditional Generation X students at most business schools in the past (Stieger, 2015).

Rankings

First of all, it's important to state that there might well be several potentially positive effects that derive from rankings. But there are certainly some potentially negative impacts too. On the positive side, rankings may impact the change processes at schools. Rankings may support schools' strategic processes, above all when it comes to concentrating their resources where they believe these may be of most use. Accreditation processes – the leading ones being offered by EFMD (Brussels), AACSB (Tampa, Florida), and AMBA (London) – may seemingly also lead to these types of benefits when it comes to innovation, but they have, regrettably, in the end a negative impact. In the first instance, the accreditation (or reaccreditation) process involves a lengthy and expensive preparation of materials. It is possible that the subsequent feedback provided to the schools, based on written reports, as well as information that might have been gathered during the visits that constitute an integral part of such accreditation processes, might lead to improvements when it comes to how a given school might want to evolve its strategy. However, this is simply not worth the great expense and effort that is expended by the school. Thus, although the process of ranking and the inherent accreditation processes might have positive effects in relation to quality improvements, these will be limited, at best.

School rankings are, of course, important when it comes to a student's choice of schools and are particularly helpful for those choosing to study overseas. Students may not have access to much other specific information about particular foreign schools. Of course, when it comes to those relatively few international schools that already have a stellar reputation (e.g., the leading US schools, such as Harvard Business School or Wharton, or the European schools IMD, INSEAD, London Business School), published rankings might perhaps not be needed. However, there are now specialized firms that provide prospective students with background information on a wide range of schools (e.g., Keystone).

Changing Strategic Capabilities

When it comes to strategic direction, business schools face the challenge of coping with three key stakeholder groups – each in essence faced with their own trade-offs – in addition to an overall trade-off regarding the relative importance of each of these stakeholder groups. The priorities of these three groups are:

• The business school itself: relevance – rigor – enrollment
• The faculty: research – teaching – consulting
• The students: rigor – salaries – networking (McMillan, 2016).

Over time, a relatively greater emphasis on the priorities of the student stakeholder group has evolved, at the expense of the faculty stakeholder group. And, within the emerging reality, the newly dominant student stakeholder group has developed a greater preference for networking, moving somewhat away from rigor.

These changes suggest that the business school of the future might be developing an emerging strategic structure that focuses on areas such as communication, two-way pedagogical approaches (take+give; listen+feedback), cross-disciplinary project implementations, effective use of web-based technologies, and so on, and at the expense of more traditional capabilities to deliver when it comes to axiomatic disciplines. Perhaps this shift in strategic capabilities might also impact trade-offs when it comes to the other two stakeholder categories, with relatively more focus on teaching by faculty, and relatively more concern paid to relevance when it comes to the priorities of funding institutions.

So, a focus on the management of competing demands will increasingly be key, especially when it comes to the teaching that is delivered on campus. But we shall also see that the successful management of the business school itself will be based on the successful handling of at least three other key dilemmas. Success will depend upon maintaining a balance in how these dilemmas are dealt with. Here they are:

- Research and teaching (pedagogy); "two sides of the same coin." They are equally important for a school's success.
- Innovation and focus on existing school strengths. New cutting-edge capabilities must be developed all the time, while continuing to focus on the utilization of existing strengths, developed in earlier times. So, it is a matter of a dual focus; "today for today and today for tomorrow."
- Web-based (ICT-based) learning at home and discussion sessions on leading-edge dilemmas at school; i.e., "blended" learning. This implies individual home-based study, typically when it comes to more basic materials, and learning in groups at school, typically when it comes to discussing key dilemmas.

According to a recently retired senior McKinsey consultant, Mr. Trond Riiber Knudsen, formerly head of this company's global marketing prac-tice, a lot changed in the world of business in 2009. The predominant business model, which had been in vogue up until then, came under severe criticism, triggered by the severe world economic crisis that started in 2008. This led to a search for new ways of managing. There was a strong feeling that the major mistakes of the past should not be repeated (high levels of unsecured debt primarily linked to real estate; a senseless focus on growth without proper links to customers' values; the emergence of fundamental shifts in consumer values, away from a more traditional post–World War II value set dominated by banking and finance, and so on) (O'Sullivan, 2015; Gilder, 2016).

So, what else supports the claim that 2008 or 2009 might represent a distinct turning point? There are two fundamental reasons, as we see it:

- The demise of the classical economic model, and the dramatic world crisis that came about not least due to deficiencies in this classical model
- A period of acute underachievement in business and social progress in the first two decades of this century, with the old operating system not working as well as it had worked previously. This has the potential to create additional bureaucracy, which may slow us down and make systems more rigid, rather than giving us more speed and flexibility.

Let us now briefly discuss each of these in turn:

The failing economic model. As Alan Greenspan observed, "almost every industrial country found it difficult to overcome the financial crisis in 2007–2008 . . . why did money and banking, the alchemists of a market economy turn into its Achilles heel?" (King, 2016). The central players in industrial economics, above all corporations, led the search for alternative ways to stimulate growth when more traditional monetary measures no longer worked. Of central importance here was the drive toward more innovation and entrepreneurship. And, gradually, many governments and policy-makers followed, offering tax incentives and other stimuli to encourage innovation. In time, an added focus on the so-called network economy emerged, together with new corporate success stores: Google, Facebook, Amazon, and the like. Legislative measures were relaxed or, in several instances, simply not put in place, to stimulate this trend. Hence, the new economy has gradually been able to "take off." Clearly, we have not seen the end of this trend. The emerging business school of the future is clearly part of this.

The need to keep things simple. Confucius once said: "Life is really simple, but we insist on making it complicated." Most of us, as individuals as well as in our organizational roles, tend to complicate things, often unnecessarily so. And this seems to apply to many business schools too. Many of us, including business school leaders, may actually experience a degree of comfort with this level of complexity. Is this OK? My sense is that there are at least two dysfunctional effects resulting from this, which are perhaps interrelated. The first is that excessive complexity can hamper speed. In today's context, with ultra-rapid technological and communication developments, slowing down might definitely hamper a business school's ability to adapt. Also, excessive complexity tends to be synonymous with excessive bureaucracy, another factor that tends to slow down business development and can curtail faculty and staff initiatives and motivation levels.

Morieux and Tollman have discussed this issue in the context of business organizations, but their findings apply to business schools as well. According to their argument, the problem may not be complexity as such, but too much "complicatedness." In today's competitive world, the winners may be those business schools that are able to exploit complexity to create competitive advantage. Excessive complicatedness, on the other hand, is bad. The proliferation of over-complicated organizational structures, procedures, and rules put in place by many schools to deal with the increased complexity of their contexts today proves the point. Such complicatedness tends to be dysfunctional, and impedes schools' performances (Morieux and Tollman, 2014).

To "frame" the phenomenon of complexity, Morieux and Tollman list six simple rules for managing this dilemma:
• Understand what your people do.
• Reinforce integrators.
• Increase the total quantity of power.
• Increase reciprocity.

- Extend the shadow of the future.
- Reward those who cooperate.

The first three address how individuals in a school might apply their intelligence and energy to fight dysfunctional complicatedness; the last three address ways in which groups of faculty and/or staff might be mobilized to battle excessive complicatedness through cooperation. Teamwork is particularly key to enhancing an organization's performance. Different viewpoints may thus complement each other, to ameliorate "getting stuck" in the same old ways of doing things.

This brings us to the speed of decision-making processes. Kahneman, and several others, have addressed this. The so-called System 1 implies fast, intuitive thinking, while System 2 implies slow thinking, in essence a "monitoring" of System 1, i.e., attempting to maintain some control. It follows that relying as far as possible on System 1 in decision-making processes tends to enhance speed, while System 2 might slow things down. But the two systems are, of course, complementary when it comes to ensuring solid performance. While relatively simple strategies should be given preference, since these might lend themselves better to more intuitive decision-making (System 1), it is also necessary to "turn all stones," i.e., engage in proper analysis (System 2) (Kahneman, 2011).

Let us now move to another phenomenon that might lead to unnecessary complexity, namely the use of difficult language and jargon, a central problem in much of academia. The famous British physicist James Gingell, for example, stresses the importance of translating scientific jargon into understandable English (Gingell, 2015). There is certainly an unfortunate tendency for many academic writers to "invent" their own language, terms, definitions, etc. Business schools might have an important task here in working toward a more widely shared, relatively straightforward use of language, given that complexity bias due to jargon is a serious issue in many business schools. Snyder (2012) deals with this by setting out a series of lessons that complicate societal matters, others that may complicate life for individuals, and a final set that might unnecessarily complicate the world order. The level of complexity created by specialized language and jargon may indeed constitute a threat to the effectiveness of business schools.

In sum, we have seen that there are a number of ways to confront excessive complexity in business schools:

- To apply the simple rules of Morieux and Tollman when it comes to the workings of school organizations. Above all, this implies new organizational forms, such as networks, and fewer formal rules and controls. And there would be fewer departments and hierarchies.

- To strive for relatively more of System 1 – fast, intuitive decision-making, as discussed by Kahneman – but with a balancing of this with System 2 decision-making, for quality and control.
- To embrace teams, for enhancing the quality of outputs, by also allowing for relatively more intuitive decision-making, as proposed by Kahneman, and Morieux and Tollman.
- Finally, we saw that specialized language and jargon can lead to unnecessary complexity, and also to dysfunctional complications (Snyder, 2012).

So, we have considered four different ways of coping with excessive complexity in schools, with the intention of restoring more performance-enhancing simplicity. There are undeniably other ways to achieve this. While certainly not simple, we should remain optimistic, and can definitely agree with Ernst F. Schumacher (2010, p. 12) when he states: "Any intelligent fool can make things bigger, more complex, and more violent. It takes a touch of genius – and a lot of courage – to move in the opposite direction."

A New Context for Today's Leading Businesses

Many business school organizations are indeed radically different now when compared with the pre-2008 era, both in terms of their design and in terms of how they operate. Still, there is no doubt that "new" knowledge is needed to cope with these new realities, both at the macrolevel (e.g., emerging economies, such as the rise of the intangible economy; Haskel and Westlake, 2018) and at the business level (networks and learning processes).

So, a new reality for business schools has emerged, founded on a more robust, solid business model. What is the evidence for this? While not totally clear, there seems to be a political shift toward "the right" in many societies, and also an increased societal focus on issues such as those mentioned above. These broad societal macroshifts thus seem to be impacting how business schools are changing their focus. Cost efficiency has become particularly key. And new offerings are emerging, for example, with a focus on health and safety. To stimulate these shifts, fundamental advances also have emerged in the ICT sector, and developments in ICT have, in turn, stimulated such shifts. A new area of interconnectedness and worldwide communication has come about. We might say that our world has become "more compact"! Clearly the impacts of all of this on business schools of the future may be significant.

Given the context of this book, it is significant to observe that the post-2008 economic realities have led to a set of newly emerging educational needs for many companies. We will consider ten of these here. It should be noted that our reference group will be senior management in corporations. Clearly, many of the more basic educational needs that businesses have grappled with in the past are still there. We shall not discuss these needs here. But, the new context and the emerging educational needs that are coming up will be particularly relevant for the new cadre of senior managers.

A caveat should be provided before we proceed further with our discussion. The ten emerging factors that we shall discuss all seem to be critical, and they do not appear in any particular order; the sequencing that I have chosen does not signify a hierarchy of importance. Rather, what might be relatively more important for one type of business school may turn out to be less so for others. Furthermore, there might possibly be additional relevant factors, although it is impractical to expand further on such a list here.

1   A Need for More Fundamental, Discipline-Based "Trend" Analytics

We might to some extent be going back to basics when it comes to this, in the sense that a renewed emphasis on mathematics and statistics could become ever more significant. The discipline-based application of large-scale data analysis (big data) is now becoming possible, given the tools on offer through a more powerful ICT, and the skills to manage this will be increasingly in demand in today's complex world. But there are also other emerging analytical approaches stemming from the new digital reality. Relatively straightforward tools for finite problem analysis and for finding solutions are now more common, for instance. But this could generate a need for more basic programming skills, so that the senior executive might be able to actually do things, and be more involved. There would, in contrast, be relatively less need to develop "softer" skills within, say, the leadership area. What is emerging is more of a quest for being able to do things, to be involved, in contrast to simply discussing things. The course offerings in today's leading business schools will need to reflect this. The curriculum would look quite different!

The analysis of big data and so-called cloud computing have created a fundamentally new field, opening up opportunities for the analysis of truly huge data sets! While the relevant algorithms for analyzing particular emerging problems already exist, the capacity to analyze the data to "solve" such problems has only recently become available. The new CEO of Microsoft, Satya Nadella, described this shift better than many others in his 2017 book *Hit Refresh*, in which he stresses how new technology is likely to lead to more attractive offerings to consumers. But this, in turn, would call for revised marketing approaches and new modes of distribution. Thus, what we have come to define as marketing is likely to take on entirely new forms, according to Nadella. There is the potential for particularly significant new avenues to relevant new knowledge to be found when it comes to more dynamic pricing approaches (different prices to be applied to different contexts, and also changing over time), as well as new routes to markets (different outlets or routes for various types of customers, each with their different needs). The field of marketing is definitely experiencing a renaissance due to this data "revolution" (Marmara, 2017). What is particularly important, however, is that senior management better understand the ramifications of cloud computing. A sufficient depth of knowledge will be required at the top of the organization to integrate new findings arising from this "revolution" into their business strategies. All of this would, of course, have implications for leading business schools, in terms of both what might now be taught and faculty competences.

2   Avoid Excessive "Complicatedness" to Gain Speed

As already touched upon, the issue is, of course, not to try to avoid complex business settings: the schools that are able to successfully tackle high complexity might be those which become truly profitable. The issue is, however, to avoid excessive "complicatedness." Morieux and Tollman offer several simple values for managing without getting complicated – understand what your people do; reinforce integrators (teams); increase the total quantity of power (empowerment); increase reciprocity (again, teams); extend the shadow of the future ("today for today and today for tomorrow"); and reward those who cooperate (Morieux and Tollman, 2014). Kahneman has come up with an analysis of how executives think – fast when it comes to merely routine issues, and slow when it comes to addressing unstructured issues (Kahneman, 2011). This too might help us to focus on speed, in the sense that "slow thinking" should only be applied when appropriate. What definitely seem to be on their way out are excessively complex organizational structures as well as overelaborate control procedures. New learning will be called for here: revised approaches to organizational decision-making, as well as to the delineation of "lean" control approaches. The modern business school should be able to squarely address these issues.

3   Focus More on Projects: "Do It" Rather than "Talk about It"!

It is more important than ever for business people to develop the appropriate project skills, such as working effectively with others, perhaps specialists in other fields, as well as being able to work virtually in an effective way. How might one become better at hands-on problem solving, for example, by obtaining greater exposure to nonconventional settings to build up one's capabilities for facing the relevant new realities? One way to do this is to engage in "consulting" projects in entirely new areas, shedding light on how to become more effective when it comes to handling emerging and complex projects. For instance, a recent MBA class at IMD spent one week working in a leading hospital, tackling capacity bottleneck issues, so typical in this type of organizational setting, and another week working with start-ups at the Technical University of Lausanne (EPFL) to gain insights into entrepreneurial projects, learning how to scale up new businesses quickly and well. The need to learn more about ways to run complex projects effectively is, of course, key for most people working in corporations today, and should be reflected in what business schools are now offering. Projects to introduce new products or services – quickly – might be particularly key. How to work effectively in "flat," often temporary teams might be critical here. And, how does one develop the skills to bond teams more effectively, for example, through the development of trust, or by communicating more effectively? Coming up with effective ways of addressing these types of issues is key for today's leading business schools.

4   Innovation

Innovation is, of course, even more key when it comes to growth (Gilder, 2016). For a successful economy, a strong focus on innovation is essential. This might be manifested in a business school's teaching by a focus on a rich set of examples of start-ups and new ventures. However, established companies might also provide examples of this strong drive for innovation. Here, we focus in particular on how capabilities to innovate in larger established companies might be improved. Specifically, how can large companies become more like new ventures in their drive to innovate? And how might this be done at a relatively early stage? Given the high pricing that is typical for successful ventures at a later stage, it might be particularly critical for a large firm to get in early, to thus avoid paying too high a price. But, how can this be achieved?

We will now turn to the emerging issues which will drive the key educational needs of established companies as they look to become more successful in venturing. An entirely new set of teaching and research agenda items is opening up for the business school of the future:

- How might one develop a better capability to seek out "disruptive" forces, so that a more realistic foundation for an innovation might be established? Accurately identifying disruptive forces will be key, and such disruptive forces might be emerging technologies, new consumer groups, emerging legislation, etc.
- How might the large firm become better equipped to conduct a "lean" analysis of early movers, i.e., early start-ups? Clearly, most large firms "analyze to paralyze"! And, the conventional wisdom is that early stage start-ups tend to be associated with relatively more failures, which is not particularly welcomed in most large firms. When a start-up has evolved further, however, it might then have proven itself to a greater extent. It may now have evolved to become something beyond simply a good idea, and there might also now be some actual business revenue associated with this venture. This may be a more comfortable situation for many large firms. But the cost of acquiring the venture at this later stage may now have gone up dramatically. How does one develop the relevant analytical know-how to make a judgment call in this instance? An ability to analyze the power of disruptive technologies, to assess potential competitors, and to appreciate potential customers might be key.
- The classic established firm tends to be rather hierarchically organized, largely focused around various aspects of the established business(es). New ventures might be seen as rather peripheral, often perhaps as a counterpoint to internal R&D. However, coming up with new internal R&D successes is becoming increasingly difficult – both costlier and perhaps based on relatively too little creativity in the R&D teams of most large, established firms. Creative minds may hence be attracted to independent start-up settings, rather than to what they might see as excessively bureaucratic larger organizations. So, how can the larger firm improve its capabilities to become more like these new ventures? How might the organizational culture be changed, to perhaps become one that considers the total business engagements of the firm as a portfolio, no longer allowing the firm's dominant business activity to take the lead? How might new ventures be seen within the organization as relatively more important? Often the initial founders might be given a continuing stake in a venture, to signal this. But how then might a culture based on less than 100 percent ownership in all of a firm's businesses be established legally as well as workwise? Finally, how might proper financial analysis be conducted to assess the alternatives of investing in a venture versus in an internal R&D project, and how might future follow-on financing needs be assessed?

5   More on Venturing: The People

As discussed above, new competences will be needed when it comes to assessing a new venture, particularly when it is at an early stage. Also, there will be a need for new know-how in the field of finance, in particular, to assess the dynamic finance needs of ventures, and relative to internal R&D projects. The modern business school might be expected to be able to "deliver" on these issues.

We will now take a look at what might be seen as the key characteristics of the people who typically drive new ventures, and how we might develop our ability to assess the strengths and weaknesses of a potential entrepreneur Do they sufficiently understand the technology, for instance? Are they properly motivated, i.e., sufficiently passionate about an idea? And, what is the track record of this entrepreneur? They might have experienced previous failures. Would this be an alarm signal, in that the entrepreneur might be seen to lack essential abilities, say, regarding marketing or finance? And, perhaps particularly hard to assess, is the prospective entrepreneur potentially too greedy? Are they being entirely honest about the prospects for the venture, in that they might arrive at a stage when they primarily emphasize a project's upside, minimizing the significance of key risks? How can these types of assessment skills be developed, especially in large firms? A school's organizational behavior offerings should clearly make room for this.

6   Management of the Balance between New Business and Established Business

Managers need to carefully coordinate the flow of projects and/or revenue-generating business to ensure a healthy balance sheet. To illustrate this, let us consider a consulting firm, for example, one operating within the field of management consulting. This firm might perhaps have a backlog of business projects. When the firm's consultants work on these projects, then the backlog tends to go down. Only if explicit efforts are made via marketing to bring in new projects will the backlog remain. But these marketing efforts do not necessarily result in immediate income; this is only forthcoming at some later stage. In contrast, work on specific projects today will result in immediate income. Thus, for a healthy consulting firm it is essential to establish a balance between project execution, to bring in revenue today, and marketing to secure future business success. There must be a balance between "today for today and today for tomorrow."

Research done by the consulting firm Boston Consulting Group (BCG) has established that most corporations, to remain successful over time, should also maintain a balance between new business and established business, i.e., a balanced portfolio of businesses (Haanaes, 2018). Paradoxically, relatively too much new business might lead to financial problems. Similarly, this would also be the case for a firm that had relatively too much established business, namely, financial problems at a later date.

So how do we manage to balance a portfolio of new and established businesses? Perhaps the body of knowledge required to succeed here might be quite similar to that needed to achieve successful corporate venturing within an established business, otherwise known as "intrapreneuring," as discussed in Section 4 of this chapter.

It is also worthwhile considering the implications of this balancing of new and established business activities within a portfolio when it comes to executives' career development. Young talent might, for instance, be given the key task of running new businesses, while more experienced managers might focus on the running of the more established businesses. Perhaps a similar agreement might be made when it comes to the distribution of management tasks in family-owned firms. Members of the family's younger generation might run new business activities, while the older generation might run the more conventional businesses (Lorange, 2019a). We shall discuss this process in more detail in Section 7. For now, suffice to say that new knowledge might be needed to run businesses with different degrees of maturity in a single balanced corporate portfolio. There are obvious implications for business schools' strategy when it comes to the teaching of these topics, as well as teaching on the topic of family business, which we shall turn to next.

7   Family-Owned Firms

It has been established that family-owned businesses often lead to more sustainable societal and national economic success (Kammerlander, 2016). Such firms might be characterized by a longer time horizon, stronger management commitment, and a more harmonious profile of coexistence within societies within a country. However, a lot of new knowledge might be needed by its managers to ensure that a family-owned firm is managed professionally. Let us consider four such factors, all hopefully to be addressed in emerging courses on the management of family-owned firms:

- Management transition between family members. We have already touched upon this indirectly in the previous section, with the suggestion that the next generation initially focuses on new business, which might lead to them gradually taking over the running of the entire firm. It is as if establishing a harmonious transition process might be both important but also difficult. How might a family's pool of complementary capabilities and skills be put to work?

- This brings us to the domain of governance in family firms. How might this be more effectively organized? Should the family firm, for instance, have a board? Or should it have a family council? Should family members receive compensation, not only as executives or board members, but also as owning family members (e.g., dividends)? How might various family members be able to pay their income tax, if they "only" receive dividends?

- A family office. When a family's financial holdings grow above a certain minimum size and diversity, then it may make sense to bring in professional managers to run the bulk of a family's activities, and to establish a so-called family office. How might the establishing of this be done? And how should such an office be run? What might the role of the family then be, if any? Should the manager of the family office receive a bonus? There are clearly many issues here, all requiring new knowledge.

- Social investing/"active" philanthropy. Many families typically have particular social interests, and they may also be inclined to provide financial support to particular social causes. Such activities may contribute to the building up of goodwill for the rest of the family business, and thereby be of potentially high value to the family. Selectively done, such social investing might also turn out to be financially rewarding. But how? More knowledge is clearly needed regarding the development of such "for profits" philanthropic activities.

The implications of all this are clear. A radically different set of teaching and research offerings will be called for, and the modern business school should meet these demands.

8   Cyclical Businesses

Let us consider first what might perhaps be the most well known of all cyclical businesses, ocean shipping. The phenomenon of freight level cycles in various segments of ocean shipping is well known, and amply researched (Tinbergen, 1934; Lorange, 2020). There are, of course, cycles in many other industries too, such as in stock markets, in real estate, in banking, in various types of commodities, and in most capital-intensive businesses (e.g., steel, oil, paper). There are two simple rules for making money in such businesses:

- In/out. This means that one might attempt to get in at the low end of a cycle, to buy cheap. One would then attempt to get out toward the top of the cycle, to sell at a profit. Thus, it is important to recognize that a trading activity is key here, i.e., the buying and then selling of assets in such a way that it creates value. The timing must be right!
- Long/short. This implies that one might attempt to enter into a long-term time charter when a market cycle is near the top or, in the case of other types of cyclical business, to secure a future high price/cash flow. In contrast, when the market is low, one would tend to go short, i.e., be ready to reap an advantage when the market turns up again later.

There is a fundamental body of knowledge that involves developing a better understanding of specific market cycles. In the case of shipping, it is important to be able to cope with supply/capacity changes, say, due to the lay-up of ships, new building orders, shifts in forecasted economic trade patterns, etc. Lead indicators are also applicable when it comes to other cyclical businesses. Thus, it is becoming increasingly important to take onboard new knowledge regarding expected relevant cyclical movements.

It goes without saying that for most so-called asset-light businesses there is typically relatively less cyclicality, i.e., less of an opportunity to apply an "asset-play" strategy, based on "in/out" or "long/short" actions. For such businesses, revenue streams are developed through the development of networks. Typically, there is often a large number of members in such networks, who, as a group, contribute to a (usually) predictable cash flow. Companies such as Google or Amazon come to mind. How such networks can be effectively managed is still relatively unknown, but it will be increasingly key. We will go on to discuss this in the next section. For now, the emphasis needs to be placed on a better understanding of key business cycles becoming part of the modern business school's agenda, in both teaching and as a research topic.

9   Asset-Light Growth and Political Factors

We have already seen (in Section 4) how successful innovations drive this type of corporate growth, and also that growth may be particularly accentuated in family firms (see Section 7). When considering the world's most valuable firms, measured by asset value, we see that high growth is perhaps the key determinant to value creation. Companies such as Amazon, Facebook, Google, Uber, and Microsoft top this list. And, it is interesting to observe that, while growth is the key driver for value creation, profitability as such does not seem to be as important. Companies such as Amazon, Tesla, or Uber have yet to turn a profit (Haskell and Westlake, 2018)!

Another key characteristic of these firms is that they be asset-light, as discussed above. Many of the classic asset-heavy firms, such as the major automobile companies or the major oil companies, are no longer on the list of the world's most valuable firms. This issue has been discussed by Libert, Beck, and Wind (2016) as well as Haskel and Westlake (2018). A better understanding of how to operate in this emerging asset-light business domain will definitely become key. We shall return to this in Chapter 10.

Let us now turn to the question of how to more accurately integrate key insights regarding the economy, competition, and governments. There are, of course, well-known bodies of knowledge here, relating to the analysis of macroeconomic growth trends among nations, trade development, competitive analysis, and political governance. Competitive analysis has long been a central part of the knowledge domain of senior executives. Macroeconomic growth trends and trade development, on the other hand, have tended to fall within the domain of a corporate economist, or perhaps some macroeconomic consultants, and, unfortunately, top management have often operated in a void when it comes to these issues. A closer link to economics and political sciences may be called for. When it comes to understanding governments politically, there is often a more or less total lack of top level executive understanding. Rather, top level executives often follow conservative dogmatic doctrines.

Perhaps a better understanding when it comes to some of these factors might be gained through some relevant heuristics:

- The Greek historian Thucydides hypothesized that when a new power emerges and is challenging an established power, then war tends to result (and it is assumed, of course, that the economic strength of such an emerging power is real!) (Allison, 2017).
- In his book *The Rise and Fall of the Great Powers*, Kennedy postulates that a nation's economic growth cycle tends to precede the same nation's pattern of military spending. This might allow for a better understanding of "winners" and "losers" (Kennedy, 1987).
- Chua makes the point that the strengths of various tribes in given countries tend to indicate the degree of political stability within a country. With unrealistic alignment among tribes then there might be political disruption, particularly if a strong tribe is left out (Chua, 2018).

In general, these types of heuristics might assist senior leaders to better understand key sociopolitical factors which would normally be outside their domain. We would expect that such issues might now be covered in the business school of the future.

10   Coaching

The Olympic Museum in Lausanne contains a large and impressive display of past Olympic gold medal winners. It is interesting to note that most of these high performers have been working closely with a designated coach, so as to receive advice regarding how "good might become even better."

How might such effective coaching be further developed in the context of modern corporations? New knowledge is needed here too. We will now look at a few suggestions:

• The coach. How might one be able to "teach" without being considered an imposter, i.e., without being rejected? To be able to draw on a broad body of knowledge is key: reputation and experience definitely matter! Perhaps the military might provide us with relevant insights here. The armed forces are built on teaching new managers about war. Teaching and coaching is key for readiness, since actual wars seldom happen! Senior officers thus tend to be good at coaching their more junior counterparts. In companies such as Nestlé, for instance, older managers are good at coaching their younger counterparts. To be able to teach with speed is key.

• The person that is being coached. Here, open-mindedness is particularly key, with a strong skillset built on an ability to listen, to be non-dogmatic, and to be enthusiastic. Again, such an ability to receive information would be a key element of an effective coaching process.

This entire area has not received much attention in most leading business schools so far. An exception might be the pioneering work carried out at INSEAD by Kets de Vries and Rook (see Kets de Vries and Rook, 2018). We anticipate that there will be a growing demand for more effective ways to address the issue of coaching. It may well be that the development of a more clinical teaching capability will emerge!

Conclusion

There is a broad set of emerging knowledge that is becoming key for the business schools of the future. Leading today's emerging corporations requires that senior management take action to acquire this knowledge, and business schools must be ready to support them. This may be particularly challenging, given the fact that the bulk of these new competences will need to be obtained from sources typically outside the domains of classical senior management practice, as taught today. And, there is substantial new learning that will need to take place. This also implies that a corresponding "unlearning" (including within business schools) will need to have to happen – to free up cognitive space! Much of what might now become less important includes so-called softer skills, with a focus on "talking about" particular phenomena (sociological). Today, more actionable know-how is called for (anthropological)!

We have pointed out several fundamental reasons why so many business schools struggle to implement what would be necessary changes, and why they may be skirting around much-needed innovation:

- an overabundance of rules and regulations, which may make it difficult to introduce change; to innovate may even be seen as illegitimate in some schools!
- too much complacency, among professors as well as staff, with too little willingness to "see" and react to impacts arising from change signals from the market
- too much structural complexity, often as a result of an overambitious international strategy.
- too weak a vision at the top, in respect of the changes needed and the necessary drive for innovation; rather, day-to-day firefighting may be the chief occupation of schools' leadership teams!

In the last part of this chapter, we highlighted a set of at least ten complementary bodies of knowledge that might be expected to be needed in business schools over the coming years. Most of this increasingly fundamental knowledge is new to the business school of today, even though it typically might be found elsewhere, in full or at least in part, in practice and/or in other parts of the curricula in many universities. We have identified the emerging educational needs of companies, calling for considerable change in business schools' offerings.

In the following chapters, we will look in more detail at these issues. The aim is to come up with a set of prescriptions for the leaders of the business school of the future on how to address the changing requirements of the business world.

2   Evolution of the Conventional Business School

In a recent book, two colleagues and I reviewed in detail what one might consider conventional business schools (Thomas, Lorange, and Sheth, 2014). Not surprisingly, we found that business schools have become increasingly prominent over the last four decades, in terms of the esteem in which they are held in business and in society in general, in terms of their reputation for research focus and pedagogical preeminence, and also in relation to their general standing in universities. It should also be noted that many of these institutions now have a global reach. Furthermore, while there are examples of institutionally free-standing business schools, most of them are attached to universities. However, from an institutional governance perspective, they have become relatively independent from the rest of the universities to which they belong. Thus, there is ample space for institutional innovation. But is this happening? As we shall see, it does not appear so. Indeed, business schools might typically be considered conservative.

The so-called US business school model seems to be winning out, with a relatively heavy focus on research, dominated by well-trained professors, generally with an axiomatic focus, and with curricula built up around semester-long courses but that are often not logically integrated. While this business school model largely developed in the US, there are also clear traces back to Europe, but only here and there. For instance, it was Alexander von Humboldt who first organized an academic institution along axiomatic lines – Berlin University in 1809 – with discipline-based professors doing both research and teaching, supported by assistants and embedded in axiomatically focused academic institutes.

But back to today. A key premise is that research and teaching should be closely linked, but are they? While there are, of course, many good examples of such strong linkages, there is also an abundance of examples where this does not take place, as we shall see.

The pedagogical approach to learning is often relatively standard in this conventional model, typically involving large classes taught by one professor over a full semester, i.e., "his" or "her" course. There is often relatively little interaction between professors and students, the most prominent exception to this perhaps being the so-called case study discussions pioneered at Harvard Business School and now widely adopted. In general, however, classroom experiences are one-way, with dissemination of knowledge flowing from the professor to the students and with relatively little focus on the experience-based knowledge that individual students might have accumulated during their own work practices. The average student also tends to be relatively young in age. Are we seeing efforts to try out new approaches to learning? Generally not.

Running a business school in today's world is extremely expensive, both when it comes to paying competitive salaries to professors and staff and in terms of coping with an ever-increasing number of administrative tasks, involving faculty and staff, institutes, admissions, alumni, the financial side, etc. The emergence of accreditation agencies has also become increasingly important, adding extra administrative burdens on staff (and more costs). EQUIS/EPAS (from EFMD, Brussels), AACSB (Tampa, Florida), and AMBA (London) come to mind as the most preeminent of these agencies. The standard student tuition fee would normally not cover all these costs. Thus, public-sector organizations, such as governments, regions, or/and local municipalities, have had to become increasingly active in funding most modern business schools. Stipends for the students must also be provided in many cases. But are these public-sector institutions providing financial support with no strings attached? Regrettably, I would say, typically not. There is often public-sector influence on issues such as governance, appointments, curricula, and even the research carried out (not least through public-sector grant processes). Is the public sector sufficiently competent to manage this? Again, I would assert, not always.

We might also question whether most business schools are sufficiently focused on running their activities in a way that delivers top-quality business education. Again, my answer would be, not always. Senior faculty are, of course, particularly key here. Their training is at the center of this, as they will have undergone strong doctoral programs with a cutting-edge focus on particular axiomatic research dimensions, as well as having learned effective business skills. In their professional lives, research productivity is seen as particularly key, with great emphasis placed on publishing single-authored articles with research results in so-called A journals, which are refereed, of course. Promotions and tenure processes are also typically heavily driven by research productivity and quality. But is this system working as well as it might? Not always, unfortunately. There is insufficient interaction with the real world when it comes to pursuing applied research, and there is also a shortage of top-quality doctoral programs. In addition, the publishing process is relatively slow. Is there scope for faster, web-based publication? What about cross-disciplinary research, carried out by teams of academics, or efforts to achieve a broader interaction and synthesis, say, through book publishing? We might also ask whether pedagogical innovation is being sufficiently rewarded. In general, are today's academic value–creating processes still optimal? Clearly, there is an issue relating to the availability of competent professors. Ideally, today's professors should possess both pedagogical insights and practical experience, even though this is typically not part of the preparation given during doctoral programs. We might also look to address the shortage of qualified professors, encouraging the recruitment of faculty members with more balanced backgrounds.

As a rule, today's modern business school is functioning well, despite questions that might be raised here and there. However, it faces some key challenges as it prepares for the future. A few of the issues we will examine are how one might complement the skills and strengths of the traditional business school and what a constructive evolution might look like. This might give us some insight into the shape of the business school of the future.

Emerging Competition

As we know, new competitors are emerging and are starting to challenge the traditional business schools. Some of these new entrants are serious providers of high-quality business education, but at a more reasonable price, as well as providing more flexibility to participants/students and offering more relevant curriculum offerings. There might also be entirely new entrants, offering MBA degrees, for example, but with an insufficient focus on quality. There is also another group of new entrants that includes consulting firms, accounting firms, and other executive program providers. Typically, these providers will have a more intimate knowledge of actual business practices. This last group of entrants may be particularly active in the executive education program space.

So, what are established business schools doing to protect their position? I believe that the most effective way to do this would be to undertake internal reforms to become more relevant in the eyes of customer-students. This would include more relevant curricula, more flexibility, more professors working at the cutting edge, more inspirational and effective pedagogy, and so on. These issues are at the heart of the argument introduced in this book.

There is, of course, another way in which to protect and promote the value-added of any individual school, which is to acquire so-called accreditation. I have already touched on this in Chapter 1. As previously noted, the leading accreditation organizations are currently AACSB, EFMD, and AMBA, ranked in this order when it comes to their perceived prestige. To be accredited by one of these agencies, a school must fulfill several criteria relating to academic staff, research focus, internationalization of student body and faculty, and size of programs offered by the school. Having such an accreditation is important, particularly when it comes to a school's marketing efforts. Accreditation might thus be a sine qua non when it comes to participating in the top league, most particularly when it comes to selling MBA programs. Clearly, there are limitations to such accreditations, which may act to preserve the status quo or even discourage innovation, but despite their limitations, accreditation processes might indeed represent an effective barrier to new competitors. Understandably, therefore, organizations such as AACSB, EFMD, and AMBA receive broad support among more traditional business schools. For a more detailed discussion of the strengths and disadvantages of accreditation, see Lorange and Thomas (2016).

Evolution of the Modern Business School

Let us now take a look at the evolution of the business school. In recent years, there have been a number of insightful publications on this topic (e.g., Thomas, Lorange, and Sheth, 2014; Khurana, 2007; Spender, 2016). These publications are in agreement on at least three major trends or evolutionary stages. The initial stage is the traditional execution of what we might label the "trade school," which is practitioner oriented and focused on "how to do it"; the second stage is the so-called scientific business school, which draws heavily on more established scientific disciplines in the sciences and social sciences; the third stage incorporates modern information technology and the modifications resulting from this in most of the disciplines taught in business schools. Another very useful review of what might be seen as the main evolutionary stages of higher academic institutions has been published by Ritzen (2010). His analysis focuses on the evolution of Dutch universities since 1945 but is equally applicable to business schools. He identifies five stages:
• the academic institutions of tradition;
• the democratized academic institution;
• the bureaucratic academic institution;
• the professional academic institution;
• the innovative academic institution.
The original developmental stages were mostly European, built on a symbiosis of good business practice and what was then cutting-edge theory. In Latin European countries, such as France, strong links were developed

between the business schools, generally labeled *haute études commerciales*, and the local chambers of commerce. In the Germanic tradition, the business schools tended to be labeled *Wirtschaftshochschulen, Handelshochschulen*, etc. A common aspect of all of these early schools was a strong link with best practice, often manifested through students pursuing two tracks in parallel – academic studies and practical work. In many ways, these institutions were built on the so-called *Fachhochschule* (or "trade school") tradition. In the US, the early composition of most business schools was also grounded in solid business practice. Wharton, considered to be the first business school in the US, was a typical case in point.

Next, a strong focus on so-called scientific foundations, most notably quantitative disciplines, including economics, came to dominate the evolution of the majority of business schools, with US business schools generally taking the lead. Topics such as operations research (OR), economic modeling, and statistical decision theory became prominent.

Later, a growing sense of the emerging importance of the rest of the world led to a focus on more global activities. Many leading established business schools expanded in "new" geographic directions. One such example is INSEAD, which was originally founded in Fountainebleau, France, and which later opened new campuses in Singapore and Dubai, as well as having significant activities in the US. Powerful new business schools have also grown up in many of the emerging economies, notably, among others, CEIBS in Shanghai, Singapore Business University, and the Indian Institutes of Business. While not yet entirely clear, there seems to be a growing trend to refocus on best business practice in many of these schools.

There is also, however, another parallel evolutionary trend, involving what might be seen as the predominant culture and relating to the basic set of values that truly drive faculty success (in teaching and research). In this case, we are not talking about an entirely new trend but one that has emerged in parallel with what has been discussed above. Here, too, there are major evolutionary stages. In the early days, there was a strong emphasis on classical academic excellence and good practical experience. Successful professors on the faculties of business schools would often already have impressive business careers on their curriculum vitae during this initial stage, and this was generally the case worldwide. A second stage was the emergence of faculty members trained in more basic disciplinary areas, such economics, OR, finance, or behavioral sciences. The career path for successful faculty members increasingly became one of "publish or perish" by increasingly focusing on research that might lead to the publication of articles, ideally single authored and in refereed axiomatic journals. And, increasingly, a successful professorial career would have to be focused around this research. To "diverge" into the practice of business would be not only a risky dispersion of energy but also a sign of a "lack of commitment."

Another evolutionary phase now seems to be emerging, perhaps as a reaction to the above, namely, a reemphasis on the importance of effective teaching to complement cutting-edge research. Increasingly, research and teaching came to be seen as two sides of the same coin. Once again, good practical experience also became key to complement the latest theoretical developments. Increasingly, professors might now be recruited from a more diverse set of backgrounds, not only from leading business schools' doctoral programs but now also from management consulting practices, leading business companies, family businesses, and so on.

One of the world's leading scholars writing on business school education today, Professor R. Khurana at Harvard Business School (HBS), offers the following pointers regarding how the reality of a business school's context might be changing (Holstein, 2013):

First, when it comes to the changing reality, there are now more than 900 business schools in the US versus only 140–80 law schools and around 130 medical schools. However, there are definite signs of decline when it comes to the perceived value of the traditional MBA, the key offering of most business schools, and applications are down. Other programs, such as a one-year executive master's, specialized degrees, part-time degrees, and online offerings are faring better. The sheer cost of tuition might have something to do with this – at HBS it is US$54,000 per year, for instance.

Second, faculty members at many business schools may focus their research and teaching in a way that helps them to get promotion and to obtain tenure. This might not, however, produce significant cutting-edge management knowledge. The general credibility of business schools in the eyes of leading businesses might suffer as a result of this trend.

Third, while many typically bright students place a high value on obtaining an MBA degree, this might traditionally have constituted a higher priority for them rather than the actual learning involved. As a result, business may become disenchanted with the relatively low level of knowledge they are getting with these new hires, again with a potential loss of credibility. The needs of major clients, i.e., today's leading global businesses, seem to be changing. Businesses may in the future require executives with skills to build coalitions with governments, with nongovernmental organizations, and with social enterprises. Perhaps a better understanding of the different roles of governments might be taught. Would newly minted MBAs meet these requirements? Furthermore, given that the majority of students have a preference for careers in financial services, consulting and/or entrepreneurship/start-ups, how might business schools train and encourage students to work in more traditional global businesses?

Finally, how can business schools cope with the gravity shift that is taking business away from the US and toward non-US companies? There are many examples of non-US global leaders in their industries, such Infosys (India) and SAP (Germany) in technology services; Tata Cars in the manufacture of inexpensive automobiles, and several European auto-motive manufacturers who are leading the way in automotive innovation. A number of Chinese and Asian companies lead the way when it comes to high-tech electronics (e.g., Huawei in China, Samsung in South Korea). It is essential to be able to actively build business schools that are winning institutions and create real opportunities! An experimental mind-set is key, coupled with an external focus. A better understanding of where a business school's new boundaries lie will contribute to success and this will include knowledge of how a firm might both compete and cooperate with NGOs, its competitors, and suppliers in organizational networks, outside the more classical hierarchical organizational structure. The busi-ness school of the future must position itself within this context. While we can clearly see that this might be very different from the past, the exact point where the heaviest emphasis might lie is perhaps not yet that clear. The multipolar business school is, however, emerging, and this is what we will see more of in the future.

Should the business school of the future be free-standing or part of a university? This issue represents a truly contentious dilemma. No answer may be entirely correct – there are trade-offs, pros, and cons! Let us first review some of the arguments for a free-standing business school.

A free-standing academic institution may perhaps have more autonomy when it comes to following administrative procedures and thus experience fewer delays when it comes to issues such as faculty appointments and promotions by not having such decisions subject to review by the university board. The same might be said when it comes to the authorization of a school's budget, for example, to launch major fundraising campaigns for new facilities, major research initiatives, or other such matters. Perhaps the largest negative issue related to being part of a university is being obliged to pay a financial contribution to the university. It is a fact that many well-known business schools generate considerable surpluses. It might, therefore, be tempting for the university to "tax" its business school, despite the fact that investments in expensive physical facilities, such as laboratories, would not be required by a business school. Less lucrative departments within a university, say from the Arts and Sciences, might also need to be "subsidized." The business school might understandably object to being treated as a "cash cow" in this way. It might argue that its funds should be fully reinvested in new research or salary increases to stay fully competitive. Typically, such arguments are to little avail, however.

The major argument for a business school to be part of a university is that it will be able to draw on a broader disciplinary resource base. Stanford Business School, for instance, draws in particular on Stanford University's engineering school, as well as on its medical school. The Lauder Institute at the University of Pennsylvania draws on the Wharton School as well as the School of Arts and Sciences. At Imperial College London, its relatively small business school is heavily focused on entrepreneurship and draws substantially on the strong science base in the rest of this university, and so on.

There may be potential downsides to becoming too close to the typically academically better-established disciplinary areas that a university represents. Let us return to what Professor R. Khurana, the leading Harvard Business School professor, observes: "In an attempt to develop academic legitimacy, especially at the research-based business school, the faculty began to emulate the arts and science faculty. The social scientists hired into business schools established their careers by applying their specialty, but not by producing general management knowledge; instead, they just reiterated their previous perspectives. The economics hired into business schools acted even more like economics one they were then. The same goes to sociologists and psychologists" (Holstein, 2013).

So we see that there are arguments on both sides. Perhaps, however, the added potential for speed and greater flexibility that might come with being a free-standing unit counts for more in today's world, with its rapid pace of change. This may be the preferred mode for the business school of the future.

Let us now consider how a number of key emerging challenges might be handled by such institutions. We will briefly offer suggestions as to how today's business schools might have to evolve in six key areas to "make good even better"! We will come back to each area in more detail later in the book.

Seven Key Challenges

The Faculty

How can a more balanced approach, to research and teaching, to knowledge dissemination and class discussions, having both an axiomatic and cross-disciplinary focus, be achieved? Will this new breed of faculty be more or less permanently attached to a particular business school, or might they be shared across several? To be a good teacher is perhaps a natural ability that some "have," and others do not. But there are a number of ways in which more effective teachers might be developed. Accepting "mentoring" inputs from others would be one way. There are other developmental issues that might be nurtured in a good teacher. First and foremost, a positive attitude is key. Some might view teaching as something that takes time and energy away from their research. To see teaching and research as two sides of the same coin, and not in opposition to each other, would be a key motivational requirement. A passion to teach would be complemented by an equally strong passion to learn, where research might play an important role. Hence, we see that the two passions might be mutually reinforcing. One might gain further insights about a phenomenon through teaching, complementing one's research. Perhaps it might be so-called soft skills above all that would be a part of a committed teacher's repertoire. To listen better, to engage in effective dialogue, to give useful, stimulating, and positive feedback, where appropriate, might be part of such a repertoire of skills. The teaching/research duality might be particularly critical for meaningful teaching involving such soft skills dilemmas!

The faculty culture would be key here. Unfortunately, faculty culture can sometimes be described as "me, me, me." But a more of a team culture would probably be called for, i.e., "we, we, we"! How might more of such collegiality be created (Sahlin and Eriksson-Zetterquist, 2016)?

Outsourcing

Primarily used to "capture" a better quality of know-how, but also to save on costs. How can the modern business school become more relevant, particularly by drawing more on external resources, professors, guest teaching practitioners, and administrators? The risk of diminishing cost efficiency is, of course, important here, but it should not stop such exchanges. Enhancing quality would be relatively more important than making savings on costs!

The Learning Side

What can be done to strengthen the modern pedagogy, say, when it comes to placing more focus on discussions of cutting-edge dilemmas, on reflective learning, rather than on more superficial approaches. Also, the physical (classroom) layout may have to change, from catering to a one-directional mode of communication delivered by a faculty member, typically in a large horseshoe-shaped auditorium, to more two-way discussions in smaller "flat-floor" auditorium with tables. A quote from Churchill comes to mind here: "we are impacting the buildings, and these buildings are impacting us!"

The Student/Participant

The modern business school may increasingly be faced with the challenge of attracting highly talented students/participants, who typically already hold senior positions in the public or private sectors. A different curriculum might be called for: one that is more flexible, with workshop-based discussions of key dilemmas in school, complemented with studies at home that contribute to the understanding of more basic materials. There would probably also be more focus on follow-ups once the formal course of study ended (lifelong learning). Relevance, as experienced by the student, would be absolutely key!

Culture

This often tends to be faculty-dominated and relatively closed in many of today's business schools. Furthermore, there is often a strong focus on control. Later on, we will consider approaches that might be introduced to develop more open cultures, including different physical landscapes, faster feedback, less control-oriented testing, etc. The role of a business school's dean or president may be particularly key here, as we will see.

Marketing

Classical marketing, through brochures, advertising, even word-of-mouth, is now, in large part, a thing of the past. Rather, it is now all about social media and more two-way interactive marketing. The individual student is at the center, in contrast to the "mass marketing" of the past. So, while classical marketing basically treated large groups of consumers as homogeneous, and attempted to impact these groups through insights from so-called consumer behavior, the current trend is to interact with each individual consumer, drawing on one's understanding of what makes each given consumer respond. Much of this would take place through an interactive process.

New Technology

Digital technologies, in various ways, are here to stay. In total, the accumulated effect of all of this is that it offers a new way of learning.

The learning methodology is new, i.e., significant pedagogical innovations.

From the students', i.e., the customers', point of view, why is the advance of this digital technology revolution so significant? In my opinion, there might be at least three major reasons:

- It is demanded by today's students. For them, the integration of digital technology signifies that their school of choice is at the cutting edge. It is simply a matter of being up to date for those business schools that wish to remain current.
- Digital technology adds flexibility for the modern student, who is typically coping with several parallel career paths. To combine a full-time job with study, for instance, might be more realistically achieved and will be even easier when virtual learning, individually at home, and at the student's own pace, becomes more widely adopted.
- Different students learn at different rates, of course. While more conventional classroom teaching generally treats all students in more or less the same way when it comes to the pace of learning, the virtual approach would allow each student to follow his/her own pace. Some students simply learn faster than others, and some students may wish to pursue more in-depth, more advanced knowledge acquisition in a given area than others, who might be content with simply internalizing the basics. Virtual technology would allow for this. Speed of learning, and the extent to which a student wishes to delve into a topic are easily achievable the virtual way!

Digital technology will also have potentially positive effects on the business model of the business school of the future. The traditional learning approach, with a professor lecturing in the classroom, clearly has its limits when it comes to scalability. The professor would basically have to be in class, and there would be little opportunity for them to leverage their time and competences, except, of course, by offering larger classes (which might be unattractive to students and offer rather limited learning, being essentially one-way and passive from the point of view of the student). With digital technology, however, the professor might become involved in virtual modes of learning, where their core competences might be shared more broadly and with a much greater opportunity to diverge. Clearly this might offer an opportunity for "the business school of the future" to remain cost-effective. The explosion in the cost of higher education in general might thereby be contained.

Artificial intelligence (AI) can be seen as a fundamental technology, which is empowering people who learn or various objects that may need to learn (cars, for instance). The key is that one would be learning one thing, rather than getting better at other things. So, current human learning focuses on one thing at a time, and AI can expand that learning. Deep learning, coming out of the field of neurology, is at the center of this. At the human level, we are capable of pattern recognition, i.e., perceptions regarding object recognition. Parts of one's brain can be focused on recognition, and thus also become better at related phenomena. Analogically, in AI a similar approach is simulated, allowing various objects to observe certain patterns and learn from this. For example, take one area of the medical field. AI can empower radiologists, for instance, to find tumors. This medical tool makes this process more precise, and less time-consuming.

While there has been a lot of progress when it comes to AI, we are still far from being able to come up with an artificial general intelligence. We humans are probably always going to be key, even though more repetitive tasks may generally become part of the new AI domain.

The advent of computer literacy, as exemplified by the Generation Y-ers (and, indeed, Z-ers too!) has had a profound impact on schools' decision-making processes. Above all, things are happening much faster! Time is of the essence, as we discussed at some length in Chapter 1. But this might have particularly strong impacts on relatively "slow" decision-making processes, such as the so-called Nordic or Japanese decision-making processes, where quite a lot of time is spent upfront by all key stakeholders in discussing what might be an appropriate decision. Then, when the decision has been made, implementation can be decided on quite quickly. A long "me, me, me" process is subsequently dropped, in favor of a "we, we, we" process. With a relatively long "me, me, me"-based discussion phase, however, there is no benefit in terms of time. A professional cadre of experienced executives would have to find their way through this, by asking questions primarily for clarification rather than debate, taking on board the fact that compromises mean a "win" for all, rather than "winners and losers." In this way, a shortened timeframe might still yield good decisions.

Unfortunately, some Generation Y executives may fail to see the need for a blend between a prior truncated "me, me, me" style and a posterior "we, we, we" style. Their bent for speed might lead them to focus solely on a "me, me, me" approach, which could easily lead to poorer decision-making. This dilemma, often not explicitly recognized, deserves further attention.

In sum, we can see that there is an array of new challenges or dilemmas facing the typical modern business school. We will go into more detail about these in Chapter 7, but let us briefly summarize these here:
• The key role of being innovative, "in the small" and "in the large"
• Leadership: top down and bottom up

- Research and the latest in business practice
- Top-line growth (more students) and good bottom-line performance (economic results)
- Learning at home and at the business school
- Basics (facts) and cutting-edge dilemmas
- Small (workshops) and large (classes)
- Local (campus) and global (at customer's site, anywhere)

Thus, there are a good number of ways in which the business school of today can adapt to the future. As noted, it is important for us to view this as an evolutionary process – hence, the so-called business school of the future is, as such, nothing more than an evolutionary extension of today's successful business school. And this future will be dominated by Generation Y students – those who have grown up with ICT-based support from a relatively young age – or even Generation Z students – those who have grown up with the personal computer, unlike most students up till now (Generation X), who have typically adopted these technologies relatively later in life. The implications for the business schools of the future might be expected to be significant due to the different attitudes brought to the table by this new generation. We will return to the main differences between Generation X and Generation Y later.

Pedagogical Innovation and Changing Learning Styles

Change is always difficult, but there are ways to achieve it and still keep valued members of staff onside. The former CEO of a large asset management firm, headquartered in San Francisco, told me how he "solved" a possible dilemma with an 84-year old senior asset manager, who was still held in high esteem by many key customers and who was also strongly set on continuing to work. The potential problem, however, was that he no longer fit in with the more modern culture that the CEO was determined to create. The CEO built a small organization around the veteran high performer, and then, in parallel, let new organizational entities grow "in the periphery" around this unit. He likened this to an old city, where the historical city center remains visited largely by tourists, while newer parts of the city would be established in the periphery, housing the current service and manufacturing sectors.

I have experienced an analogous situation in my role as dean of a leading business school. There were a few particularly well-established professors who were encouraged to continue their brand of academic value creation as before, including the teaching of "their" well-established courses, the use of established pedagogical approaches, and the provision of designated research support, etc. These "gray emi-nences" were, indeed, popular, and they added a lot to the school's prestige and reputation. However, the bulk of the faculty was newer hires, encouraged to be experimental when it came to their research and choice of pedagogy. Above all, so-called blended learning tended to be a central feature for this group. These younger professors would thus largely represent the future of the school, and were able to deliver their own blend of academic value creation without being hampered by the traditional ways of the older generation of faculty. We indeed saw a perfect analogue of the old inner-city center with a new and dynamic side, with the senior broker in his own cosmos and the emerging organi-zation around him. A harmonious organization was thus created, with the more established traditional culture functioning in symbiosis with the newer more dynamic organizational culture. This is potentially another trait of the business school of the future, namely to build on those elements that have value, rather than sweeping away everything to do with the past.

There is general agreement that one of the most significant challenges for managers and entrepreneurs in an increasingly rapidly changing world is to meaningfully articulate central business problems and challenges. These are often known as "key dilemmas." In terms of delivering this kind of learning, it might best take place through a combination of self-study on the more fundamental aspects of a given topic, complemented by extensive face-to-face discussions of more subtle aspects. The professor might provide important inputs here, and these, together with the discus-sions that take place between participants, drawing on their unique prac-tical backgrounds, will contribute to a deeper understanding. But, the key question still is: how "deep" is this new understanding? Clearly, this can only take place if several factors are in evidence:

- The professor must truly be on top of the topic to be able to bring forward pertinent issues in a clear way. This is essential in gaining the respect of the participants. They should also be actively engaged in research on the given topic. A broad practical experience might also be key.
- The professor must be able to inspire the participants in such a way that a better understanding through listening might take place, as well as through an inspiring dialogue. They must de facto possess many of the same qualities as a good orchestra conductor!
- The participants should ideally come from diverse backgrounds, in terms of relevant experience, age distribution, gender mix, and nation-alities. Only then might truly meaningful learning take place, leading to a more balanced understanding.

- The class size must be small enough to allow for meaningful interaction between relatively few participants. Close eye contact is key! There has been a great deal of debate about this. Traditionally, perhaps most especially in the Germanic regions, the concept of *Fachhochschulen* has been long established. This essentially stands for a blended learning approach, through practical work at a company and more cutting-edge discussions at school, the latter often being attended in evenings, weekends, and/or on specially assigned days. This approach is particularly effective when it comes to achieving a combined effect from learning at work, at school, and among colleagues. Concepts from school might be tried out immediately in the real world.

For many business schools, this last approach has found a major outlet in executive MBA programs. At CEIBS (China Europe International Business School, one of Asia's leading business schools), for instance, its EMBA program has become by far the largest in its portfolio of program offerings. The employer must consent to a student attending this course, and "allow" the student to be in class at CEIBS two working days per month. In addition, students will, of course, have to spend evenings and weekends on independent study. The program takes two years. Similar EMBA programs can be found at many business schools, including at IMD and at the Lorange Institute. To combine studies and work while maintaining a student's career track is particularly attractive.

But, even with all these factors in place, it may well be that sufficient in-depth learning might not result. Would there be too much reliance on the more free-flowing workshops, with perhaps too much undirected energy at play? Would there also be sufficient learning through self-study? Might at least some students fail to understand key content in sufficient depth? Might some students actually skip self-studying? And, back to the workshops, what would be the difference between truly reflective comments by a student and more popular, superficial solutions? Would there be enough time to truly "sit back and reflect"? Would enough time be set aside to allow one's thoughts to truly develop? Or, would the fast pace and time pressures in the end making the learning process weaker? We do not pretend to have satisfactory answers to all of these questions, but at least four issues present themselves:

- As previously noted, the professor must be highly proficient at what they do, ideally with cutting-edge conceptual understanding, derived from research and practice, and with a strong propensity for listening and debating. One of the interesting outcomes of many workshops is that these typically generate good ideas, insights, and concepts that indeed might be considered cutting-edge and, at times, even produce entirely new thinking! The professor, already an expert on the particular topic under discussion, might thus be encouraged to write some of this up. Such action research might then find its way into more practitioner-minded journals, or/and become part of new books and/or teaching notes, rather than being published in so-called A journals, which would typically report on more traditional research. Whether one might denote these types of activities as research or not is perhaps beside the point. Write-ups of these "happenings" might support a more in-depth understanding of a particular key cutting-edge dilemma. Hence, this would be valuable. At the Lorange Institute, plans have been under discussion to provide financial support for this type of activity. At this relatively early stage of the Institute's life cycle, however, this type of research support is not yet available.

- The students/participants should ideally already possess some relevant knowledge. Thus, the average age of a class may typically be higher than was previously the case, say, forty years or more.

- Providing incentives for students to excel can be a spur to higher levels of achievement. This might be on an individual basis, such as high achievers qualifying for a "Dean's List," becoming a Baker scholar (Harvard Business School), or "best in class." These might be nonscholarly incentives too, such as being consistently on time to class, so as to qualify more easily for popular electives (CEIBS).

- The school might also introduce competitions between groups of students, for example, when it comes to projects (at CEIBS, for instance), or for excellence in offering the best analysis of a student consulting project (IMD), and so on. One of the challenges, or potential problems, when it comes to such group work might be that one or more team members might elect to take it easy, i.e., to contribute less than their full weight. Managing this type of "free-riding" constitutes a challenge for the faculty member.

- For an individual student/participant, specific feedback tends to be particularly motivating. Relevant feedback on an exam or an assignment can be particularly beneficial. But such feedback must be detailed enough to be seen as useful and "to the point." The competence of the person giving the feedback is thus key: this will only work if the student/participant respects the authority of the person giving the feedback. Junior teaching assistants might typically not have acquired this status. Timeliness of feedback is also important. Delays here might have considerable dysfunctional effects on learning and motivation.

- It goes without saying that the process of giving effective feedback will require considerable mental effort. This is typically quite demanding, in the sense that the professor cannot know beforehand what direction a class discussion might take. The professor will need to be highly attentive and alert, and will have to draw on their entire body of knowledge and experience.

- Advanced seminars and workshops have, of course, been traditionally offered at many business schools for a long time. Workshop classes should be relatively small in size, to ensure that everyone is given a realistic opportunity to take part in active learning, and so that no one can "hide"! These smaller groups are particularly well suited to discussions of key cutting-edge dilemmas. This type of workshop may have its roots in the so-called Harkness Tables, which were developed at the Philips Exeter Academy in the US in the 1920s. The central idea was that the participants would learn from each other. The professor in charge would act more as a discussion moderator. This pedagogical method, in which students learn from debates, stimulated by a professor, goes back much further, of course. It is the backbone of the so-called tutoring approach that has been followed at Oxford and Cambridge for hundreds of years. Here, the classes might be even smaller than those typically found in today's workshops, with as few as three or four students per tutoring session.

- Clearly, our rapidly changing world gives rise to many new dilemmas and paradoxes, to which no finite answers exist, at least not yet! So to explore such phenomena through open-ended discussion might make particularly good sense. The advent of social media and ICT-based support might make this approach even more appropriate, in that the more basic background materials might be studied by each individual student at home beforehand. So, while workshops as such have been around for a long time, the modern version of such workshops has evolved!

- Finally, there must be sufficient time allowed for reflection. It is important to avoid the learning process becoming too tense, or something resembling a "sausage factory"!

It may, of course, be difficult for typical academic institutions to change direction. There is one major reason for this: they tend to be rather conservative. They typically become better rather slowly and, similarly, also to decline in quality rather slowly. But there are at least three factors that might impact this:

1 Joint ventures between schools may represent one way of accelerating progress. Two elements of differing schools may come together and in combination lead to a quick accumulation of relevant new know-how, as well as allowing the school to sidestep any attempts to slow down such developments by potentially conservative faculty members. (There are, of course, other potential organizational challenges in making two organizations work together in a joint venture, which

might lead to delays. We shall not discuss these here.) CEIBS, for instance, has made use of a joint venture approach quite widely, by having several programmatic joint ventures:

- 2 with Harvard Business School
- 2 with IESE (Barcelona)
- 1 with Wheaton

2 While joint ventures may represent a good way to improve a school's quality, there are at least two major ways in which to destroy a school's perceived strengths. One is to do with a change in leadership. A new leadership team might, perhaps, be naturally inclined to try out new things – "to do things differently" – even though things might have functioned quite well up until now. The result could have negative repercussions, leading to a loss of established focus, a diffusion of organizational energy, and, ultimately, a loss of reputation. We see many such business schools which used to enjoy a strong position in the rankings, but which may no longer feature.

3 The leadership, faculty, and staff at schools facing decline may not be able, or willing, to face up to this. Perhaps there is an element of denial at work! This failure to acknowledge new realities might, perhaps ironically, lead to a future acceleration of decay. Old ways of doing things, which ought to be revised, are being retained instead.

Generation X versus Generations Y and Z

We have already briefly referred to Generations X, Y, and Z. Let us now come back to a discussion about some of the more the apparent dichotomies between Generation X and Generation Y students (Stieger, 2015). These labels have become popular in describing individuals' aptitudes in relation to the personal computer, or even the degree to which such individuals would see the PC as an essential part of their working world. However, those students who have only started to make use of the PC relatively late in their lives would be labeled Generation X. For them, the PC would perhaps never become a truly intuitive tool, but merely a way to reach higher efficiency. If the PC had never been invented, most of these people would probably not care that much!

Generation Y, however, typically consists of individuals who were introduced to the PC early on in life, as students and/or at work. For Generation Y'ers, the PC would turn out to be an intuitive tool, essential for getting tasks done, whether it comes to knowledge acquisition, to writing or calculation-oriented tasks, or to interactive tasks, at times bringing the individual closer to a virtual reality. So, for Generation

Y'ers, today's PC is a "must have." To consider a world without such devices would be totally unthinkable.

Some experts have now identified a Generation Z. These are young people who have grown up with their mobile devices – the iPhone, the iPad – and the personal computer. Rather than relying on more traditional means of communication or expression, say, through hand-written notes, these individuals typically relay information by texting on their iPhone and/or iPad. While there might not be a huge difference between Generation Y and Generation Z, there is a definite difference in degree. The latter archetype is going totally all the way when it comes to relying on these devices. Perhaps this mind-set might be particularly well illustrated through the phenomenon of downloads. Rather than watching movies or TV programs on a TV set, they will download them to view at their convenience. Music too is typically downloaded, shared, and consumed in this way.

The implications of this shift from Generation X to Generations Y or Z regarding the way students learn could be formidable. Studying at home will potentially become much more effective. And students may now be sufficiently well prepared when it comes to covering the basics to be able to later engage in interactive discussion-oriented modules around key dilemmas. We may thus be more realistically in a position to shift from the more traditional, essentially one-way learning approach, with the professor lecturing to the students, to a more interactive learning approach.

Learning Spaces

The concept of distance learning has become increasingly accepted as a legitimate way to study. Strictly defined, the student acts entirely alone, including taking various tests, which would be available on the computer as part of a particular program of virtual studies. Occasionally, the student might interact with a tutor using virtual means, i.e., over "distance." While this model of learning potentially offers significant benefits, such as allowing for more flexibility for the student according to when they have the time or inclination to learn, and definite cost-effectiveness benefits through scalability, there would also be a limitation in that a program of study would be conducted, in essence, in a setting of isolation. For this reason alone, continuing to organize workshops where students and tutors can regularly meet will be particularly key.

Another driver of the change in learning approach relates to the increasingly fast and general degree of change.

We live in a world where the emphasis is, increasingly, on "learning to learn," so as to be able to pick up on new issues, and to drop ("unlearn") what may have become obsolete. Argyris denoted this "second loop learning," in contrast to the traditional single-loop learning (Argyris, 1978; Gilbert and Lorange, 2001). The "new" pedagogy hence focuses on discussions of the latest business issues in a learn-to-learn context. There may be no "answers" today, but, rather, a student might identify several dimensions to track, and in this way to ultimately learn how a given dilemma might play out – i.e., an experience of "learning to learn." With the current pace of change, things should be so different a few years from now, that to learn to learn will become essential, in contrast to the classical internalization of "truths."

At the Singapore Management University (SMU), the president, Dr. Arnoud De Meyer, has concluded that to work on actual open-ended projects might be an effective way of achieving this mode of learning. He has introduced cutting-edge projects of this type in a number of this institution's courses. Some of these projects might find tentative solutions, others not. What is key, however, is the broad realization among students that to learn to learn is key! Even though there may be a solution today, this may not necessarily be valid some time hence.

At SMU, they are building a designated building to implement this way of teaching. The teaching rooms are relatively small, and the floors are "flat." The intensity of the pedagogy when working on these types of projects is, of course, high, to the extent that there are even shaping cubicles for those students who find it necessary to work on it around the clock. The design of the space encourages mobility and a sense of interaction, even going as far as introducing details such as all chairs being on wheels in entirely "free" and flexible seating arrangements! We will return to SMU in a case study later in this book.

It might be useful to elaborate on a distinction between anthropology and sociology at this point. There is an abundance of literature regarding what might be considered effective practices for leaders of business schools. Many of their authors discuss "how things ought to be," essentially based on observations from the "sideline," and often in contrast with what actual leaders of business schools might say. There are of course exceptions (see Fragueiro and Thomas, 2011; Canals, 2012; Iniguez, 2011; and Watson et al., 2011, also make valuable observations). We might compare these two approaches to sociology versus anthropology, to talking about phenomena versus being part of the setting that one discusses. Tett (2015) has indicated four key aspects of social anthropology which largely confirm the value of this approach:

- A bottom-up vision, i.e., (in my words) the key to understanding how a business school might actually work.
- Listen, look, and compare this to what people actually do, i.e., the key to better understanding!
- Look at the totality, i.e., again, it would be the workings of the entire business school that matter, not merely an individual faculty member/group/department, a particular research program, or a given course.
- Compare different societies and cultures. For me, this would imply that one might benefit from understanding the strengths and weaknesses of several business schools, not just one.

As Tett also says, there often tends to be more than one valid way (Tett, 2015).

In the following section, I will discuss several key success factors, which I expect to be part of "the business school of the future." I find it interesting that many of these are quite similar to what Field Marshal Montgomery proposed in his memoirs (Montgomery, 1958):

- Concentrate your resources. For instance, Montgomery argued against having two parallel fronts in Western Europe in 1944–45, one toward Southern Germany, headed by General Bradley and one toward the North, headed by himself. (As events turned out, he was correct – the counteroffensive by the Germans in the Ardennes became very expensive for the Allies!)
- "Strategy means choice," which implies that one often has to make relatively hard choices to determine where to employ one's strategic resources, typically also concentrated. So, to do too many things at once, say, through "letting all flowers bloom," might not work. There are many examples of this. A particularly good one might be the proliferation of activities at Sony in the 1980s–90s (Tett, 2015).
- The importance of developing an overall plan, which would be more than a series of individual actions, good as each of these might be!
- Speed is key, both in military campaigns (Freedman, 2015; Sked, 2011) and in business (Tett, 2015). Endless discussions without decisions, overly complex organizational structures, etc., might slow things down too much (Lorange, 2002).
- A need for clear leadership from the top. Here too there is a strong similarity between effective military campaigns and effective business school leadership. There is, of course, an absolute requirement to emphasize the bottom-up side of leadership in military campaigns. Soldiers must be treated in such a way that they are motivated, with strong morale, etc. But there needs to be a counterbalancing force, and effective top-down leadership is essential for such a balance to take place. We see a similar need for such a top down/bottom up balance

in business schools, where faculty members are key, and in business organizations too.

- There must be a firm belief in the strategy, i.e., that it will ultimately succeed. This is true in military operations as well as in business. Ultimate success is typically a matter of accepting a long-term time horizon. Actions in the short-term should be taken with this strong long-term belief in mind, i.e., "today for today and today for tomorrow" (Lorange, 2002).

So, it is important to recognize that what seem to be central strategic principles for success in the military field might also equally apply to the strategic success of business schools of the future. Perhaps this underscores the fact that leading business schools might also find themselves in a "win/lose" situation in the competition for survival!

Some Shortcomings

This chapter points out several of the key challenges facing today's leading business schools. We will summarize these here, acknowledging the inevitable repetition. We hope that this list of problems will not lead the reader to believe that today's business schools are incapable of evolving into institutions that are better equipped to cope with the future – indeed they can! Our aim will thus be to point out directions that these evolutionary paths might follow, i.e., to complement rather than disrupt! So, let us now list some of these typical dysfunctionalities:

- Often an abundance of rather petty political debates, and also a lot of committees, meetings, open-ended discussions, etc. So, in the end, the key task of research and teaching suffers. This is clearly to be avoided.
- The faculty is often organized along established axiomatic disciplinary lines. Research, as well as accepted pedagogy, typically follows this tradition, which includes conventions such as "my course," one-way learning, "me-me-me."
- Business school culture is quite typically bottom up, with a strongly articulated faculty. In contrast, there is typically relatively weak top-down leadership, often due to the leaders being elected by the faculty, with a relatively short period of service. This can lead to a slow-functioning culture, faced with a challenging task to adapt to changing conditions, and with a relative scarcity of new innovation.
- Silos are another significant "problem" (Forssell, Fälting, and Kvarnström, 2017; Williamsson, 2017). As previously noted, we have seen that so-called silos often lead to dysfunctionalities, and we have advocated the abolishment of axiomatically focused academic departments. Tett has also found that silos might lead to significant

dysfunctionalities, and claims that "large universities were often beset by tribalism" (Tett, 2015, p. 7).

- Tett (2015) comes up with five suggestions for how to ameliorate the dysfunctional side effects of silos, and these are generally in line with our own findings.
- Rotate staff and create "meeting places" – i.e., coffee bars, open office spaces, etc.
- Avoid pay and incentives that might lead to more of "me, me, me" focus.
- Pay attention to information flows, so that the bulk of executives might get information, avoiding partial flows to certain groups or departments. Nestlé's introduction of its so-called Globe ICT project is an example of this, based on a worldwide common set of performance criteria, definitions monitoring, and common database and reporting (Killing, 2002).
- Let people experiment with alternatives. Let them suggest "how to make good even better"!
- Use technology to challenge the silos. At Kaba, for instance, several waves of electronics have changed the original concept of lock, leading to new organizational entities, in R&D, manufacturing, sales, and so on (Lorange and Häberli, 2016).

It should be noted that there can be positive aspects to silos, too, above all that added organizational stability might be created (Campbell, Heriot, and Finnay, 2006). I am, however, of the opinion that the potential positive effects would typically not out weight the negatives.

There are, of course, other shortcomings that we might have pointed out. However, let us pause here, and move, in Chapter 3, onto a discussion of how we might cope with the issues that we have identified here to support today's leading business schools to adapt to a better future.

3   The Faculty and the Dean/President

In this chapter, we will look at how the faculty, with its dean or president, can create superior academic value in the business school of the future. We will see that flexibility, adaptability, and speed are even more important today than ever before. An ability to innovate effectively will be the key feature of the business school of the future. We will focus on a networked organizational structure as our organizational approach of choice, which implies a lot of outsourcing.

A modern curriculum will naturally play an essential role. We will look at how to develop such a curriculum, and also how to implement it. This will, of course, involve input from faculty, and we will also consider how to develop a team of part-time faculty members in the business school of the future.

The dean's or president's input will also be crucial, involving a clear top-down style, but also "listening with big ears." The choice of an effective new leader will, of course, be particularly critical, and we will discuss this in the final section of the chapter.

Speed and Flexibility: A Networked Approach

We have seen that the business school of the future has many of the same characteristics as those typically found in other types of organizations organized according to the so-called network model. For instance, the business school of the future will draw on professors from a wide range of backgrounds, some from more traditional business schools, others from consulting firms, leading businesses, or even from practice. Bringing these diverse resources together will be key. At the Lorange Institute of Business, for instance, this is physically managed by having a large table situated in the school's lobby. Visiting professors and administrators meet here for effective, face-to-face communication. Coordination tasks are thus typically handled easily and promptly!

The requirement for speed, flexibility, and adaptability also seems to be better handled in a network setting. While parts of a network might disappear – people as well as cooperating organizational entities – new groupings might relatively easily be formed, all with a relatively high degree of speed. In contrast, the classical fragmented way of organizing a business school, with academic departments and research centers (this applies to most universities too, with their separate faculties for economics, law, humanities, theology, etc.), is probably becoming too slow and inflexible. A network organization may increasingly yield more speed and flexibility.

The concept of speed is linked to the need for a school to develop a modularized curriculum of study programs. It is important to allow for flexibility for a participant when it comes to carrying out their program of studies. Most students will also have a job, often full-time. So, for them, it will be important to be offer flexibility when it comes to taking the various actual modules. Hence, some students may actually take a relatively long time to complete a program of studies. For other students, in contrast, the overall time spent might be less. Thus, it will be up to each individual to decide on how much time an overall program of studies will take. There should be no fixed rule for this. That there might be a rather liberal maximum time for the completion of a program would, of course, not diminish this flexibility regarding the choices made by students on how long they might need to complete their studies. An indicative maximum time limit would merely be established to counteract excessiveness, and to instill some sense of an overall commitment to finishing.

We have argued that speed and flexibility might become even more critical for business schools than before, i.e., for the business school of the future. What does this mean? Partly, it is an issue of being able to react faster, to learn faster, to acknowledge mistakes faster, to make corrections faster. This might have to do with a diverse set of issues: the curriculum, appointments, marketing, etc. Partly, it may have to do with being able to register results faster, such as being able to register research outputs "now," versus having to wait for a distant future, to come up with course offerings that might yield positive feedback relatively quickly, and so on. To strive for speed would thus typically also imply a cultural shift. Many academic institutions might be characterized by a swathe of highly complex processes needed to reach consensus, by numerous committees, debates, etc. The dilemma with all of this is that while it might ensure a higher likelihood of broad buy-in at the end, it might take too long a time! On the other hand, a more top-down approach might result in more speed, but perhaps at the risk of broad acceptance of a particular decision.

This brings us to the dilemma of more speed versus less speed! We saw that there might be a trade-off between speedy top-down actions and less speedy bottom-up processes, the latter perhaps increasing the likelihood of broad buy-in. There might also be a trade-off between more speed, to get operational things out of the way, versus less speed, to gain more time to reflect. Kahneman (2011) has made some excellent observations on this topic, as has Eriksen (2001).

It goes without saying that imposing a strict time regime when it comes to starting and ending class sessions is key. Assignments and exams should also be typically managed according to a tight time schedule. So-called home-based or take-home exams should be delivered on time, for instance, and feedback must be delivered to students on a timely basis.

The faculty represents the core resource of any leading business school. However, the totality of capabilities and competences that a faculty represents might be adequate for one particular situational setting but not for another. Evolutionary needs might make a particular group of faculty more or less obsolete in the future, even though it would be fine today. Therefore, bringing new capabilities to a faculty today, and letting go of capabilities that might no longer be central, would be a key task. For this reason, we propose that extensive use of part-time faculty may be preferred. It might simply be easier to change a school's capabilities in this way; it would be faster and result in relatively less organizational hassle. But beyond this added emphasis on visiting/part-time faculty, what might it take to evolve a school's faculty capabilities? Again, the dean or president would be at the heart of such changes, in line with their vision for what they might try to develop as "their" business school of the future. Hiring new talent would be key. Promotions and terminations would also need to be effectively managed. To facilitate all of this, and, in particular, faculty terminations, the school's salary policy would need to be clearly delineated. Equally, bonuses (i.e., lack of such) and feedback discussions with faculty would be critical. These are all top-down initiatives that would be driven by the dean or president.

Departments and department heads might, of course, play a role here. But since a particular department might have a rather myopic view on these issues, one might not expect an effective renewal of faculty competences from this quarter. Sheer vested interests, to protect what the department head considers to be a particular department's role and axiomatic traditions, might add to this. The appointment of progressive department heads by the dean or president might, of course, make some difference.

Increasing a school's visibility in the academic community is vital for attracting new talent. One way to do this is to arrange research symposia, to which cutting-edge scholars might be invited. At CEIBS, for instance, each of its five academic departments holds such symposia every year.

Leading scholars are invited to present papers, five in total at each event. This increased visibility can help to attract new faculty members, as well as providing an opportunity for the visiting scholars to teach at the school. Schools also typically arrange social gatherings in connection with major academic conferences. While widely appreciated, one might question whether this practice increases the visibility of a school to be better positioned to attract faculty – probably not! Still, this is a common practice!

Many business schools are finding that it is becoming increasingly difficult to attract a sufficient number of qualified faculty members who are at the cutting edge research-wise as well as experienced in practice and teaching pedagogy. Ideally, they should also have an ability or interest in working effectively in cross-disciplinary ways. Very few, if any, would meet all of these criteria! With the increasing degree of specialization, the ideal of having "in-house" full-time leading-edge professors to cover all topics, therefore, is becoming increasingly unattainable. Of course, there are potential cost issues too.

An interesting development here is that many business schools are increasingly making use of visiting faculty members. At the Lorange Institute of Business, we may have taken this to the extreme, by exclusively engaging faculty on a part-time basis. However, we have attempted to build up a relatively stable network of strong part-time faculty who typically visit for short periods of time, and only when needed. Also, when a particular faculty member has been visiting the Institute for a number of years, then it may be time to replace them, since they might not be likely to offer a stream of strong new thoughts but continue to draw on what has already been provided. We might then invite another world-expert faculty member to visit, to introduce a unique set of new perspectives on a given competence, as reflected in their most recent research and pedagogical activity. With the general acceleration of knowledge that is taking place, it may be even more important to rotate faculty, at least to the extent that the school always has a cutting-edge faculty base in place, i.e., always on top. New faculty members would be expected to bring with them the latest advances in research and practice. Thus, achieving top quality is the driving force behind establishing networks of part-time faculty. Given the fact that some business school will only need to draw on given faculty members when needed, this might clearly also lead to cost savings. While this is obviously important, the driving issue would be to enhance quality and relevance.

So, a networked approach is key when it comes to coping with the faculty sourcing dimension. It clearly becomes important for the person(s) responsible for inviting this diverse group of part-time faculty to be fully aware of what might be "available" when it comes to relevant faculty members on a worldwide basis. Connectivity with leading institutions and faculty groups across the world thus becomes key.

As we know from network-theory approaches, the coordination of most networks tends to take place with relatively few leaders at the top, often with only one or two. This, when applied to networking in business schools, might lead to a risk of one-dimensionality, even a lack of variety in faculty recruiting. The majority of network leaders might end up driving the momentum of a network too far in a particular direction. I can clearly see the potential danger in the case of the Lorange Institute, where my own biases, as exemplified by a certain age-based network of contacts, unique academic interests, etc., might have led to such biases in choice. Given the acceleration of knowledge, and with new managerial discoveries now increasingly coming from leading practitioners and service supporters (such as consultants), and no longer only from academics more or less exclusively, it follows that one may now be able to recruit to one's network from a much broader basis than before. Practitioners and consultants may thus complement the classical academicians. And faculty members might need to possess different skills from those classical professors might be expected to have, say, perhaps more "orchestrators," listeners, being open to two-way communication, etc.! Thus, the emergent faculty network might become distinctively different from what one might find in ordinary business school faculties – more variety, more diversity in competences, a broader set of skills!

Why might this type of faculty profile also be seen as meaningful from the vantage point of the majority of individual faculty members? For many of them it may imply now being able to learn more current, relevant issues from the students/participants. The workshop mode is a key to this. Here, the relatively small size of each class, with each participant contributing their unique work experience and relatively more seniority and age (e.g., at the Lorange Institute, the typical age is forty-two years, on average), the professor might realistically pick up a lot from the students. There also is cross-learning between these participants themselves, not only to/from the professor. For many faculty members, this combination of cross-links might represent a true inspirational experience. Professors might feel that this is something that might not readily be experienced as part of the typical "one-way" teaching found in more conventional, "normal" business schools.

We have already agreed that, with the virtual explosion of what constitutes the state-of-the-art in many fields, it may become increasingly difficult for professors to remain at the cutting-edge more broadly, or within their particular fields. This, we have argued, might call for an expanded reliance on visiting professors, who might be mobilized to become part of a particular learning setting within a relatively narrow field where they might be experts. On the other hand, they will not be required to be involved in teaching outside this relatively narrow area of core competence. Thus, by drawing on a relatively broad range of part-time faculty, the likelihood of securing cutting-edge competences across the board might be increased. As a side effect, this approach will also be more cost-effective, with less of a need for experienced faculty to sit around on "stand-by" mostly. Most faculty members may also welcome the additional career and economic benefits coming their way from extra teaching at other institutions. They might relish the opportunity to be "allowed" to show their abilities as an "orchestrator," listener, being able to "give-and-take," in short, being involved in a two-way learning process. Perhaps this type of opportunity might not be that readily available at faculty members' home schools, with their typically more traditional approach to teaching.

There are, of course, potential negatives too. One such potential drawback might be that the research component might suffer. Research is typically funded by the institutions in which a faculty member is employed. An entirely part-time faculty member might thus not be able to generate enough research funding for their work. Furthermore, the home institution, to which a faculty member is attached, may not "allow" the faculty member to "bring" these research findings with them to other academic institutions. After all, the original institution might have funded this research! And there might be contractual limitations too. The main institutions may see this as "cherry-picking" and resist this! A counterargument, however, might be that, since research findings would largely rest with individual faculty members and not with the academic institution, then the individual should also be free to make use of the research in whatever way they might wish. We will return to this topic at the end of this chapter.

A key argument for maintaining a permanent staff also relates to developing a more targeted school profile or culture, typically driven by a set of specific research competences. This type of more focused institution-building would be the preferred way for most thriving academic institutions. In contrast, "letting all flowers bloom" might not only become too expensive, but also impose potentially severe challenges when it comes to maintaining a minimum degree of quality across disciplines or departments. Examples of such specialized institutions might be London Business School, or the Norwegian School of Economics and Business Administration (NHH), both of which have a heavy focus on finance. A commitment to one's institution, beyond what might be seen as a self-centered focus by a faculty member on their own career or discipline, might also be key. This might address the potential risk of too much "me, me, me." It is also true to say that all business school organizations need to have core values, and these are typically put into practice by those faculty members who represent a dominant discipline at the school, and who are also typically present at the school, participating in specialized research seminars, etc. We will discuss this in more detail in Chapter 7.

Arguments against the Networked Approach

Let us return to the argument that the networked approach can be seen as "cherry-picking" by the traditional type of academic institution. Would schools such as the Lorange Institute, perhaps unjustly, be allowed to draw on what has been built up, perhaps over many years, and "invested" in by more classical academic institutions, to better support an individual faculty member's research, and which the faculty member might now take advantage of as a visiting professor? We would suggest that the Lorange Institute, and other similar academic institutions, would play legitimate academic roles, for two reasons:

- First, academic institutions such as the Lorange Institute often come up with innovations that might be of benefit to the entire industry, i.e., approaches which would be complementary to those practiced by a typical business. So, it may open up practical ways of demonstrating how existing and novel modes of operation can be achieved. The issue of being able to implement change at higher speed might be key here: the more traditional business schools may be at a disadvantage here.
- Second, while not yet broadly implemented, due to (as yet) insufficient financial results, the intention for the Lorange Institute has always been that it would plan to contribute faculty stipends that would support the research of participating faculty members. Stipends would be offered to the most "prominent" of the visiting faculty members in the network based on length of service, degree of teaching involvement, and who have attained a high quality of teaching, according to students/ participants' feedback as well as the judgment of the Institute's teachers. These stipends would thus be given to individual faculty members, and not to their parent institutions, reflecting the philosophy that knowledge accumulated from research "belongs" to the individual researcher (professor) and is thus not institutional knowledge. As we know, when a professor moves from one academic institution to another, the knowledge tends to move with them. It is thus worth observing that if any traditional academic institution denies their professors the opportunity to become involved in other professorial

networks, such as that of the Lorange Institute, on a part-time basis, this might perhaps be a reflection of the fact that the leadership of such traditional business schools might not "see" the complementarity between their organization and what institutions such as the Lorange Institute might stand for. It might perhaps be seen as supporting potential competition instead!

Outsourcing for Speed and Flexibility

Let us now consider several further issues regarding outsourcing (or in-sourcing) and speed.

The concept of in-sourcing of the faculty resource is key to the networked approach, as we have seen. There are, however, several other aspects of this faculty in/outsourcing that should also be examined. As suggested, the extensive use of outsourcing may lead to an increase in the quality of business school's activities in at least four different ways. The main purpose of outsourcing is, thus, quality enhancement, not savings made on costs per se. Let us now take a look at some areas where outsourcing might be beneficial and others where it would be inadvisable.

Outsourcing may allow better opportunities for a school's leadership to bring in specialist skills and to also apply pressure on entities that are performing outsourced tasks to meet deadlines. This is more of a problem when nonrepetitive tasks are to be undertaken. A good example might be the development of a school's web page. Here, highly specialized skills would typically be needed, and they will also be required when it comes to updating one's web page in a fast, relatively inexpensive way. Search engine optimization, allowing a web page to be listed toward the top of Google or other search engine's pages, would be key. Independent experts might be better placed to achieve this. In short, outsourcing can increase both more punctual delivery and better quality. There are many other examples of this, such as, for instance, it the availability of a basic IT-related service, the development of marketing materials, such as brochures, etc.

But outsourcing can also be effective in the case of more repetitive tasks. We have already discussed the use of part-time faculty members in teaching. This is, of course, an example of outsourcing. Here too, as we saw, a more consistent degree of cutting-edge quality might be achieved. The professors in question would typically be under a great deal of pressure to deliver on time – not only in terms of adequate delivery in class but also to provide a timely delivery of assignments, prereadings, exam questions, grading, feedback, etc. If not "up to speed" on delivery, the professor in question might risk not being asked to teach again! There are also additional basic tasks that might lend themselves to outsourcing, such as taking care of a school's accounting, cleaning, canteen/restaurant services, etc. Again, we see the leverage that management might gain, by having the option to discontinue a particular in-house service to replace it with a better and more timely service.

Outsourcing in a Networked Organization

It is, of course, essential to maintain a high degree of professionalism in one's own organization. This would typically involve functions that might not readily lend themselves to outsourcing. Functions which are strategically important should not be outsourced. In a business school, such key functions might involve sales, program development, customer relations, academic follow-ups vis-à-vis professors and students/participants, the management of exams and grades-keeping, etc. These in-house functions need to be handled in a consistent, risk-free, and professional way. A networked organization needs to be particularly carefully managed when it comes to these core activities that might be seen as the skeleton of a school's own competences. This implies that attracting and to retaining the skills of a core of top-quality administrative staff members is of vital importance. While these may not add up many people on a school's permanent headcount, they must be of absolutely top caliber! Only then will they be able to perform their role as links to the nonpermanent members of the network. A generally high caliber of personnel in a network would help hold it all together.

Creating a Slimmer Organization

Outsourcing can help business schools to maintain a low break-even point. This would safeguard a school from having a disproportionately large fraction of fixed financial commitments (salaries, social benefits, pensions, etc.). Such commitments may not only be substantive, in that they might take away resources that otherwise might have been used to invest in new directional activities; they might also lead to excessive bureaucracy, i.e., too many people in the organization that, strictly speaking, might not be needed. However, a gradual shift to a slimmer organization will take time, and it might involve considerable expense, in the form of severance packages. These may be perfectly fair and reasonable in their own right. But adaptation may be harder, slower, and rather expensive as a result.

To recap, in general, outsourcing can be a great asset in the management of business schools by offering them "economics of small scale."

Outsourcing is done to gain quality, speed, flexibility, and adaptability – not primarily to save on costs! The business school of the future might thus be expected to be considerably dissimilar to most leading business schools of today. Outsourcing is key to this, and this is driven by the need for the top schools of the future to deliver superior quality throughout, including higher-quality faculty and staff functions, when it comes to both speed and quality. As we have agreed, the motivation for outsourcing would primarily be to improve quality. But the leverage of a school's fixed cost base is important too, and this is also more achievable through outsourcing. Proactive adaptation might thus become easier, and the risk of a school's eventual decline, or even obsolescence, might be diminished.

Macroenvironmental Changes and the Curriculum

A school's curriculum is of central importance. The offerings of the Business School of the Future should reflect the business challenges that might face students and clients over the coming years, thus enhancing the capability and skills they will need to manage in this more complex world. Here are some of these emerging issues, in this case raised by Pedro Nueno, Emeritus Professor at IESE, Barcelona, and elaborated on below:

Global Macroeconomic Shifts

There are likely to be even more profound global macroeconomic effects (Nueno, 2012). For example, China's economic slowdown in the mid-2010s seems to have led to severe consequences for many world economies, underscoring the increasingly strong ties that exist between them. China's slowing economy and its shift toward relatively greater focus on the consumer has led to less need for raw materials imports, i.e., bulk cargoes, such as steel, coal, etc. This seems to have had dramatic negative impacts on the national economies of major raw materials-producing nations, such as Australia and Brazil, and also on major coal producers, such as, again, Australia. Consequently, the worldwide shipping rates for bulk carriers have slumped. This shift in China's economy, from a relatively greater emphasis on exports, based on the transportation of raw materials, to relatively more emphasis on consumer products and finished goods, has also led to a boom in the exports of finished goods from China and strong growth in the container shipping industry. This has helped to keep container shipping freight rates at a reasonably sustainable level, despite of the over-capacity of container ship tonnage.

The relatively high volatility in the Chinese stock market, coupled with the country's reporting of several key economic indicators that might be falling, has led to increased volatility in virtually all of the world's stock markets. Many developing countries, notably several African and South American, as well as most of the so-called BRICS countries, have China as their major trading partner. They will be feeling the slowdown in China as particularly acutely when it comes to the effects on their own economies.

China's devaluation of its yuan, in August 2015, led to devaluations in several neighboring countries, as well as pressure on the US dollar. The Federal Reserve decided to delay its planned interest rate increase to keep the value of the dollar from further appreciating. So, might the direct effects from these changes in the Chinese economy be on foreign companies? With the weakening of the Chinese stock market, some of the relatively small but wealthier segments among Chinese consumers may have been particularly hard hit. This will, in time, have led to a slowdown of luxury goods sales such as luxury cars, high-end watches and jewelry, luxury clothing brands, etc. Similarly, with the Chinese central government's restrictions on gift-giving, such as luxury watches, major watchmakers, above all the Swiss, may have experienced a decline.

The increased transparency brought about by social media also means that particularly negative developments in one part of the world might no longer be contained locally, but might lead to rapid global exposure, with potentially negative consequences for a company. Let us the consider the cases of so-called contaminated milk in China and unhealthy noodles in India, both involving Nestlé. Both cases led to negative economic consequences for Nestlé as a whole, and loss of reputation. It could be increasingly important for modern business schools to teach how to effectively handle such crises.

Advances in Communication Technology

As alluded to above, key technological advances, in particular those affecting modern methods of communication, are having profound impacts on business. Communication is becoming truly instant and world-encompassing, not only through the web, emails, etc., but also via TV-based news. Thus, managing one's company's reputation is becoming increasingly important, and should be reflected in a business school's curriculum! While this perhaps might be seen as a rather defensive activity, there are, of course, positive effects too. The impact of social media on modern marketing come to mind in particular. Innovations can now be more readily communicated to one's target group of customers, leading perhaps to both more top-line sales and higher profits at the bottom line (Lorange and Rembiszewski, 2014). Developing effective and up-to-date web pages has indeed become a new "science." So-called search optimization has become particularly key, ensuring that a firm's web page is displayed at (or near) the top of the list when a potential client carries out a search. This is potentially another extension to a school's curriculum.

Finally, modern communication technology implies more two-way interactivity! The potential client might now feel that a communication is more exclusively addressed to them, and that they would thus have the option to respond, to ask more questions about a service or product, etc. Thus, advances in communication technology now allow for more individualized communication, more effective, two-way interactivity, and all this at a much higher speed, often almost instantaneously! Curriculum offerings at the business school of the future should clearly address these issues.

New Regulatory Environment

Emerging legal complexities represent another development that may fundamentally change the working context for the global manager. Added requirements on compliance might be one such factor. We have seen a number of "scandals" all over the world, most particularly in financial institutions, stemming from a range of factors including what are now considered overly liberal lending practices, the introduction of complex "financial products" that were much riskier than customers might have been led to understand, the manipulation of key interest rates or outright fraud! Heavy penalties have been imposed on firms that have gone too far, as well as a tightened regime of controls. Furthermore, new requirements regarding the minimum amounts of equity required in projects financed by banks are now being implemented.

The regulation of competition is a factor that will need to be dealt with in a school's new curriculum. This may increasingly represent a dilemma. On the one hand, we have seen a clear trend toward cooperation in networks, often with former competitors, perhaps to come up with a broader line of offerings, faster and/or at lower cost, and/or to better serve certain customers and/or suppliers, i.e., co-creation. But, on the other hand, legally it may be becoming increasingly difficult to follow this evolutionary practice. New regulations may, for instance, set clear limits for how such competition might take place, particularly when it comes to what might be considered coordination on price-cutting. Hence, while close relations are key, for example, one's key customers, it may be illegal to pursue such arrangements too far. A potential downside might be, for instance, that some customer-initiated innovations might in the end not take place. Understanding the limits of cooperation in emerging networked economies thus becomes key. The public sector is also, to an increasing extent, coming up with guidelines and regulations for business to follow. In the future, failing to comply may result in penalties, not only for an employer's firm, but also for the employees themselves. It follows that senior executives will increasingly need to spend time on such regulations.

The dean of Yale's School of Management, Dr. Edward A. Snyder, has produced a set of emerging curricular "requirements" in a different way, although basically complementary to Nueno's (2012):

- a need to keenly understand markets and competition
- how to lead, including in networks, and internationally!
- understand and navigate in an increasingly complex world, across cultures

A recent attempt by the faculty of IMD, one of the world's leading business schools, to identify what might be seen as a cutting-edge curriculum, has resulted in a seven-point agenda for how today's corporations might be transformed (Anand and Barsoux, 2014), and thus, how IMD's program offerings might be evolving. All of these transformational agenda issues may be seen as global. Here they are:

- presence, i.e., going global
- value generation, i.e., working with customers all over the world to create value and not be locked up in creating value for a particular customer segment or region
- leadership development, i.e., to develop leaders who might be effective in any parts of the world, i.e., relate to customers anywhere
- solutions, i.e., to provide more than a product, but an entire service!
- agility – to bring an entrepreneurial drive into the company, often by breaking it up into several smaller units, but with common direction
- coinnovation, i.e., to establish a strong network with strong partners, so as to come up with the strongest innovations, in competition with other networks
- sustainability, i.e., to bring various key stakeholders together to stake out a common, most viable strategic direction, acceptable to all other stakeholder groups

Needless to say, for a school to be able to deliver on all of this, a more flexible way of organizing will clearly be needed. This would typically also imply more cooperation between schools themselves, and perhaps also for a student to orient their studies to several academic institutions, which will discuss later in connection with the so-called MOOCs phenomenon (Bisoux, 2017).

In Sum: A More Relevant Curriculum

Let us now attempt to pull together the core issues relating to how more relevance in a business school's curriculum can be achieved. Needless to say, developing a relevant curriculum for the business school of today is a major challenge. Relatively little has been done to attempt to empirically establish what might be managerially relevant when it comes to curriculum changes and delivery. There are, however, exceptions (see McMillan and Overall, 2016). There have also been many critical contributions regarding curriculum shortcomings (see Bennis and O'Toole, 2005; Maerki, 2008; Minzberg, 2004). It is, of course, widely claimed that an explicit curriculum design/revision should drive the renewed curricular focus (Bisoux, 2017). In practice, however, a business school's body of professors, both established and newly appointed, would probably play a major role in shaping what is actually being taught. Although a faculty member's research productivity seems to represent the most typical major criteria for hiring and/or promotion, there is relatively less emphasis placed on the contribution that they might be able to make in terms of relevance through their teaching. The net effect of this, of course, is that a business school's curriculum is quite often impacted by such randomness.

How might this situation be ameliorated? At IMD, we tried to address this by encouraging all our faculty to come forward with their latest contributions to research and/or pedagogy (including new case studies) at our annual Orchestrating Winning Performance program. Here the professors would also be able to interact with a relatively large set of leading executives, typically a headcount of approximately 600 to 800, from different functions, companies, genders, and geographies. The interaction between academia and practice that resulted from this was intended to stimulate a further constructive reshaping of the school's programmatic offerings, to make these managerially more relevant. Another source of inputs to curricular relevance was IMD's various business advisory councils and its board. However, it should be admitted that the resources that both individual executives and the board members represented were probably not used to the full. It is, however, encouraging to observe recent attempts to synthesize IMD's capabilities to impact significant transformations in companies, by channeling research outputs and faculty insights into the seven key areas listed above (Anand and Barsoux, 2014).

At the Lorange Institute of Business, where the approach is to exclusively make use of part-time faculty, central delivery of the curricula might perhaps be designed in a more explicitly holistic way. For instance, faculty experts could be invited to join the Institute for relatively limited time periods and to contribute in the areas of their own cutting-edge competences. It would all "add up" to the desired curriculum, driven by the set of faculty members that had been selected.

In practice, however, there are some potential difficulties to overcome. The choice of faculty members could be impacted by the specific network contacts of the business school's faculty administrator (in the case of the Lorange Institute, initially I, and later on, Dr. Philip Boksberger, the my successor). There would thus be biases when it came to shaping the network, with, in our case, relatively stronger contacts with faculty members in the strategy and behavioral science fields, versus relatively few when it came to more quantitative areas, such as finance or economics. Also, largely to save on costs, professors were initially invited in from relatively nearby, with gradually more coming onboard, but exclusively from Switzerland. Both of these factors, however, might also have led to unintended biases in the curriculum at the Lorange Institute.

Seeking a greater variety of inputs from an active business advisory council would thus be key. Those who represent leading business practice might be particularly valuable as potential direction-providers. Leading consultants might likewise be highly effective. The composition of a school's business advisory council would thus be critical, perhaps more so now than ever before.

How might a business school's curriculum evolve, then? Would there, for instance, be a relatively optimal balance between required course offerings and electives, or, as often seem to be the case, is the curriculum so rigidly structured that it might come across as too "heavy"? Are new topics well represented, such as, for instance, communication based on social media? Are some of the more "classical" axiomatic disciplines such as, for instance, economics, accounting, or finance, becoming so dominant that "softer" topics such as leadership, entrepreneurship, or marketing are given insufficient emphasis? These and other related questions might legitimately be raised. They might at times be seen as implying some degree of criticism. So, what might be done? The next section identifies several means of coping with this.

Changing Direction

First, we know that a curriculum might be broken down into knowledge components, skill components, and value components. The first tends to be related to the basics, which are often relatively classical axiomatic materials. The second might be related to the "softer" side, often captured through cutting-edge dilemmas. And the third would have to do with the basic values that a school might stand for, such as focusing on educating its students to primarily serve a particular type of business, say, finance, manufacturing, or shipping, or to develop certain types of skills, such as entrepreneurship, or to prepare its students for state-owned, public-sector positions. It would most likely be the dean or president, through their top-down actions, that would impact this, through key appointments, for example, course heads, teaching assignments, promotion and termination of professors, or channeling research funds. Regrettably, many deans or presidents seem to be unwilling to influence the curriculum, however. They might even see such an act as meddling in their faculty's own affairs, even infringing on academic freedom. This might lead to a slowing down or even stagnation of a school's efforts to adopt a curriculum to be well prepared for the future.

Second, one might ask whether a particular curricular direction might actually be attainable, given a school's faculty profiles. Change faculty profiles, through new hires, promotions, and retirements of "old hands," might be difficult, however, even though it may be called for. In many academic institutions, these tasks are largely delegated to the various academic departments. The problem here, however, is that a given academic department might typically be inclined to recruit and/or promote faculty members with a similar profile to its current dominant staffing. Thus, this would not be an effective way to recruit to meet the requirement for a modern curriculum. Again, the dean or president might need to step in, to ensure that the new competences that might be necessary would be hired.

Third, an active advisory council or advisory board might play an important role when it comes to impacting the curriculum. Leading practitioners might be more aware of emerging needs for new directions than many entrenched faculty members. Their point of reference might be what businesses will need to succeed in the years ahead. Appointing members to an advisory board that might be able to offer concrete curricular advice seem to be key, therefore. This would be in contrast to the largely ceremonial roles that many such advisory boards currently play.

Key Role of the Dean or President

Let us now return to the critical role of the person at the top of the school. The former dean of Harvard Business School, Dr. Johan McArthur, says (*HBS Alumni Bulletin*, 2016), "Being Dean is not that different from running a nursery school. Successful nursery schools are the ones where there is a lot going on to encourage the minds and energies of all those kids. There may be a din, there's almost certainly a mess, but good things are happening." His "message" thus seems clear: top-down management, but in such a way that it leads to variety, not to the shifting of creative efforts through too many constraints set by the top.

Dr. Bertil Andersson is president of Nanyang Technological University in Singapore. When he took over as head of Nanyang ten years ago, this technical university was ranked as No. 132 by the Financial Times. Ten years later, in July 2017, Nanyang was ranked No. 9 worldwide. Dr. Andersson concedes that to lead an academic institution to success is likely to require firmness at the top, particularly when it comes to decisions that are directly related to quality, such as faculty hiring, performance reviewing, faculty terminations, among others. But, as he states, "top-down leadership, but with large ears"! Thus, he stresses that an effective top-down style also has a lot to do with listening and showing respect for faculty members. There is, of course, no conflict between this and firmness. But finding leaders who are both able to manage in a top-down way and to work in harmony with faculty is not easy. Perhaps Dr. Andersson's own background as a successful scientist might have a lot to do with this! This was also the case for Dean MacArthur, who is a respected scholar in corporate finance.

Thus, a strong academic background can clearly be an advantage for an academic leader at the top. In fact, this might help in establishing respect vis-à-vis faculty members. Clearly, when it comes to the actual leadership decisions that the president is involved in, specific academic knowledge would normally not be all that important. But a strong academic profile in the eyes of the faculty can only be an advantage when it comes to practicing "top-down leadership, but with big ears."

Let us now turn to what might be particularly important decision areas for the dean or president in relation to quality. We will first of all review the set of key areas that a leader should focus on to ensure quality when it comes to what might typically be found in more conventional academic institutions, and then to do the same for the business school of the future.

Steve Jobs at Apple was perhaps the ultimate master of "borrowing with pride" (Isaacson) those aspects that he considered the "best" from other companies. When it came to the Apple laptop, for instance, he drew heavily on existing technologies, such as basic computing (above all, from IBM), display technology (Samsung; Toshiba), communication features (above all, from Nokia), design (inspired, above all, by Sony), and so on. And, he was eminently successful with this approach. He followed a similar path when it came to Apple's other big innovations (e.g., the iPhone).

Is this approach of "borrowing with pride" from leaders in one's own industry appropriate for successful presidents or deans too? In my own experience as the president of the Norwegian Business School as well as when at IMD, I tried to maintain good contacts with a broad section of business schools as well as with other academic institutions and keep abreast of developments. Above all, I tried to spot what types of new hirings these institutions were making, i.e., which competencies were they adding, as well as specific new courses and research programs. Scanning the literature, books, articles, and papers was also key.

I was also on the Board of EFMD, the Brussels-based accreditation entity, as well as on EFMD's Board (the Swiss federal technical university of Lausanne). I kept in close contact with AACSB, the leading Tampa, Florida-based accreditation agency. Furthermore, we had meetings on a regular basis with the top leaders of INSEAD and London Business School. These contacts, in the aggregate, gave me a good handle on directional changes that we needed to take at IMD, not only when it came to academic contracts, but also regarding pedagogy and the commercial side. Clearly, this was "borrowing with pride," and it led to success!

Why do we see so little of this? Many top business school leaders may be (or may have become) so enamored with the unique approaches taken by their own institutions that they may no longer appreciate that "good is never good enough"! They are simply no longer interested in (or able to) listening, learning, and adapting effectively.

There are, of course, limits to this approach. A school's strategy may simply be "perfectly good enough." To fine-tune further might simply take too much time and energy, cost too much, and even be confusing or distractive to the organization. It is, of course, equally critical for a president to maintain a stable strategic course, and not change excessively by "borrowing with pride," to be effective.

Faculty Development: Mentoring and Coaching

Many business schools have introduced programs whereby senior faculty members mentor and coach their junior colleagues. Why is this? The answer is simple: to strengthen academic value–creating processes, particularly when it comes to teaching, but also to develop research capabilities. There seem to be many "potential traps" that might be avoided through proper mentoring or coaching, particularly when it comes to more effective two-way interaction between teacher and students, for example, in case teaching and workshop discussions. What are some of the benefits of systematic mentoring and coaching?

For senior faculty, who would typically be the key actors, training their junior colleagues might prepare the latter to take over a relatively larger part of the teaching load. Thus, senior faculty might be "freed up." The benefits for a junior faculty member include getting up to speed faster, by avoiding unnecessary mistakes. This might also be motivational, in that they might actually feel that they are becoming better at teaching and/or research.

What are some of the potential problems with this? Senior faculty might, of course, feel that they have insufficient time or energy for this. Thus, they may not be fully committed to such a task. Junior faculty might actually want effective coaching or mentoring, but be resistant to "being told," preferring instead to build their own self-confidence by doing it themselves. Also, some junior faculty might feel that they simply cannot set aside the time required for coaching, given the many perceived pressures they face, perhaps especially when it comes to delivering on research. The sentiment that this all seems like a "waste of time" and that they "cannot afford it" might be real!

Ensuring Quality in More Conventional Academic Institutions

Performance reviews of faculty members are, of course, essential in ensuring quality in any school. They might only take place once a year, but ideally they should be carried out bi-annually. It is important that this is done face-to-face, to signal the importance of the process and also to provide the president with a better feel for the types of academic value creation that are going on. Sufficient time must be set aside for each review of, say, one hour per review. Some of this time might be spent on reviewing a given faculty member's output, but a significant part of the time might be spent on going over the faculty member's plans for the future, including the resources that will be required, as the faculty member might see it. It is perhaps wise for a second person to attend these meetings, typically an associate dean, in the event of disputes.

For business schools with a faculty of, say, more than sixty faculty members, it may simply be difficult to impossible for the president to find sufficient time for all such reviews. In these cases, the president might at least review all direct reports, for example, all department chairmen. However, it would be important for the Chairman to be provided with the plans for each department, as well as a summary assessment of each individual faculty member's performance. In-fighting and conservative momentum regarding direction at the departmental board level must be guarded against!

It goes without saying that faculty reviews will typically be time-consuming! To ameliorate some of this, it is helpful for each faculty member to submit a written plan beforehand, including a copy of research outputs as well as teaching ratings. Published outputs, such as articles or books, would be key, rather than writing projects that are "almost done"! It is also important for the president to formulate a brief feedback document, acknowledging the various outputs of each faculty member, and the extent to which the president sees this as satisfactory. An annual, or semiannual, performance bonus might also be awarded to those faculty members who have excelled.

There may be a conflict of interests arising from the faculty review process focusing on each individual faculty member, while the president may have an ambition to focus on a more cooperative culture for the faculty, i.e., a "we, we, we" focus. To overcome each faculty member solely pursuing a "me, me, me" focus, cooperative research efforts and coauthored articles or books may be given special credit. Similarly, a faculty member's efforts as a "citizen" might be specially recognized (such as advising, coaching colleagues, committee work, alumni relationships). In the end, it would be research outputs and classroom excellence that would truly matter, however.

As we have already noted, the processes of faculty hiring, promotion, and denial of contract renewals are central for enhancing quality. The president would typically want to be centrally involved in these processes. While the search for new faculty members would typically be driven by those faculty members active in a given area of recruitment, it is also important for the president to be involved. If not, it is possible that strong new faculty candidates, seen as potential competitors to those already on the faculty, might not be recruited. The involvement of the president should also ensure an openness to new directions, not already found in the existing faculty. When it comes to promotional or tenure decisions, it is equally important for the president's view on emerging high-quality candidates to be represented. Without such a top-down presence, there is also the risk that other factors might be ignored (race, nationality, gender, etc.).

In sum, we see that top-down involvement by the president to drive quality would require that they are actively involved with faculty, in terms of both faculty performance reviews and faculty recruitment, promotion, and termination. Many presidents might indeed also be quite visible to other stakeholders, such as alumni, the business sector, potential financial donors, politicians, etc. While such stakeholder interactions would be important, it is driving faculty performance which, in the end, would truly matter. Only through strong faculty performance can high quality be ensured and built upon.

The President's Role in the Business School of the Future

What would the president's role in the business school of the future be in terms of quality assurance? As we know, there would be no, or only a few, full-time faculty members at the business school of the future. Hence, the president's faculty review process would take on a slightly different form from that discussed above. We will first discuss the process of attracting part-time faculty members for the purpose of conducting workshop sessions on key dilemmas. We will then consider the actual review of each workshop. It should be noted that our discussion will follow the opposite order to that of the previous section relating to more conventional business schools.

When it comes to attracting appropriate part-time faculty members to take on the role of discussion leaders for workshops on key dilemmas, the president would again play a central role. Several considerations might be touched upon:

- Is the potential faculty member already associated with a reputable business school, consulting firm, or company? Related to this, what type of employment record does this faculty member have?
- What type of profile does this potential faculty member have? Do they work at the cutting edge? For academics, their publication record might be an important factor. For consultants and for business executives, it may be more difficult for the president to make this type of assessment. Their record when it comes to major projects or previous job assignments might provide useful indications.
- General reputation when it comes to a person's personality would also be key. Is this person relatively easy to get along with? What kind of classroom reputation might they have? Again, the president might obtain useful information about these "softer" issues from others in the network.

Given the fact that it might be relatively more difficult to assess the suitability of potential part-time faculty members, then the past experience of the president may become even more critical. Is the president part of a broader network that they might draw on? This may be particularly critical. Being an effective president in "the business school of the future" calls for a relatively extensive length of experience. They must "know" a broad set of people to be effective!

Having tentatively selected a prospective faculty member, some important steps need to be taken, namely to ensure that the faculty member in question would actually be allowed by their principal employer (if they have one) to take on this assignment. Full openness vis-à-vis the other employer would be key. Assessing the actual performance of a given part-time faculty member as a leader of one or more workshop(s) on cutting-edge dilemmas might actually be relatively easier to do rather than attempting to attract the most appropriate part-timers. The president would need to have access to student feedback, as well as an opportunity to examine preassigned readings, questions, etc. The president should then try to sit down with the part-time faculty member to go over their teaching experience, particularly as delivered in their workshops.

One important performance measure that the president could use would be the quality of assignment materials, the timeliness of assignments, the grading of exams/papers, and feedback provided to each student. Excessive delays when it comes to these issues would typically result in the discontinuation of employment of any given professor. Over time, however, a relatively stable network of part-time professors should emerge. The quality of the work of this group is key, and must be maintained, or even strengthened further. The president is key here!

A common question that is often raised is: Why would anyone actually want to become a part-time professor at the business school of the future? Let me briefly touch upon three factors:

- The pay. This is, of course, a typical motivating factor. While not usually involving significant amounts, this extra pay might still be considered as attractive.
- Stimulating workshops settings, which also might include learning. With relatively few students, all coming from different backgrounds with their own experiences to draw on, the workshop might identify new insights which might be beneficial for the professor too.
- The prestige of a particular business school of the future. To be seen as being part of this type of a conventionally determined, highly ranked institution might be important for an aspiring faculty member who might not be able to get this type of exposure in their more conventional work setting.

Quality is absolutely key. While we have a relatively clear understanding of what this would imply in more conventional business school settings, and what type of role the president might take to enhance quality, these issues are less clearly understood in the context of the business school of the future. In the end, the president's own instincts may be the key driver.

Choice of New Dean and/or New President

The issue of leadership succession at a business school is, of course, critical to its future success. A good choice or, for that matter, a bad one can make a huge difference. Relevant demonstrated leadership experience will be key. Has a particular candidate been successful before? The effectiveness of the management of the school from the top down is at stake. We will look at three issues that seem particularly relevant here. But before we do, let me state that the search for a new dean/president tends to be undertaken by the school's board of directors (governors), or by a subcommittee of this, or even by the Chairperson of the board alone. Alternatively, there might be specially appointed search committee to carry out this task. We will say more about this below:

> Issue one: Open or closed search? An open search implies that candidates apply for the job, typically after seeing it advertised in the press and/or posted on the net. While this method might have the advantage of identifying a broader set of potentially qualified candidates, the negative side is that many good candidates may be reluctant to actually apply, due to a potential fear of being turned down, and possibly due to a fear of pertinent information being leaked in a so-called confidential process.

> A closed process, on the other hand, means that the search committee would identify whom they think would be the best candidate, and then negotiate with this individual exclusively. This candidate might come from the school itself, or from outside. Typically, one would know the preferred candidate very well, i.e., there would be no surprises regarding their strengths and/or weaknesses. The downside to this would be at least twofold: one might miss out on better candidates who would potentially be available, and, there would be a real danger of "friend-buddy" preference.

> Issue two: Would this be a democratic process? This relates to issue one, i.e., whether the process is open or whether a particular candidate might be preferred a priori. Clearly, the former would be more in line with the democratic expectations we might have of today's business schools.

> Similarly, the composition of the search committee should also be carefully considered. While in the past, the search committee tended to be the board (or a subcommittee of this), today's search committee might be composed of a broader set of stakeholders, such as the faculty, students, staff, or alumni.

The search committee might even be elected. While the latter might be seen as more democratic, however, it is not clear that this would be a more effective means of finding the best candidate. There might be a lot of political maneuverings as well as special interests brought into play. Many of the faculty, for instance, might actually prefer a relatively weak candidate, to diminish the risk of this person "rocking the boat" – more about this in the next paragraph. The risk of a drawn out, "leaked" process would, of course, be relatively high with such a broad (and large) search committee.

Now let us discuss the merits of a direct election of a new dean/president. Such elections are traditionally executed by the faculty, even at times by the full professors only. In other instances, those eligible to cast a vote might include the staff, and even the students. The candidates for such elections would typically be internal. The identification of suitable external candidates would not be easy, however, using the direct election method. While the process might, on the surface, be seen as "democratic," there would be a real danger of suboptimal choices being made, due to a lack of truly good candidates, a conservatism in voting (not "rocking the boat"), as well as political considerations. This approach, therefore, while most commonly used in the past, is on its way out.

Issue three: Should a management search firm be used? There are two positive aspects to employing a management search firm: firstly, the search committee is assisted in the task of actually evaluating key candidates, including the interview process, and secondly, the search for candidates might be broadened. On the negative side, the headhunter may lack a deep understanding of what might be needed to be effective in this job. This might be particularly the case when it comes to appreciating what it takes to be an effective "top-down" leader. Being both a good academician and a good administrator is key, but not that easy to find. The new dean/president will also need to have a familiarity with the stakeholders they will need to interact with, but how might a headhunter assess this?

So, in summary, when it comes to the search for new dean or president, my recommendation would be that the search should be undertaken by a relatively small search committee, perhaps by the board itself. There might not be a need for assistance from an external headhunter. Of course, a lot of time will need to be spent on interviews and consultations, as well as on background checking. Above all, a candidate who would be able to exercise a strong "top-down" leadership function should be appointed. This is perhaps not "democratic." What matters, however, is to come up with the best qualified individual to lead the business school of the future.

Conclusion

In this chapter, we have focused on the effective value-creating roles of the faculty and its dean or president in the modern business school of the future, which is typically organized in a networked model. Speed, creativity, adaptability, and innovative capabilities are key! The modern curriculum is central here, and we have discussed ways of implementing this. The president or dean is a key custodian of top-down driven inputs, but in a nonautocratic way. A good dean or president is, of course, crucial for ensuring top quality in academic value creation. We have also seen how the choice of new dean or president is a particularly critical and challenging task.

4   Modern Pedagogy and the Modern Student

We have previously touched on the ways in which the advent of computer-based learning has introduced a major new dimension in the pedagogical world of most business schools. Some business schools now post many of their courses on the internet, often with free access for anyone who wishes to follow a particular course, and often delivered by world-renowned professors. Some business schools have developed course offerings specifically tailored for delivery on the internet, so-called MOOCs (Bisoux, 2017; Clarke, 2013). A student/participant is now able to enroll in a series of MOOCs, offered by different business schools, and thus study for a degree entirely via distance learning using MOOCs taken "at" several different academic institutions. Exams can now also be taken via distance learning. The issue of how to verify a particular student's authenticity, to avoid cheating, is now also being worked out (Wilson, 2013).

Individual learning, via the web at home, can also be carried out in combination with sessions delivered on the school's premises, providing a mix of distance learning and on-campus learning. Specific prereadings and/or prestudy materials might be distributed beforehand to the participants via the web. These might be relevant articles, book chapters, notes, etc., or the pertinent parts of these. Assignment questions might also be provided to help to guide the student/participant in their preparation. More basic or factual materials might be particularly well suited to being internalized in this way, i.e., by each student participant alone and at home, through the web.

This individualized study then allows for to a more intensive on-campus class experience later. These might, perhaps, be considered as intensive workshops, where cutting-edge dilemmas would be discussed. The focus might now be to better understand key aspects of such cutting-edge issues and dilemmas, in contrast to learning the more basic issues during the individual prereading/prelearning phase.

We will go on to examine some aspects of this revolution in pedagogy in more detail. But first we should reiterate that the successful management

72

of the business school itself is based on successfully handling three dilemmas. Success implies a balance in how these three dilemmas are dealt
with. Here they are:

• Research and teaching (pedagogy) are two sides of the same coin. They
  are equally important for a school's success in the future.
• Innovation and a focus on existing school strengths. New cutting-
  edge capabilities must be developed all the time, while also making
  sure that existing strengths, developed in earlier times, are fully
  utilized. So, it is a matter of a dual focus, "today for today and
  today for tomorrow."
• Web-based (ICT-based) learning at home and discussion sessions at
  school, i.e., "blended" learning, i.e., learning alone at home, typically
  when it comes to more basic materials and learning in groups at school,
  typically when it comes to discussing key dilemmas.

The Physical Setting

Many of today's schools no longer find the classical, tiered, horseshoe-
shaped auditorium found in many conventional business schools to be
optimal. These were originally developed at Harvard Business School,
for case study discussions, not for even more open-ended group discussions of key dilemmas. The class size would also typically be much
larger in such conventional case discussions. They are increasingly, in
contrast, considering so-called flat rooms, i.e., rooms with level floors.
These would ideally consist of a number of round tables in each room,
say five, and around each of these tables there might be a number of
chairs, say seven. Therefore, a maximum number of participants
would be thirty-five. Each participant at a given table would be able
to hear their neighbors, and to easily interact with all. There might be
an extra empty chair placed at each table for the professor, should
they need to be present to stimulate discussion at a particular table.
There might not be a traditional blackboard, but notes might be
written on whiteboards along all four walls, and/or on flip-charts.
Each participant would be in a position to take picture(s) of these
notes with their mobile phones, for rapid storage on their computers.
The professor would typically not be encouraged to show slides:
perhaps a good maximum might be around five, in contrast to the
typically large number shown by many professors in more classical
lecture settings. Instead, the professor might now focus on a small set
of key dilemmas, i.e., setting the scene for what might be discussed in
the workshop. There would, of course, not be a lectern, rather the
professor would be encouraged to move around among the tables, to

be more fully part of the learning team, with little "distance" between the participants.

There is a lot of research evidence that shows that workshop-style learning in flat rooms can yield better results than learning in more classical auditorium settings. Foldnes (2016), for example, documented such improved learning results in a recent study, on what he calls flipped classroom learning. In a follow-up study (Steen-Utheim and Foldnes, forthcoming) researchers report on positive learning effects for twelve students on a mathematics course who followed this approach in one semester and a more classical learning approach in the second semester. When interviewed, all twelve indicated a strong preference for learning in a flipped classroom, on several dimensions: commitment to status quo being recognized, feeling safe, instructor relation, physical learning environment, learning with colleagues, and use of videos when learning new content.

There is a strong body of evidence showing that the spatial layout of facilities has a strong impact on the propensity to innovate in the modern business school (Coulson, Roberts, and Taylor, 2011; Doorley and Witthoft, 2012; Laure-Fayard and Weeks, 2011). The issue of distance is key here: open space can facilitate the lessening of distance. The closer actors are together, the higher the potential for innovation (Allen and Hense, 2011; Catalini, 2012; Kyungjoon et al., 2010). These innovations have been incorporated in many of the so-called innovative centers or social science parks (Delbridge, 2007, 2014; Price and Delbridge, 2015). There is clearly strong sociological evidence behind all of this (Brewer, 2013; Buraway, 2004).

The Process

As suggested, the professor would elaborate on key dilemmas, and the surrounding context. They would steer the discussion, giving relatively clear pointers about what would be discussed. This first part of the workshop might take up around one-third of the overall session. The participants at each table would now be considered as a group. Each group (table) would discuss the dilemmas that the professor had just posed. These group discussions might take up another third of the overall session. The groups (tables) should stay in the classroom and not move into separate study rooms. The discussions and activities taking place in the room would typically act as a stimulus for productive discussions in each group. Finally, there would be a plenary discussion, taking up the final third of the workshop session. The various conclusions reached by each group would be posted on the boards on the walls. The professor would act as a catalyst and might attempt to draw key conclusions also.

Thus, it goes without saying that the professor should be an expert in the topic under discussion.

Experience shows that better learning outcomes typically seem to result from using this interactive method based on a workshop mode. More material might be covered, and faster – even when one adds in the individual time and effort each student/participant might have put into their prereadings. While we do not have precise research-based measurements or results, it seems as if two days of intense workshop-based learning activities might lead to more or less a similar result to a five-day class-based week using traditional methods!

Exams

It is, of course, important for proper checks to take place, to ensure that the intended learning has actually happened. This might, in part, take the form of a pretest. The purpose of this would be to check that the more basic materials studied individually at home had been understood, i.e., based on the self-study of the prereadings. It would assess the level of understanding of the students/participants of key issues before the workshop took place. There might also be an exam after each workshop, to test the depth of learning regarding the key dilemmas. What "feel" do the students now have for these cutting-edge issues? What is their level of understanding? By comparing the two tests – before and after the workshop – one might also get a good indication of the learning progress that has taken place as a consequence of the workshop. There might be a third element to a learning assessment; one based on oral performance during the workshop. Since the purpose of a workshop is to take-and-give, to learn from each other based on listening, open-mindedness, and feedback, the oral performance assessment should measure these elements – the ability to listen, to be open-minded, to make presentations – rather than on more dogmatic expressions of "right/wrong." The tests (pretest/exam) would typically be completed at home by the students. There would simply not be enough time to conduct these tests/exams during the workshops themselves.

As a general point, we should recognize that the traditional type of exam may not work, either as a means of testing a candidate's level of understanding or to enhance further learning. The conventional method used to conduct exams typically encourages candidates to prepare for a given exam, rather than focusing on lasting learning. Rather, it might be better to allow candidates to focus on what they have actually learned, stated in the form of various essays. This might also include more consulting-type reports, focusing on specific problem-solving issues, perhaps (and preferably) from real life.

Reflective Learning

It goes without saying that the type of learning that we have just described, workshop-based learning, might be rather intensive. But there is a complementary way of learning, which focuses on the more reflective side. A student/participant might simply prefer to "sit back and think." A less intensive way of learning might at times be a good complement to the more intensive learning experienced in workshops. While a student/participant might not be "allowed" to opt out of all workshops, they might legitimately choose to attend some in a more reflective mode. The workshop setting is, of course, the same. But a participant may elect to be more passive than they might normally be in other workshops.

Offering students the opportunity to experience the power of diversity is an important part of a business school's mission. The learning process, focused on discussions of key dilemmas, seems to yield better results when there is a certain degree of diversity among the participants, i.e., that there are different values, outlooks, and philosophies. This assumes that such differences are not the product of cultural norms of not engaging in such dialogues, found in some cultures where a high level of respect for authority would make open dialogue more difficult. Cultures in, say, Japan and/or Southeast Asia might fall into this category. It, of course, is possible that the distance in diversity between some participants would simply be too great to allow for an effective process of dialoging. Large age differences, formal job level differences, and/or formal educational differences may contribute to this.

It goes without saying that a certain degree of open-mindedness is essential among the participants: dogmatism is to be avoided. To pretend that there is a "right" answer, and that everything else is not only "wrong" but would simply not be tolerated will not work in this kind of setting. The professor, in their role as a facilitator, would typically play a key role here.

Another way to attempt to avoid dogmatic argument would be for the discussion group to develop a few shared principles for how such discussions might work. For instance, if a participant takes a particular viewpoint on a dilemma that is being discussed, they should be encouraged to illustrate their view with an example from their practice. If no such example can be given, then that particular argument might simply be dismissed. Illustrative examples could be based on a participant's own experience, on what they have read and/or experienced on social or other media. There should be no requirement for any such examples to be too comprehensive or overly detailed. This effort of linking one's argument(s) to a given example does, however, allow for a certain sense of realism to characterize the learning dialogue. Ideas that are too extreme or unsubstantiated will simply not fly.

The conventional way for a professor to teach has typically been to focus on lecturing, to cover a set of basic materials, i.e., essentially a "one-way" pattern of interaction with students. However, a two-way dialogue may now be more in vogue. This might not only be the case when it comes to case teaching, which would be largely based on faculty/students' discussions, but also in discussions of key cutting-edge dilemmas. What would an effective two-way teaching style imply for a professor? Clearly, they would need good listening skills and to know the materials in question well enough to be able to discuss various pros and cons, i.e., an ability to shed light on both sides of the various key dilemmas. Being able to then bring such discussions to a close, perhaps summarizing some of the key points on the whiteboard, would thus also be helpful.

The role of a typical faculty member is thus shifting from being an unchallenged authority on certain issues to being more of a catalyst, leading "we, we, we" discussions around certain dilemmas. But this is not an easy transition and not everyone can do it! As we have previously noted, one of the problems with this type of approach is that some participants adopt a more "passive" profile, a situation that some professors and students might consider to be "free-riding." The other participants might feel that they are unable to learn from the specific experience of a more "passive" student! It goes without saying that the number of "passive" students in any one workshop can only be a relatively small fraction of the group. However, a more reflective learning mode should nevertheless be tolerated, within limits, of course.

As general conclusion, we can safely say that modern pedagogy has revolutionized today's business school: from passive to active, from large to small groups, from classes to workshops, from classical auditoria to "flat rooms," and so on. The basics are perhaps now more effectively learned via the web at home, and face-to-face, campus-based gatherings are now more widely used for in-depth discussions of the more cutting-edge dilemmas.

The Modern Client/Student

Let us now return to the student/participant, who is key, of course! First of all, the student/participant is the client: the business school is here to serve him or her. For this reason, it may be more appropriate to use the label "participant," rather than "student." The latter may signal that they are not be the number one stakeholder! Regrettably, there is a lot of confusion about this. In some business schools, organizational behavior points toward the professor as the leading stakeholder, with the staff, the government/society, etc., also high on the stakeholder ranking, perhaps ahead of the participants!

At this point it is worth considering the typical work contract of today's leading participant. It is perhaps more difficult today than it has been for a long time to get a good job and to be on track for an attractive career. Quitting a job to go back to school might thus not be an option for many, who may be concerned that their job would simply no longer be there once the studies were over. But at the same time, many in private or public-sector jobs realize that lifelong learning is more necessary now than ever, to cope with the rapid explosion of knowledge.

The answer to this dilemma might be for today's typical participant to enter into part-time studies, to keep their job while still following a course of study. They would typically appreciate a more flexible curriculum so that job and studies might be combined. Furthermore, they would probably be in a position to commit to pursuing web-based studies at home, to prepare themselves for the more intensive workshops. Flexibility regarding scheduling each particular workshop, as well as the time it might take to complete one's studies would typically be appreciated. The key here is that it should be relatively realistic to combine the learning activity with one's job, as well as with family life. As far as timetabling is concerned, it would be up to each participant to decide on this according to their individual needs, based on their background and experience. Should accounting always be studied before finance, for instance? The answer to this clearly depends on each individual's own background.

Traditional business school programs have a fairly rigid curriculum when it comes to the sequencing of particular topics, particularly during the earlier stages. With the introduction of various electives, typically later on in such programs, there tends to be more flexibility. In the business school of the future, however, entirely the opposite approach would be taken to ensure maximum flexibility as to when a particular subject might be taken by a participant. Thus, the sequencing of topics would be up to each individual.

At least two factors might have made this change possible:

- First, a typical participant will generally have little problem in deciding which sequence of topics to take, given their considerable business experience. This is therefore typically a straightforward decision. The participant will be motivated to learn what they need to know beforehand to benefit from a given module.
- Second, today's participants generally belong to the so-called Generation Y. They are fully comfortable with the latest technology and consider this to be a natural part of their work reality. Studying

independently, at home, using computer-based materials is both effective and natural for them. A typical participant can thus be expected to work on what they might consider specific knowledge for an upcoming module on their own. In general, so-called distance learning might be more easily adaptable to Generation Y-ers than to the more classical Generation X-ers (Stieger, 2015).

Here, we come to the issue of cohorts. There will be no cohort groups in this model. Some proponents of the more traditional model for studying at a business school might consider this a weakness. But is it? In the typical workshop sessions at the business school of the future, there will be plenty of opportunity for discussion, with both the professor and the participants taking part. The key cutting-edge dilemmas that are being discussed will, of course, receive more in-depth attention from the various students, with their diverse backgrounds. And the rest of the class will benefit from their input. So, learning, in effect, takes place by learning from fellow participants, and not only from interchange with the professor. So, the traditional cohorts are being replaced with what we might label learning communities. This is what modern participants might find valuable, rather than cohorts.

Open Space (Building and Culture)

We have already pointed out that the dominant culture of the business school of the future will be more open. This increase in openness goes hand in hand with the adaptation of a more network-oriented structure. This could manifest itself in several different ways:

- Physical space: open office landscape, with most of the members of the organization sitting together. This brings a strong sense of community, "we, we, we." It might also contribute to a speedier execution of tasks, more face-to-face, rather than via written memos and formal meetings, now in a more horizontally organizational mode, rather than hierarchical. This more open culture is also closely associated with the workshop-driven pedagogical approach that we have outlined. This implies greater focus on listening to each other, communicating with each other, and having respect for each other. This is a "fast" culture, with immediate feedback and dialogue. This culture might thus also support meaningful pragmatic routines, rather than traditional bureaucracy. All of these would be "hallmarks" of the business school of the future.
- Communication: this would not only be fast, as discussed above, but also be virtual.

Unfortunately, many of today's business schools are hindered by a reliance on set routines, for instance, an excessive emphasis on specific infinite learning points, when we know that the outcomes of the cutting-edge workshop discussions might go several ways, or an excessive emphasis on a forced distribution of grades, when we know that the small class sizes associated with workshop-based pedagogy would be at odds with the relatively large class size that would be needed to apply a meaningful normal distribution of grades approach. We also saw how the concept of exams might move from their conventional control focus to one that represents more of an inherent learning activity.

So, a more open culture, as found in effective networks, is what we might ideally strive for. We have already discussed many aspects of this.

Hypotheses and Disruptive Innovations

As we have seen, the business school of the future may be able to benefit from a certain body of understanding, based on insights that the more mature student body might bring, and also regarding how our target group of participants prefer to study. In our case, upwardly mobile young executives may prefer to study part-time, while being able to maintain their full-time jobs, through distance learning at home complemented by intensive workshops at school, and with the necessary flexibility to plan these studies at the participant's own pace. Christensen (in Horn and Staker, 2015, p. xv) calls this approach a focus on hypotheses and, further, considers it key to look for anomalies that might help one to develop an even better understanding of what might lie behind a given hypothesis. For instance, in our case, we made the initial hypothesis that participants might already possess a set of the most basic business skills through previous studies and/or experiences. Unfortunately, it may turn out that at least some of these more basic skills might not have been fully absorbed (an anomaly). Accordingly, a preparatory workshop might have to be introduced. Our initial hypothesis, that the participants would already possess a set of basic business skills, might therefore have to be modified!

Christensen labels such hypotheses, which are now relatively well understood, "paradigms." And with fundamental shift in one's base of understanding, i.e., in one's hypotheses, then we may have a "paradigm shift." Such shifts more often seem to take place when new actors with different disciplinary backgrounds become involved. Consider the paradigm for an "ideal" academic institution set out by von Humboldt as far back as in 1809, for instance – disciplinary, axiomatic, research-based! It is only recently that this paradigm seems to have shifted, toward more blended learning, toward the recognition that teaching and research may be complementary, and perhaps of equal importance.

Christensen (in Horn and Staker, 2015, p. xvi) points out that disruptive innovations take place when there is no longer a trade-off, between, say, research and teaching, but when there is an opportunity to strengthen one dimension without necessarily having to diminish the other. Disruptive innovations thus take place when there is no need for such a trade-off.

But, as we have previously discussed, such disruptive innovations might more typically come about through a series of somewhat smaller, related innovations which, when taken together, might become disruptive. For instance, the emerging model of the business school of the future, with little to no trade-off between research and teaching, has come about via the cumulative effect of many relatively small innovations, including effective distance learning; workshops focusing on discussion of cutting-edge dilemmas; an improved pedagogy, including new classroom layouts; part-time professors-cum-world disciplinary experts, etc. Taken together, this adds up to what in effect might equal a disruptive innovation, where better research and better teaching go hand in hand, i.e., with little to no trade-off!

In a recent example of a disruptive innovation in business education, a promising joint venture is now in place, between the London-based world-renowned newspaper and publishing organization, Financial Times (FT) (which, incidentally, is now part of the Tokyo-based publishing group Nikkei), and the Madrid-based business university Instituto de Empresa (IE), with the FT providing cutting-edge inputs on content and IE delivering on the pedagogical side. The target group is primarily companies, i.e., executive education. This 50/50 joint venture is located in London, and already has a staff of twenty-five. The results so far are impressive!

Conclusion

The challenge of delivering both cutting-edge content and state-of-the-art pedagogy is certainly not insignificant. Professorial staff may find it hard to stay entirely on course when it comes to covering the basics as well as more recent developments. While many of today's theories might, of course, remain valid for a long period of time, some perhaps virtually forever, there is another side to the challenge of providing relevance content, namely that of being able to deliver on recent global developments, in business as well as when it comes to more macrodimensional issues. When it comes to pedagogy, we have also seen that many professors are rather conservative. For instance, many may still find it more comfortable to lecture in a "one-way mode" to a relatively passive group of students, rather than to be part of a two-way interactive discussion. Many professors may, as Argyris (1978) would say, prefer single-loop learning, rather than double-loop learning.

5   Research, Marketing, and Managing Resources

> Change is the law of life. Those who look only to the past or present are certain to miss the future.
>
> John F. Kennedy

> Research is the engine that drives (the school). It keeps faculty at the forefront of practice and therefore sustains (the school's) mission.
>
> Dr. Johan McArthur, Former Dean of Harvard Business School

We have seen that the business school of the future is likely to differ from today's top-ranking business schools. It will probably have few full-time faculty, drawing instead on a network of faculty specialists worldwide; a different curriculum with more workshops focusing are cutting-edge dilemmas; external independent prestudies, largely made feasible through the advent of modern computer technology; a diverse group of students, all with different work experiences; smaller classrooms featuring workshops with a maximum of, say, thirty-five students, sitting around round tables with seven at each (each table is a group); and a new role for the professor – listening, synthesizing, acting as a two-way communicator rather than the traditional professional lecturer.

These are merely some of the changes we foresee for the business school of the future. But where does research fit into this new archetype of an academic institution? How will cutting-edge insights be developed and disseminated? Are we running the risk of under-focusing on fundamental research in this new world? At this point, let us pause and underscore the belief that live research must always be part of academic value creation in business schools – clearly, this also applies to the business school of the future. We will argue this case in the following pages. But we will see that the way we do research, and the way research is organized is likely to change.

From the traditional power of a business school's "brand" and reputation to now the individual professor's "brand" and reputation.

There are a number of world-leading universities, for example, Harvard or Yale in the US, or Oxford and Cambridge in the UK. These top universities are often labeled research universities (Weber, 2019).[1]

---

[1] There is even a European League of Research Universities, located in Strasbourg.

This signifies that these institutions place a heavy focus on research and the pursuance of new knowledge. The reputation of these leading institutions is, in fact, largely built on the quality and quantity of their research output. And this, in turn, attracts world-class faculty. The quality of the teaching thus also becomes strong. The best students also go to these institutions. It is a virtuous circle!

The best professors typically attempt to stay at such universities for long periods of time, perhaps even for their entire careers! The so-called tenure process grants them job security, and lifetime employment, at one or several institutions, is the norm. This pattern is essentially the same for most modern business schools. Research excellence is essentially the main driver of reputation.

It is interesting to note that this trend of basing institutional reputation on accumulated research outputs was not always the dominant way. In his epic History of European Universities, Rüegg (2004) points out that, before the so-called creation of the modern university by von Humboldt in 1809, it was essentially the individual professor who would hold a reputation as a result of their scholarly works. These professors tended to move from one university to another, spending a few semesters at each place. It was thus the employability of the individual professor that determined their success. Did they produce relevant research, and were they able to teach this, and provide intellectual inspiration to students and colleagues at large? Being able to market themselves and their work was thus also important. Publications, reputation, and networking were key! Today, we might label this a virtual work reality!

Paradoxically, we see the reemergence of much of this kind of behavior today. In many types of businesses, networked organizations are beginning to emerge, typically with relatively few employees, and with those employees typically making several lateral career moves, rather than staying with one employer for their entire working career. This is the network society, with boundaryless careers and employability security only for those who continue to develop themselves. Authors such as Arthur (1994), Castells (1996), Rousseau (2015), Kanter (1995), and Kellan (2012) have amply analyzed this shift in the way in which most organizations now function.

This is the case for business schools too. We have already seen how professors now tend to be employed on a part-time basis and for relatively short periods. But how can they maintain their employability under these types of working conditions. To maintain a satisfactory level of relevant research might now become increasingly difficult. Will these changes result in faculty members' continuous development being weakened? We will argue that this is not the case.

But before we continue, it should be pointed out that the so-called tenure process, i.e., an institution grant of lifelong employment for a given faculty member, might itself have had the effect of slowing down some faculty members' continuing research efforts. Paradoxically, this very process might have led to a situation of lower employment security.

Doing Research Today

So, how might worthwhile research be pursued now? The main clue to this can be found as a consequence of the predominant pedagogical model that is now emerging – workshops focusing on the exploration of key dilemmas. There is a strong element of give-and-take for all those participating in this process, both the students with their differing backgrounds and the professor. It is likely that a lot of cutting-edge research themes will emerge from these sessions. There should be plenty of opportunities for a dynamic professor to pursue!

Carrying out relevant research should be far less onerous today. Clearly, the preparation of manuscripts, such as articles, cases, or books, is now much easier, given the advent of the modern laptop computer. Finding facts using powerful computer-based search procedures is also very straightforward, and interaction with fellow academicians on the web is likewise very easy. Strong computational power, such as so-called cloud computing (Marmara, 2017) now in vogue, makes data analysis easy too, with conventional parametric statistical distribution constraints now largely gone. There are also many databases available to the researcher.

Most importantly, today's pedagogical process represents what is in essence a laboratory, which is available to the professor for the incubation of new ideas.

What about interaction with other fellow academicians, which has been a traditional source of idea generation and a valuable sounding board when it comes to the critique of research? The business school of the future, with its network organization, is likely to facilitate more interaction with other researchers, who will tend to be more diverse in nature. Each professor will develop their own network of contacts – fellow academicians, practitioners, students, etc. This diversity within one's network is essential for good research: eclecticism becomes easier, and axiomatic thinking may be on its way out.

To create a strong network, potential members must be able to see the benefits they may accrue from being part of the network. This puts a healthy pressure on individuals to maintain a cutting-edge profile. Being able to effectively market oneself also becomes important. The classic relatively introverted or isolated researcher may no longer find their way (Arthur, 1994; Rousseau, 2015)!

The Library

The library has traditionally been the centerpiece of most research universities and leading business schools. A large, up-to-date library has traditionally been considered a key prerequisite for research. But this is changing. Journals are increasingly being published electronically. Today's cutting-edge research is being published in a fundamentally different way. It is relatively easy for anyone to log in and to get immediate access. And shorter research notes and progress reports are flourishing. The publication process is becoming less traditional and, above all, faster. The traditional print journals took a long time to be published, with drawn-out review processes, and many top journals had long backlogs. Books, too, are now widely available in electronic formats. We are already seeing that books printed on paper may be on their way out. Speed is becoming key!

What will happen to quality control in this new world? What about the review process, for instance? Clearly, there is a risk that this ease of publication might lead to a deterioration of previously high standards. New electronic journals, as well as new publishing houses, might thus perhaps justly be met with a degree of skepticism. However, when it comes to the review process itself, things might not have changed all that much. Clearly, it is easier for reviewers, editors, and researchers to interact today. Revisions can be made quickly, as can modifications in the research reported. This is all to the good. On the other hand, the enormous increase in the number of web-based journals raises the question of whether there will be enough qualified reviewers available, and whether there is actually a willingness to review this volume of material.

We are clearly experiencing significant shifts that are impacting on the context of the library. The traditional library may no longer be needed. Instead, the library budget is increasingly being channeled into database subscriptions as well as electronic subscriptions of periodicals. The library is thus increasingly becoming paperless. This change has, of course, already been made in many libraries, and many others are embarking on such changes.

Training New Researchers

Traditionally, new faculty members get trained through doctoral programs. Most of these will take doctoral candidates through a series of specialized courses, to bring the students up to speed with the state-of-the-art when it comes to relevant axiomatic theory for a given field, as well as a thorough grounding in research methodology. The candidate then typically designs a research project, which will build on or extend a body of existing knowledge. This research has to be original and to be carried out independently.

While this way of training new academicians seems to have served the needs of conventional academic institutions rather well, it does not prepare candidates all that well for creating value in the business school of the future. Little preparation is typically offered for getting the candidate up to speed with teaching. This may be a particularly serious shortcoming today, with the need for effective professors cum facilitators in discussion group settings. Here, the requirement in an effective teacher would, above all, be to be able to stimulate debate around key cutting-edge dilemmas, to listen, and to synthesize. Also, as part of the preparation for these sessions, the teacher would be required to put together relevant prereadings and test questions. Finally, the effective teacher must be able to effectively assess the extent to which each student has actually learned the subject matter, not only at what might be considered a minimum level but also at levels of excellence beyond this.

An equally serious limiting factor would be the nature of the research itself. The fact that this typically would be carried out by a candidate as an individual, and not as a member of a research team, as well as the fact that research topics tend to be axiomatic rather than cross-disciplinary, would not normally contribute a great deal to the new faculty candidate's understanding of cutting-edge topics, which benefit from being examined from several angles, and where no axiomatically correct answers tend to exist.

There is one recent and encouraging development when it comes to doctoral level training, namely for practitioners to be allowed to nominate problems from actual business practice as thesis topics, typically problems with which the candidate might be personally involved. Doctorates of this type might be called a DBA (Doctor of Business Administration), while the more conventional doctorate is typically called a PhD (Doctor of Philosophy). It should, however, be noted that leading business schools, such as Harvard Business School, grant the DBA degree for more classical doctoral training – a confusing pattern when it comes to such labels.

Faculty Career Development

Young faculty members are traditionally recruited to business schools partly on the basis of a series of job interviews and partly on the basis of the prestige of the institution which awarded their doctorate, as well as the reputation of their advisors. The new faculty member is then assigned a few courses to teach which they might expect to keep as "their" courses for a number of years. The bulk of the young faculty member's attention would then be spent on doing additional research, typically as an individual, which would be published in refereed journals. Publishing in so-called A journals tends to carry more weight as a preparation for promotion, and, thus, in the end, is preferred.

Again, it is hard to see how this process might actually stimulate new pedagogy around the discussion of cutting-edge dilemmas. A faculty member, considered as successful according to conventional measures, might, on the contrary, have neither the incentive nor the competence to deal with these practical cutting-edge dilemmas. So, to actually be able to recruit faculty members who are both ahead of the game when it comes to topical insights as well as pedagogically could be very difficult. The resulting shortage of the type of high-quality faculty members that would be needed in the business school of the future is thus a problem.

We suggest that young faculty members should increasingly be encouraged, through an understanding of relevant research (in teams and not necessarily using conventionally published materials), as well as through the development of relevant workshop sessions, to strengthen their employability. To be able to convey this to others is also key, i.e., effective marketing!

Funding

Traditionally, much of the funding for a faculty member's research has tended to come from the institution in which they are employed. This might be in the form of outright research grants, payment for research assistance, lessening of normal teaching load, etc. There would also be grants from sources such as governmental bodies, foundations, and corporations.

With faculty members now increasingly becoming self-employed, and responsible for their own employability, they will, of course, no longer be able to expect academic institutions to finance their research. Rather, the fees charged for the delivery of specific workshops should be high enough to cover a research component. The business school hosting a particular part-time professor when giving a workshop at this academic institution may also provide a specific research grant. The role of independent foundations would perhaps become even more central, assuming this scenario of the development of the business school of the future. Governments too might be expected to contribute. The development of this dynamic, flexible, knowledge network-of-the-future would depend on this.

But there would be typically be limitations too. While much of the research that is going on in academic institutions is not excessively expensive, there are, of course, exceptions. Technical universities, in general, may find that the move toward flexible employability for faculty members might be less prevalent, and that the process of awarding tenure (lifelong employment) will largely prevail. Laboratories and scientific testing instrumentation, for example, can be particularly expensive. We might find that the move toward this academic archetype of the future might be more difficult and typically take much longer to evolve in such institutions.

Marketing

Social media has, of course, revolutionized the marketing dimension for business schools. In the past, a business school would typically be marketed largely based on its reputation, gained over a long period of time. Also, in relatively isolated local/regional markets, regional word-of-mouth and alumni were key! Admittedly, business schools might make use of advertising, and even have brochures. But, in general, it was clear to most prospective students which would be the best (local) business school to attend.

However, there have been a number of changes. We have previously suggested that today's emerging school choices might be more driven by prospective participants or students who already have a job in the private or public sectors. And, as we have seen, there are now numerous ways in which the business school can innovate to make the learning experience more relevant for this emerging target group – pedagogy and curriculum design comes to mind, in particular. We have already discussed the web, and how this has impacted pedagogy and culture, but is the web likely to have a strong impact on a business school's marketing too? With a clear participant/student target group in mind, with innovations in place that are relevant for this target group, and with web-based communication of these changes to the market, we might expect to see the number of new students increase, even though the tuition fees might be high! The steps in the innovation process are highlighted in Figure 5.1.

Marketing or communication via the web does typically imply a two-way process: not only sending messages to the individual targets, but also receiving feedback (questions, comments, suggestions, etc.) from them. It therefore also follows that the business school will need to have staff members capable of handling such feedback and requests – and well briefed members of a school's organization should be able do this. We

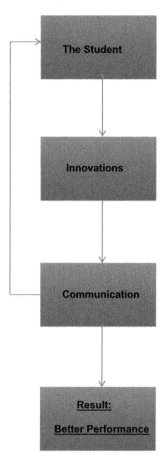

Figure 5.1 The innovation process. (From Lorange and Rembiszewski 2014).

are seeing the emergence of a new more sophisticated breed of marketers within the staffing team of the business school of the future!

Marketing may also be enhanced by using the services of independent firms which carry out so-called study program search activities for large groups of schools. Keystone A/S is perhaps the most prominent of these. A student may use their database to search for particular study programs, and thus be able to identify preferred business schools. Prospective students can also indicate whether they want more data about and obtain specific contacts within particular schools.

We have already briefly discussed accreditation agencies, such as EFMD (Brussels), with its accreditation programs EQUIS and EPAS, AACSB (Florida), and AMBA (London). There is no doubt that these types of accreditation bring significant marketing benefits – they can "signal" quality to the potential participant or student. These accreditation agencies place value on the efforts of those schools who pursue relevance through innovation, rather than being "stuck" with what might have worked in the past. Participants or students who are active on the web will, hence, be well placed to pick up on key innovations, and will typically not be too concerned with what may have been good practices of the past.

Have brochures and advertising now lost their value? Not at all! Brochures and advertising will continue to be important, but rather to raise general awareness and to provide specific information about the potential choice of studies and institution. These types of marketing materials might, above all, be focused on how a business school positions itself in relation to particular values, such as which types of innovation it is implementing. The typical limitations of such brochures and/or advertisements are that the "messages" given are often rather general. Most schools will want to stress that they are highly international, for instance, and also, perhaps, that they are "cutting edge." For many prospective students, this may be too vague. A web page would, on the other hand, be focused on more specific features of programs at a particular institution.

Role of the Dean or President in Marketing

One key implication of the new reality in today's business school – indeed, it is a condition for the effective functioning of an academic institution – is that the person at the top, the president/CEO, must be a "driver" of any attempts to promote the school to potential students and faculty.

Clearly, there is strong potential for web-based marketing to be driven from the top. The leaders of the business school of the future would have to be comfortable as, in essence, "interactive marketers"! In this context, to become an effective senior business school leader, a number of issues seem key:

• Be consistent when it comes to implementing all aspects of adminis-
trative processes, so that they all reinforce the basic mission of the school. If not absolutely essential to the operation of the school, a routine should be dropped! Regrettably, many schools are stuck with outdated procedures that can relay unintentional messages to the organization as well as to prospective students.

- Be consistent when it comes to dealing with colleagues, ensuring that they are focused on teaching and research, and not allowed to be distracted by other tasks. A faculty member should be made aware of this focus and be encouraged to adhere to the school's mission to "always make good even better." This has several implications both for effective marketing and for the general management of the school. The CEO/president should be guided by what is best for the school, and not take decisions to gain popularity with specific faculty members/ group, or even to curry favor. They should not necessarily agree with the last person to call into the boss's office. It is also important not to be intimidated in face-to-face dialogue with specific faculty members. Be consistent, open-minded, listen attentively, but do not necessarily agree with someone outside the overall context of the school's mission. It is key to attempt to establish a sense of predictability regarding what others might expect. In the end, the main objective is to follow a course that will lead to the "best" outcomes.
- Act in a way that instills a sense of urgency and speed. This would typically be required to counterbalance bureaucracy and slowness. Members of one's organization might well welcome the avoidance of procrastination when it comes to the resolution of any problems. Of course, spending too little time weighing the pros and cons is clearly undesirable: decisions should be based on reflection, not rushed, but still taken promptly. Being able to let faculty members go is key!
- The leader of the business school of the future must "give" more than they "take." Instilling sense of importance, even excitement, about the mission of the school in faculty members, is vital. And effective web-based marketing, again, depends on this! As we know, web-based marketing opens up more direct lines of communication to individuals. A business school's leader would thus be able to communicate directly with individuals. The school's mission is perhaps a particularly appropriate topic for this type of communication, and offers an opportunity for the leader to build up a their profile as someone who "gives" more than they "take"!

These four issues represent not only sound managerial practice, but they are also central for effective marketing, both when it comes to the earlier online marketing stage and when it comes to student interviews on campus later on.

One big issue for a leader of the business school of the future might be to identify those people likely to resist the strategic direction that has been taken. It would be useful to be able to isolate such resistors. However, this might be difficult, in that such resistors could be acting as spokespersons for larger groups, often with a considerable amount of power. Healthy debate based on different points of view is, of course, to be desired. And so is a faculty member's right to disagree! But there is typically a fine, but clear line between such debates and attempts to slow things down, or, in some cases, even to sabotage the strategic plan. At the end of the day, a decision has to be taken. This is then what should serve as the guide for all. The time for debate and discussions would then be over. Regrettably, this sense of maturity is often lacking in many academic organizations. It would be a key task for a business school leader to develop such an efficient organizational culture. This, however, would require consistent inputs from the top, typically over long periods of time. Good decision-making is thus top down and bottom up! Web-based marketing, therefore can only be meaningful in such a balanced context. Effective marketing can only take place if an organization is unified!

Role of the Dean or President in Leadership

We can illustrate this with an example taken from another type of professional organization, a modern hospital. The head of a small regional hospital in Hønefoss, Norway, sees his key role as one of facilitator, to ensure that his team(s) of medical doctors are able to spend the majority of their time with their patients, and not have their energies depleted by government-imposed bureaucracy or/and other bureaucratic routines. The results of his approach seem convincing – his doctors are able to spend 90 percent of their time with patients versus less than 50 percent for doctors on average in Norway. There is a clear analogy here with one of the main responsibilities of the president/dean/CEO of the business school of the future, namely to push for innovations that allow their key resource, faculty members, to spend the bulk of their energies on teaching and research. In short, faculty members are at their best when teaching and researching, not spending their time in endless meetings and/or being "forced" to work on, in essence, rather peripheral routines (Berg, 2015).

Innovations in Marketing

Let us now return to the issue of innovations in marketing, which we have already seen as being critical as part of web-based marketing. Innovations are, of course, key – without meaningful innovation it is difficult for a business school to pursue quality, or even improve on this. And marketing would surely suffer! Christensen (1997) has offered a useful typology regarding innovations:
• Those necessary to maintain one's position – let us label them "maintenance-driven innovations." These types of innovations are typically

relatively small and can be expected to occur more or less routinely in any business school with the ambition to remain sustainable. We will not discuss this type of innovation further here – the fact that these need to take place is more or less obvious.

- "Performance-enhancing innovations," to "make good even better," so that the business school might make progress when it comes to delivering on its value-creating activities. Examples of this might be more effective marketing routines to attract stronger students, improvements to the curriculum, better routines for supporting faculty, novel pedagogical approaches, etc. These types of innovations are typically key for effective marketing! They would typically require a considerable amount of effort on behalf of the senior leadership. Their impact can often be great. They are typically pulled off with some degree of speed, and are usually based on what the organization is already doing, i.e., they are incremental.
- "Disruptive innovations." These are typically truly significant "game changers," i.e., they imply entirely different ways of carrying out specific tasks or combinations of these. There are several good examples when it comes to disruptive innovations relative to marketing. For instance, the company Facebook now provides quite detailed data on consumer profiles, allowing for much more targeted marketing, in contrast to, say, more general advertising campaigns. Or, through analysis of so-called big data through cloud computing, one might be able to come up with new "routes to markets," guiding one's marketing and distribution. These are indeed disruptive innovations in marketing! Such disruptive innovations would not be incremental in nature. They tend to be developed by members of the organization who are typically not heavily involved in these tasks at the given point in time. Often, the time horizon is long. The boss might often be responsible for enhancing such game-changing disruptions: they should, at least, not resist them!

In a previous study (Lorange and Rembiszewski, 2014), we found that disruptive innovations of this type are typically rare, or even nonexistent! Rather, we found that visionary leaders might be central in orchestrating a series of performance-enhancing innovations in such a way that, when taken together, they would "add up to" what in effect would be a disruptive innovation. This is what we have experienced at the Lorange Institute, too: we certainly introduced many performance-enhancing innovations. However, I also clearly had a driving vision in the role of president, which led to a combinatory effect produced by several of these relatively smaller innovations, adding up to what in fact might be considered disruptive innovation, namely the overall new business model of the Lorange Institute of Business. Bringing this kind of message into one's marketing is key!

To give an example of the kind of innovations that may form the the centerpiece of a modern business school's marketing efforts, we will look at some of changes introduced at the Lorange Institute. These performance-enhancing innovations, which are all centrally featured in the Lorange Institute's marketing, are as follows:

- A relatively stable network of top part-time professors
- A workshop-driven curriculum structure
- Pedagogy based on discussing key dilemmas, in small classes and in "flat" classrooms
- Extensive outsourcing – so as to be able to more easily/quickly adapt, as well as to ensure top quality
- Web-based studies (of the more basic materials)

In conclusion, marketing would now play a different and a much more central role in the business school of the future, mainly due to the emergence of the web, and the many implications of this.

Managing Resources

It is important to acknowledge that achieving good enough results relatively quickly is generally better than aiming for perfection, which might take a significantly longer time and require much more effort. One rule of thumb suggests that "with 50% of effort one might achieve 90% results, while the next 50% of effort would be needed to achieve the remaining 10%." Therefore, good enough results might be achieved with only a little less effort than it would take to go for perfection. Hence, a key leadership issue in most leading business schools is to try to determine what might be considered "good enough." One should then go for this, and as quickly as possible!

It goes without saying that the energy of the business school's professors and staff is a crucial resource, and it must not be squandered. Here are a few examples of ways in which this might be managed:

- Maintain some stability in the curriculum of each workshop, including its assigned reading materials, assignment questions, exams, etc., to allow a professor to save some time/energy on the preparation needed. This shouldn't, of course, be taken too far, in that enough time must always be spent to ensure that a particular workshop remains cutting edge. It is important to avoid any laziness on the part of faculty members that might prevent the maintenance of a cutting edge. In such instances, another part-time faculty member might be brought in, to ensure that the latest thinking is introduced, based on the latter's most recent research. This balanced, but innovation-driven approach must come across in one's marketing!

- Meetings. While it is important to maintain an open atmosphere in modern networked organizations – for example, the work stations of senior management might be located in the lobby – it is equally critical that meetings are kept under control. They should be limited to essential meetings only, and with strict time limits. Meetings whose purpose might be rather difficult to assess might be had over one's lunch break!
- Benefit from the "trading table" style of having all key people together around one large table. This is something we do at the Lorange Institute, where this table is located in the lobby. Key issues can usually be easily settled face-to-face, i.e., faster, with less formality, and without using up unnecessary energy.

This might be a good point to say something more about the information flow issue. Writing as early as February 1967, Herbert Simon saw the functioning of the modern business school, as well as the design of its organization, as essentially a series of trade-offs when it comes to generating various patterns of information (Simon, 1967). For instance, what type of information would be needed to do good research as opposed to the type of information required to provide insights into good practice, i.e., the creation of new scientific knowledge versus what might be needed to advance a practical profession? Although he was writing this at a time which was too early to fully comprehend how many such trade-offs might be effectively handled without sacrificing one for another, many of his arguments are equally valid today, even though the concept of blended learning had not yet been developed.

Simon's delineation of knowledge requirements for research (and, I would add, cutting-edge teaching) also seem particularly critical, namely, on the one hand, access to the knowledge base of business, including employing faculty with business experience, incorporating consulting and field resources and, on the other hand, access to the knowledge base of science. Simon seems to see these two sources of knowledge as being essentially opposite to each other, involving a trade-off. As we have agreed, however, today they might be considered together, i.e., complementary. It would be difficult to conduct meaningful workshops based on cutting-edge dilemmas without both the bodies of knowledge of science and practice! We might even say that this dual knowledge might be a "requirement" for good research!

Simon recognized that cross-disciplinarity would be key. Combining disciplines from science and the professional world, say from more practical professional schools, may be as hard as mixing oil and water, but if this integration of science and practice is not managed, the management of a business school seems particularly difficult to achieve. It seems critical to manage information flows in such a way so as to achieve this, and cross-disciplinarity will not last, unless managerial energy is being put into maintaining it. We would reiterate that getting these types of values across in one's marketing could be key (being cognizant of what most prospective students are likely to see as essential) rather than the all-too common marketing as usual!

Conclusion

This chapter has focused on marketing, including those marketing messages which relate to a school's managerial approaches and organizational values, which prospective students typically find of central value and which should be part of a school's core marketing message. However, our concept of what might be considered effective marketing in the business school of the future differs consistently from that typically labeled as marketing in many more conventional business schools. The emergence of web-based marketing, taking over from the more traditional brochures, advertisements, and networking, allows for a two-way, more interactive marketing approach. The CEO/president/dean will increasingly become a key player in this, and a top-down, participative style will become more critical than ever. It is particularly important for a school's leadership to stimulate innovation, especially when it comes to effective marketing. A modern business school might perhaps find key innovations its most effective marketing instrument!

To be an effective leader of an academic institution, such as a modern business school, the dean/president needs to be an effective facilitator, a stimulator of their organization and of its members. The leader must thus be comfortable with a "we, we, we" style, rather than the typical highly profiled "me, me, me" style found in many top leaders. Above all, leaders must be comfortable seeing themselves as fundamentally committed to marketing what might be a wide array of institutional strengths, without taking the credit in person.

6   Innovations and a Change Culture

We have already discussed the key significance of innovations, above all in terms of being able to come up with a viable business model for "the business school of the future." We have also seen how critical such innovations can be when it comes to being able to launch effective web-based marketing. We also know that the president, dean, or CEO plays a key role when it comes to driving innovation. The difference between the more typical relatively small innovations and more fundamental disruptive innovations is a particularly key distinction here. This chapter considers the role of innovations in culture change and ways of making "good even better."

Culture Change

A good example of the importance of initiating cultural changes is that of Microsoft Inc. When its present CEO, Satya Nadella, took over in 2014, the company had stagnating sales growth and a flattening out of profitability. He set out to change this culture, which perhaps might be characterized by phrases such as "good enough," "we know best," "past success shall also take us into a good future," and so on. The new cultural mantra emphasized more growth, not being trapped in past successes (Windows technology), and embracing emerging technologies, such as cloud computing (Nadella had previously headed up Microsoft's cloud computing division). Perhaps the most important cultural traits of all were even closer contact with customers, as well as more open-mindedness (Wingfield, 2014; Nadella, 2017).

Many of these challenges are relevant to business schools too. It seems particularly critical to continue to evolve one's organizational culture, particularly in predominantly knowledge-based settings, such as a typical business school, where the culture can easily become stale. In this sense, both types of knowledge-based organizations, whether we are talking about Microsoft or a business school, face essentially similar cultural challenges. And, the person at the top, whether it is Mr. Nadella at Microsoft or a dean or president of a business school, would be key in driving cultural change (Weightman, 2010; Ashton and Hudson, 1998).

As we saw in Chapter 5, most innovations are relatively small, and represent incremental improvements to what is already working. Furthermore, they take place at a relatively fast pace, relatively frequently, and the key drivers of such innovations are on the front line, i.e., the group of executives closest to the customer, and thus presumably with best understanding of the types of innovations that customers would welcome (Lorange and Rembiszewski, 2014; see Figure 5.1). In a business school setting, faculty members and staff members who work closely with customers are the ones instigating these smaller innovations. As we have seen, a number of relatively small innovations might be combined into larger innovations, i.e., into what Christensen (1997) calls "disruptive." Typically, an overarching vision from the senior leadership of the organization is required to make this happen. It is therefore key that top management have such a vision in order for several relatively small, straightforward innovations to be combined into one relatively large, disruptor, i.e., into a game changer!

It is thus a combination of bottom-up and top-down forces that allow such disruptive innovations to take place. The many smaller innovations – we labeled these "performance-enhancing innovations" in Chapter 5 – typically come about as a result of efforts by line executives to give their customers an even better service, i.e., from the bottom up. Putting these innovations into a larger pattern in effect creates a disruptive innovation, and this is typically largely a top-down activity. Maintaining a realistic top-down/bottom-up balance would be a key task of the person at the top. They must thus have a strong vision. In many cases, unfortunately, the top-down element is too weak or even entirely lacking! The dean, president, or CEO would, in essence then, be a problem solver bogged down in details, rather than a visionary.

It thus seems key for top management to have a relatively clear view regarding "the end point." Let us illustrate this with an example from shipping. This kind of top-down vision is evident in the case of Gerry Wang, president and CEO of Seaspan, the world's largest independent owner of container ships. He gradually came to believe that there would be a strong demand for a class of significantly more fuel-efficient ships. His ongoing interaction with his major clients, several of whom were the world-leading container lines, led him to this. He simply wished to be in a better position to offer more fuel-efficient container ships to his key customers. So, his top-down vision regarding the need for a game-changing innovation came about largely through customer interaction

(Lorange, 2020). The technical team at Seaspan, led by Peter Curtis, Chief Technology Officer and COO, then came up with a series of relatively straightforward innovations, "making good even better," to several technical features of a large container ship: improved aqua dynamics, better use of materials science to reduce weight, more efficient main propulsion, lighter/more efficient auxiliaries, new coating with less underwater friction, more efficient propeller and rudder, and so on. The result was the SAVER generation of new container ships, with 30 percent less fuel consumption at twenty-one knots speed than a conventional container ship, within the 10,000 TEU capacity group. A perhaps unintended effect of this innovation, a combination of "in the small" and "in the large," bottom up and top down, was that the economic lifetime of this type of shipping asset would become significantly shorter than its technological lifetime. A modern large container ship might now be economically competitive for, say, around ten years. However, the technologically determined lifetime would typically be much longer, say, around twenty-five years. This older generation of ships would still be perfectly able to plow the oceans, even though their rather high fuel consumption would make them economically obsolete.

Culture Change and Economic Obsolescence

The business school of the future is not exempt from the accelerated physical obsolescence that seems to come about as a result of innovations, analogous to what we saw in container shipping. We will consider the effect of this in four specific areas: the delineation of the campus, the effect on IT, the reconfiguration of library facilities, and the evolution of one's website. So, let us start with the delineation of the campus!

We have seen how the business school of the future might aim to adopt new pedagogy intended to focus on discussions of key dilemmas, with workshop sessions conducted in relatively smaller classes. As we saw, this might also lead to a call for different types of classrooms from those typically found, namely, so-called flat rooms, where relatively few students or participants would be seated around circular tables, so that they might more easily interact. Thus, the traditional auditoriums, horse-shoe shaped and tiered, with the participants seated in larger spaces, would now become obsolete. Many of these auditoriums might, of course, still be in good shape, but they are perhaps no longer optimal, given the emergence of the novel pedagogy.

A similar effect can be observed when it comes to a school's ICT. We have already touched on this. With the new workshop format, built around interactive discussions of key dilemmas in class over relatively short, concentrated periods of time, the participant would need easy access to preparatory readings and background materials. New software would thus be needed to meet these emerging demands. At the Lorange Institute, we have invested in the software package "Moodle" to meet this emerging requirement – another consequence of innovations! Much of the "old" software, on the other hand, has become prematurely obsolete.

Let us now turn to the library, which has traditionally been a key part of the typical business school. Participants would usually go to the library to borrow books, look up facts that they might need, or merely to find a quiet place to study. Today, however, the classic library has more or less gone. Participants now have access to central databases and can quickly download what they might be looking for. Facts can easily be found on Google or elsewhere. And most studying takes place at home. Thus, the classic library may no longer be needed. At the Lorange Institute, our library collection of books is in stored in crates in the basement! Less floor space is needed, as a result.

Let us finally consider the website. As noted, a website is a now major vehicle for marketing and communication in most business schools. Prospective clients, corporate as well as individual participants, examine a business school's website to get a more complete "feel" for its latest innovations. Given the accelerated pace of innovations, relating perhaps to curriculum, pedagogy, staffing, etc., a school's website will need to be updated on a more frequent basis. The website's design would, in fact, have to incorporate this requirement for rapid updates, to "capture" emerging innovations. The "old" website would soon become economically obsolete!

The general effect of the innovation process would be that economic obsolescence would now typically set in much earlier than technological obsolescence in many key areas. This will, of course, have significant implications for investment levels and resource needs. Modern institutions are much more capital intensive, due to the fact that major investments now have a much shorter economic lifetime! This is not only the case for business schools but can be seen in many other areas too. Shipping banks, for instance, which finance modern container ships now have to take into account a significantly shorter economic lifetime for financing such projects. This might be further accentuated by the much lower residual value of the older ship asset, since new generation of ships which are economically more efficient are now likely to be introduced in their place. This would largely result from the innovation process.

In the business school of the future, a similar effect would take place, with significantly higher levels of funding being required to finance these new investments. Public spending would typically also have to increase. For those business schools which are privately owned, their owners would have to be prepared to come up with additional funding. There is also likely to be an increase in tuition and other charged fees for all business schools as a result of these new investments, all stemming from the innovation process. As previously discussed, there might be "savings" from outsourcing, but these could easily be offset by the additional capital spending now required due to innovations.

Top-Down versus Bottom-Up Change

We have previously touched upon the "top-down" and "bottom-up" interactive leadership exchange that will need to take place in the best academic organizations, as typified by the leading, future-oriented business schools. We will look at this in more detail here.

Some suggestions for change will come from a business school's staff, both professional and administrative. Faculty may provide inputs based on their research, as well as their classroom experiences. Research-based inputs would provide clues regarding potential new directions to take, particularly when it comes to a business school's curriculum. Faculty may also have received inputs from participants as well as from corporate clients. Some suggestions may thus come from their experience in the classroom, and some might come from dialogue with clients. A school's advisory council might also provide inputs. We will denote all of these as "bottom up," in line with what has been discussed previously.

Many of these bottom-up inputs are formalized through faculty meetings. These may be virtual, such as those held at institutions such as the Lorange Institute, whose part-time faculty members are, of course, located in many places around the world. It is thus typically easier, simpler, and less expensive to bring them together in virtual faculty meetings. A key purpose of such meetings is to "capture" relevant bottom-up inputs from the faculty.

The administrative staff may also have potentially relevant inputs to contribute. Others may come from questionnaires completed by corporate clients and/or participants. Others may come from interaction with prospective customers, corporations, and participants. The typical open physical structure of the modern business school may also contribute to the more effective generation of valuable bottom-up inputs, from students/participants and others.

In contrast, we have the top-down dimension. The most critical top-down dimension is a clear vision by the leader, including such matters as the main direction in which the business school is headed; the broad areas of research that are being pursued; and the key target student/participant groups. It seems particularly important for the top leader to leave room for renewal: their vision should be a key driver for the types of innovations that are being pursued.

In Chapter 5, we discussed the importance of complementarity between solid top-down leadership and strong bottom-up contributions, particularly when it comes to marketing, when it comes to innovations: bottom-up determination tends to lead to many relatively smaller innovations, so that "good can become even better," and top-down vision is essential for putting it all together. In more general terms, the two sides would influence each other – not only through interaction, but also through iterations – an evolutionary pattern of change might thus emerge!

Clearly, there must be a balance between the top-down and the bottom-up forces, to ensure a meaningful outcome. Too strong an influence from the bottom up might easily lead to a continuation of the status quo. Faculty would then be motivated to carry on more or less as before. Administrative staff could quite easily continue with their set routines. In short, such business schools might soon become rather stagnant and conservative. There would typically be a lot of innovations taking place, perhaps leading to a false sense of comfort for faculty and staff. The problem is that these innovations would not add up to something more fundamental. This picture is unfortunately not atypical.

Another potential issue is that the faculty in many business schools is empowered to elect its leaders. This may also lead to a status quo situation. In addition, the leader's term in office may be too short to allow for meaningful changes to take place. And the election process may in itself lead to the choice of a leader who would be unlikely to spearhead changes, but who would be inclined to "leave the faculty alone."

In contrast, an overly strong and dominant top-down force might be equally dysfunctional. In this case, the leader might end up operating in isolation, without being able to ensure the necessary support of faculty and staff. While they might indeed have visionary ideas, these could largely end up as good ideas only. In this situation, there would be a lack of a balanced approach.

What other factors might typically disturb a productive balance within a school? A common situation that arises is that, for various reasons, the top-down side stops functioning as planned. This might, for instance, have to do with the incompetence of the leader, a lack of prestige, poor decision-making, an ineffective attitude, a dysfunctional decision-making style, etc. The result might be a vacuum at the top, which often leads to an overly strong bottom-up reaction. Regrettably, it can take a very long time to reestablish a balance. A frequent result is that periods of imbalance typically also lead to periods of conservativeness, with relatively little renewal and innovation.

Let us briefly look at two other potential sources of bias, both of which might have dysfunctional effects on a business school: potential biases resulting from the idiosyncrasies of the leader, impacting the top-down dimension in particular, and disciplinary biases from groups within the faculty, impacting the bottom-up dimension above all.

We have seen that the business school of the future might typically take the form of a networked organization. And we know that the leader in a network can have a particularly strong impact on the overall functioning of the network. So, what happens if this leader has particular biases? For example, they might favor certain faculty, give preference to particular types of business, companies, or even countries, or have a particular disciplinary bias. We know that past experiences shape the characteristics of a person's decision-making. Hence, the leader's past experiences could have an impact on their choice of faculty members, curriculum delineation, etc. Thus, the business school of the future might only be the business school of the future when seen from the leader's perspective! Needless to say, the more diverse experience that a leader has, the more likely it is that biases will be ameliorated.

Each academic discipline is typically built up around a specific set of axioms that, when taken together, define the discipline. Examples might be economics, finance, or organizational behavior. To complicate matters, a discipline is typically an agglomeration of various subdisciplines, each built up around their own axioms. Economics is typically split into macroeconomics and microeconomics, finance into corporate finance and capital markets, organizational behavior into organizational design and behavioral science, etc. A typical fallacy for many faculty members within a particular discipline is to consider the axioms on which their discipline is founded as all-important, while axioms that fall outside this are often seen as less key, or even irrelevant. It follows that strong biases might develop here, embedded in such disciplinary preferences. Of course, there are advantages to a discipline focus. Learning and research within a particular discipline is typically easier than cross-disciplinary research and learning. A strong discipline-based momentum might thus be desirable, particularly in some fields, and faculty members are likely to be attracted to such groupings. A business school's momentum might then be enhanced in this way. The other side of the coin is that this represents specific disciplinary biases that one has to live with, which, in turn, might lead to less tolerance for a broader diversity of thinking.

Ethics

There are, of course, several potential ethical dilemmas associated with the emergence of what might be the typical business school of the future. Let us briefly touch upon three here:

- Potential for cheating by participants. With exams increasingly taken online, with greater flexibility for participants who can take courses from different institutions (MOOCs), and so on, there may be an increased possibility that cheating will take place. Might others take the test on their behalf? Might some participants claim courses are not finished? An overriding issue here might be the one of claiming credit. Without having finished a course, credits would generally not be granted. Procedures to address these issues are, however, well on their way!
- Research quality. With research increasingly becoming the responsibility of individual academics, how will quality control, above all when it comes to the choice of methodology, analytical approaches, data sources/sample sizes, etc., be ensured? Traditionally, these factors have been handled by business schools, through research seminars, paper discussions, departmental reviews, etc. But now, with professors increasingly becoming independent, no longer faculty members in any given business school, the temptation to take shortcuts which might compromise the quality of research could become a problem.
- Plagiarism. Similar arguments might be raised when it comes to publishing (of articles, research based or practitioner oriented), books (including textbooks), cases, and perhaps also in teaching (by not properly acknowledging colleagues who might have developed specific elements of teaching materials).

Regrettably, the evolution to a more open-minded, network-based structure in business schools of the future could lead to the emergence of potentially dysfunctional phenomena, such as those described. Perhaps, therefore, an even more explicit code of ethical conduct might be called for, for professors and students alike.

Making Good Even Better!

Constantly attempting to strive for this seems key. For instance, one example of this in which I happened to be involved began a long time ago, when I was the head of the Lauder Institute, University of Pennsylvania (from 1988 to 1990). One of the issues we faced was to find new ways for students to learn dramatically more within a given time period, so as to obtain both an MBA and an MA (in a language) in two years. New pedagogy, focused on achieving a better command of the foreign language chosen through more active student participation was developed. Later, at BI, where I was the president from 1989 to 1993, this process was continued, with the introduction of shorter, more modularized courses with more of a broad, cross-disciplinary focus. In line with this, the number of academic departments was reduced from nine to three! At IMD (which I headed up from 1993 to 2008), the process continued with a dramatic increase in workshop discussions around key dilemmas, often carried out in so-called flat rooms, which would lend themselves particularly well to face-to-face student interaction. During my next six years at the Lorange Institute of Business, many of these dimensions came together, perhaps in clearer ways, not the least because of the nonexistence of a permanent faculty body, which elsewise might have represented prime resistors to such changes.

Horn and Staker have introduced a particular concept for making good even better, which they have labeled "discovery-decision planning" (Horn and Staker, 2015, p. 268). This consists of the following four steps:

- What is the desired outcome? In our case, this might be, for instance, to come up with a more effective pedagogy.
- What are the key milestones relating to outcomes. In this case, a "false" milestone might be that better pedagogy is introduced while the number of students remains relatively high. Thus, while it might appear that a particular milestone has been reached, this may de facto not be the case!
- There must be a plan, and an intention to test this. How are the actual goals, e.g., a foreign language proficiency or a deeper understanding of a particular business dilemma, being achieved? This might be tested by exams, and the results might also be compared over time.
- How might we implement the change? This might involve smaller classes and more tutors. If not, the alternative might result in a lot of action with little or no result!

So, we can see clear parallels between the discovery-driven planning process proposed by Horn and Staker (2015) and my own "journey," from 1988 until today, to "make good even better"! In both cases, the overall aim is to achieve more tangible improved learning. But, the broader reality is that here too we may be talking about innovation. The approaches taken, both when it comes to the actions I took to make "good even better," together with Horn and Staker's four key steps, seem to have led to significant innovations.

In conclusion, innovations clearly come both from the bottom and from the top of an organization. Maintaining a good balance can lead to particularly key discipline-based innovations. As regards the impact of innovation on assets, while their technologic lifetime might still be accep-table, their economic lifetime may no longer justify continued use. Some types of assets, such as libraries, might disappear altogether. Obsolescence may occur earlier than ever before, with an accelerated rate of innovation leading to faster obsolescence, and to a call for more investment. A lot of capital would definitely be required to fund the business school of the future!

A Change Culture

What we have been proposing implies fundamental change from well-established traditions in many business schools. How might such changes realistically come about? We will see that it will become critical for an effective culture of change to exist at any given business school. And we will propose five key elements for such a change culture in order for it to be effective.

Before discussing each of these topics, however, I should point out that most business schools, and indeed most academic institutions, such as universities, are rather conservative. Effective change may be hard to come by. The five cultural factors that I will suggest have been arrived at not only as a result of what we experienced at the Lorange Institute, but also more generally from observations made and experiences had during my more than twenty years in leadership roles.

First, let us consider the business school's value propositions when it comes to how it might function as an organization. Two aspects of this are particularly critical: first, do the members of a given business school organization work as a team, rather than as a collection of unrelated individuals? Would it be more appropriate to discuss the organization as functioning in a "we, we, we" modus, rather than in a "me, me, me" modus? Does its members work together to achieve joint goals as a team, with subteams being part of this? Or, is it the case that the members of a school's organization work essentially on their own, pursuing their own individual goals. If this were the case, despite various members of such an organization having strong professional qualities and credentials, it is possible that the totality would not represent more than the sum of the individuals, i.e., not a team effect, where the totality is more than the sum of individuals (2+2=5 or more).

Second, it is important that the members of a business school's orga-nization are able to work together in an essentially "nonpolitical" way. Unfortunately, many academic institutions, business schools included, contain plenty of people and factions that work against each other, often with seemingly endless unresolved debates. The result can be devastating when it comes to impacting on performance. Too much energy can be spent on politicking and in endless faculty and committee meetings, which are just a few of the potentially negative effects. To be able to reach "closure" in such meetings about which specific approach might be followed can prove difficult, or even impossible. The culture would thus easily become one of maintaining the status quo, i.e., no change!

Lessening the so-called silo effect, occasionally labeled "kingdoms," can be addressed with relatively fundamental job rotations. Staff members might therefore expect to find themselves responsible for different decisions over time, different functions, and in different countries. Without an explicit policy of rotating assignments one might run the risk not only of kingdoms becoming overly strong, but also of a slowdown of professional development. We have seen this practice being successfully employed in many countries' diplomatic forces, for example. Business schools have a lot to learn here. A strong human resources function, linked to top management, would be key for this.

How would we deal with dysfunctional silo effects in network organizations? Networks would a priori be less stable than the more traditional, hierarchical organization. Thus, the risk of dysfunctional silo developments will be relatively low. Only when networks become too stable might we see the emergence of silos. However, if this occurs, an occasional shift in the composition of a network might be advisable.

Third, let us now once more consider the leader at the top. We have discussed the importance of a balanced set of inputs from the leadership of a business school, i.e., a "top-down" force, to counterbalance the "bottom-up" force that would come from the bulk of the business school's organization. We argued earlier that there should be a proper balance between these two forces. In general, the bottom-up side might be relatively more conservative, more focused on pursuing the status quo, as we have just discussed. Thus, a strong bottom-up orientation typically tends to imply relatively less change.

The top-down dimension, originating with the business school's leader, might be less conservative, however. A strong top-down force might thus be key to change. This relies, of course, on the top leadership, i.e., the dean or the president, being committed to significant change. Their mission may well be to preserve the status quo, and/or they may not have the strength to "push" for significant change. They may simply not have enough organizational "power," or "clout," to do this, or may lack a proactive vision.

How can the dean or president develop their "feel" for the role, to be more effective in initiating change? We will make the following observations:

It is of primary importance that the person at the top has strong credentials, a good education (ideally from (a) leading institution(s)), a strong publications record, a successful academic career so far, etc. Also, as part of their early days in the new job, they might ask each key member of their organization to prepare a list of key changes for the leader to pursue, as well as a number of "nonstarters," i.e., nonimportant factors. This would allow the new leader to more easily come up with their own realistic agenda for change. Above all, this might strengthen their will to lead and resolve to go for changes at the top – "the will to manage," as Marvin Bower might have said (Bower, 1966).

Finally, it is important that the person at the top acts in such a way that they are seen as an integral part of the organization. They might, for instance, make appointments that the majority see as "good" for the institution, and make decisions accordingly, rather than letting decisions be heavily influenced by whomever was in their office last. Faculty reviews might also be critical, sharing the commitment from the top to support individual faculty members in their quest for better research and/or teaching. Time spent on effective marketing, resulting in stronger enrolments, as well as effective fundraising, might also be beneficial at this stage. Above all, the top leader's ability to inspire the rest of the organization is key. They must be willing and able to "give more than they take." High visibility and an action profile are essential!

Fourth, the agenda for change must be relatively clear and realistic. Progress toward achieving specific agenda items should ideally be measurable. In academic jargon, the strategy should not only be clear, but also widely shared. The implementational process should be measurable, and progress on this must be shared. As previously discussed, it is important for a strategy to be widely understood and accepted within a business school's organization (as a result of the inputs from the organization's members requested by the dean or president). In addition, the dean/president will, of course, contribute some hopefully solid inputs to the strategy, not the least based on their previous experiences. And, finally, a board and/or an advisory committee may also come up with valuable inputs. Stakeholders serving on a school's board and/or advisory committee might typically come from business and might thus be able to contribute elements to a school's strategy which may be particularly relevant when seen from business stakeholders' points of view.

Fifth, let us discuss the need for the availability of financial resources. There are five aspects to this, where the availability of sufficient financial resources might be particularly critical. It is, of course, particularly important for the dean or president to be able to allocate discretionary resources for effective change implementation. The first area is to stimulate faculty research. Here, it is vital that funding is channeled to projects that will enhance the business school's strategy. Individual faculty members may have their own research priorities, which might be inconsistent with those of the school. In such cases, research funding from the school might be lower than if there were consistency with the strategy.

The dean or president might, however, prefer to be relatively cautious when it comes to limiting research funding, or even eliminating projects that might not really fit strategically. A faculty member's track record for "delivering" research outputs on time and of good, publishable quality, is probably more important. Research can only lead to meaningful results when a faculty member has the energy, commitment, and competence that is needed. Financial funding is thus probably relatively less critical.

Second, funding pedagogical efforts might also be key. Developing teaching materials, such as cases, might require an input of financial resources. Developing teaching materials for the purposes of blended teaching might also prove expensive and call for research associates to apply unique skills.

This brings us to the third change factor, namely to be able to make investments in one's website and in other social media. This seems to represent a particularly effective way to communicate with external stakeholders, particularly present and prospective customers (students) as well as with alumni. Innovations, especially those stemming from the school's investment in research and in pedagogical development, might be particularly well suited for effective communication via the website.

Fourth, there is often typically a need to invest in a business school's physical facilities. "Flat rooms" might be needed. The bulk of the classic, tiered, horseshoe-shaped auditoria that many business schools have are probably relatively less useful today, with the added focus on "new" pedagogy. While the typical business school of the future might need broadly similar physical space to what we have become accustomed to today, there is probably a need for investments focused on making the transition to flat rooms. Thus, the physical space in most of today's settings might look quite different under these new circumstances.

As a fifth and final point, there would typically be several more straight-forward requirements that faculty members would have to "deliver on," including a strong commitment to a school's fulfillment of its "promise" to its customers. For the participant, this would imply thorough faculty preparation for class sessions and, even more importantly, an ability to "deliver" effectively in class. Mentoring of younger, less experienced faculty by more experienced colleagues might also be important, again to improve the effectiveness of class delivery. This does, of course, assume a strong commitment from both junior faculty members and the more mature members when it comes to allocating time and energy, as well as careful management of each individual's ego (open-mindedness, nondefensiveness, listening). A willingness to do the necessary preparation of exams, grading, giving feedback, etc., would also be key. With the "new" pedagogy, these types of factors might become even more important.

In the end, perhaps the most critical cultural trait of a faculty member is their willingness to be "a good citizen." This implies that they would be willing to spend time and energy on matters that might benefit their school, i.e., a "we, we, we" team effort, for example, meeting prospective customers, working with alumni, engaging in PR, etc., rather than furthering their own interests in a narrow sense.

The Business School of the Future: Is There More to Change?

During a visit to South Africa, I was struck by the vivid contrasts. On the one hand, this country has been blessed with an abundance of valuable natural resources. It also has a strong, relatively young workforce. On the other hand, the economy doesn't seem to work that well, i.e., there is little economic progress. Many other countries have similar problems. Why is this, and what might business schools do to contribute more significantly to change in this type of situation?

The former CEO of Barry Callebaut, the world's largest chocolate manufacturer, headquartered in Switzerland, has offered the following suggestions to business schools to address this type of dilemma:

• Rules: Could there be alternative rules and purposes for business? Perhaps many of us have come to see phenomena such as organization, obedience, crime, and corruption through our own set of lenses cum rules. But there might be other ways! Teaching and research focused on this issue could be very effective.

• Feedback: How might feedback be given in such a way that it leads to more effective learning and improvement? Perhaps feedback might take on a much more central role in the learning process? One might place relatively more emphasis on "handholding," teaching through cases, and learning by doing. A lot of changes at the business school level would be required for a modern business school to be set up to provide this type of feedback-based learning in an effective way.

There is a further fundamental dilemma. We know that there is a certain body of knowledge embedded in a business school, vested in the professors at a given school. This knowledge is leveraged when it comes to offering courses and seminars of various kinds. But how might one build new knowledge, rather than simply leveraging the status quo? How could research support be given to individual faculty members to develop and build such new knowledge? And how could this lead to the strengthening of a team's knowledge, which would be more than the new knowledge possessed by an individual alone. What would the incentives and leadership principles be to develop a "we, we, we"-based new knowledge culture, in contrast to a "me, me, me" culture?

Conclusion

We have seen that an organizational culture that is open to change will be essential in the business school of the future. A "we, we, we" team culture will be key, in contrast to the narrower "me, me, me" culture, sadly so typical in academia today. We have also seen that a winning culture will have several key components, both when it comes to the behavior expected of most of the members of a school's organization and when it comes to the leader at the top. An effective top-down stance will be crucial. Furthermore, there must be a balance between top down and bottom up!

Many people might agree that a "we, we, we" culture, rather than a "me, me, me" culture is preferable. But, with the pressure placed on most faculty members to deliver research that is publishable in so-called A journals and by individual faculty members rather than in teams, it should come as no surprise that a "me, me, me" culture might prevail and drive out a more inclusive, cooperative culture. To succeed in this type of academic climate, a faculty member's research efforts might have to take precedence over teaching excellence. Many schools give more credit for the former when it comes to, say, promotions, allocation of performance bonuses, etc. It is often research activity that counts relatively higher.

We have also seen how excessive "politicking" might be dysfunctional. The energy of each member of a school's organization must be put to good use. In the end, a commitment to "good citizenship" is called for. This safeguards the best use of a faculty member's energies.

Finally, we have seen that the realistic availability of resources, particularly financial resources, would be another key condition for change. Competitive salaries, bonuses, research funding, etc., are all essential requirements to attract and keep key faculty as well as other central members of a school's organization. An ability to invest in ICT, social media, and in physical facilities is also key. We shall discuss these issues in more detail in Chapter 7.

7 Eight Cutting-Edge Dilemmas and Strategic Projects

As will have become clear, the leaders of business schools of the future will be faced with a series of fundamental dilemmas as they come to design a strategic plan for their organizations. In this chapter, we will go into more detail on eight such key dilemmas: aiming for cutting-edge research and leading business practice; finding a balance between research and teaching; producing revenue growth (top line) and profit growth (bottom line); introducing learning at home and workshop-based teaching at school; learning through relatively small workshops and in relatively larger classrooms settings; focusing on a local and global strategy; and, finally, pursuing so-called degree-granting programs for individual students and in-company programs, i.e., for corporations. In each case, it would not be a question of attempting to pursue one policy or another, but to go for a balance between two sides! And while we see the eight dilemmas identified above as particularly central, there are definitely other ones too, which we will allude to in our discussion. But now, let us first address each of the eight key dilemmas that we believe to be particularly central for successful leadership of the business school of the future.

1 Cutting-Edge Research and the Latest in Business Practice

State-of-the-art knowledge, informed by research as well as by best practice, should be the key drivers in building a business school's reputation. A good understanding of both research and practice is equally important when it comes to securing the school's leadership, through new hires, promotions, and terminations – both of more traditional academicians and to attract and keep leading part-timers and practitioners on one's faculty, either as permanent faculty members or guest lecturers. Research activities that are being carried out by individual faculty members might also be guided by how such contributions might fit into what the school is aiming for as its cutting-edge body of knowledge.

It is important to be explicit regarding what might constitute state-of-the-art when it comes to the various knowledge disciplines that a leading business school must draw on. An understanding of this might come about, in part, through awareness of what is going on in research – where is the research frontier? But an understanding of best practice might also be an indicator of where the state-of-the-art might be. With the rapidly increasing body of resources that seem to be being channeled into the expansion of knowledge from the business sector, a keen awareness of the latest developments is essential. It therefore seems wise to keep a close eye on what is going on in best practice, as well as in cutting-edge research. Exposure to the leading edge of both research and practice might in fact be seen as highly interrelated. While it would be difficult to provide a comprehensive list of what might represent best practice when it comes to research and/or business, I shall merely highlight the following examples:

- Big data analysis via cloud computing, to come up with better routes to market, as well as other innovations.
- Artificial intelligence (AI), to develop new work procedures where people might be more or less substituted by machines.
- Cognition, so that more effective communication might take place, particularly better listening.

There is a dramatic acceleration of research efforts contributing to what might constitute new knowledge these days. Research is being undertaken with increasing intensity and at many more institutions all over the world. These theoretical research efforts, together with what might constitute best practice, are evolving rapidly. Innovations may be at the heart of this, particularly when it comes to focusing on relatively newer firms, typically driven by emerging technologies and business incubators, linked to universities and private enterprise. Research may often be at the center of the development of these firms' business models. Here, many traditional and well-established corporations might be at a disadvantage, in that they may not so easily and readily be able to benefit from research.

In sum, a leading business school might be faced with an exceptionally dynamic and rapidly changing concept of what constitutes "the-state-of-the-art." It might perhaps be difficult, or even impossible, for a school to be "on top" of all, or even most, new knowledge fields. It is also true that staying up to date in a relatively wide range of knowledge fields might also become increasingly difficult for a particular professor. These considerations were one of the reasons that led us to settle on preferring to draw on a relatively stable network of visiting faculty members at the Lorange Institute. In this way, we hoped to be better positioned to access the latest knowledge when it came to bringing relevant cutting-edge content into the school. This kind of flexibility is best achieved by being able to draw on the best available faculty specialists from all over the world, visiting for relatively short periods of time to work on what are their core areas of competences. It should be noted, of course, that the cutting edge might be represented by more traditional academicians, as well as leading practitioners.

A network of part-time faculty would ideally be relatively stable. Only then might one secure real commitment from the faculty, which would be necessary to ensure that faculty members were willing to "invest" in the cutting-edge concepts that they would "bring" to the school. However, the network should never become too stable! New professors might thus be recruited to contribute new cutting-edge theory and/or practices. Conversely, some faculty members might simply not live up to the expectations of a school's leadership when it comes to remaining cutting-edge. The bottom line is that this network of primarily part-time professors would provide a more realistic setting for a business school to remain at the leading edge, most especially through careful faculty renewal. The school's value proposition should thus always reflect the latest in research as well as the in best practice.

2   Research and Teaching

Research and teaching may be considered to be "two sides of the same coin." The body of knowledge generated through cutting-edge research, or through best practice, should be disseminated to course participants as quickly and as fully as possible. That there is little or no time gap between discovery and dissemination is an essential marker of a top-quality business school of the future. In contrast, in many ordinary business schools there might be a considerable gap between discovery and dissemination!

It often is the case that the researcher who has been driving a new discovery through their research is in the best position to track what has now become cutting edge. The dissemination of what constitutes cutting edge, in research as well as in teaching, would thus ideally be delivered by the same person. Regrettably, there are many exceptions to this practice. In particular, it seems to have become an emerging norm for research to be carried out by one person (or team), while the teaching is done by another. It is possible that some faculty members, typically at professor level, consider the research side to be relatively more important than dissemination, and that teaching/dissemination is therefore often delegated to lecturers, frequently part-time employees. The latter would typically not be active participants in the research. This split of the research from the teaching function is likely to lead to a greater "distance" between the discovery and dissemination of the latest research findings. This could be seen as a sign of a lack of quality in some business schools. And even though some professors might favor this split between research and teaching, the fundamental duality of research and teaching remains the same, i.e., "two sides of the same coin." This is what we would see as best practice in well-performing business schools of the future.

3   Top-Line Growth and Bottom-Line Growth in Performance

A recent research project (Lorange and Rembiszewski, 2014) found that, in the case of leading Consumer Goods Companies (British American Tobacco was the featured case study), it was possible to sell more of a product or service and at a higher price provided that three conditions were in place:
• a clear identification of the target group of consumers
• the successful introduction of innovations that the target group of customers might welcome and be willing to pay for – these would typically be incremental changes and would emerge at a relatively fast pace
• effective communication of these innovations to the target group of customers, typically via social media
The latter point would also allow for two-way interaction between any member of the target group and the company, enabling further clarification of the significance of specific innovations to the customer. Under these circumstances, one would then typically be able to sell more, and at a higher price, within reasonable price limits, of course. The implications of these research findings could be at least twofold:
• Top-line (sales) and the bottom line (profits) would both grow – there is not necessarily an issue of trade-off between the two.
• Discounting, to increase sales, would thus also typically be dysfunctional.
Taking the above into account, leading business schools might consider an analogous approach. Here is a how this might be approached: a first step might be to clarify a business school's primary target groups. Certainly, it might be rather difficult to come up with just one or a small number of significantly focused target groups. We will discuss this issue further later in the chapter. But it is important to at least make some broad assumptions regarding a school's key target group(s) of student(s)/participant(s)/customer(s). In the case of the Lorange Institute, for instance, there were two major customer target groups – executives with

a median age of around forty who wanted to undertake part-time study to obtain an EMBA degree while continuing to work, and executives, usually from relatively small corporations, in need of corporate development programs. Typically, these companies would be too small to operate their own corporate training centers.

It is key, therefore, to come up with innovations that might be seen as valuable by each of these target groups. Some innovations might be seen as beneficial to both target groups, while others might be of primary value to only one of the groups.

Here are some cultural preconditions for stimulating relevant top-line and bottom-line new thinking:

- Do not underestimate the power of letting people try new things when they are working on projects! Innovations typically come about through people with strong commitment to the organization. Thus, individuals should be encouraged to try out new approaches as long as they are likely to lead to benefits for the target group(s). It is important for a leader to be broad-minded enough to give the "benefit of the doubt" to particular projects, even though some might seem to be "off the wall"!

- Strategy means choice! A school's leader should not be tempted to "let all flowers bloom." Thus, a project which might not have lived up to its initial expectations might be discontinued after it has been allowed to run for some time. Some of these activities might be considered marginal, and cutting them out would mean that a school's relatively scarce resource might be redeployed on new efforts. Key faculty would typically be the scarcest resource here!

As we have noted, it is particularly important to communicate, perhaps by social media, the specific advances that are being made. In a well-run school, one might expect solid growth to take place – new students, new client companies, more loyalty to the school from its customers. At the same time, the financial results might well improve too, partly because of the higher tuition fees that might be more easily justified to the customer base! So, we would expect to see a healthy level of development – growth in activity levels, together with strong economic results, from both the top and the bottom line. All of this should be communicated on the web.

Another way to approach this challenge might be to emphasize the maxim "today for today and today for the future," i.e., to focus both on current strengths (major impacts on the bottom line) and on innovations (major impact on the top line). Maintaining a good balance between these two would be a strong determinant for the ultimate success of a business school.

4   **Basic Learning at Home and Workshop Learning (Understanding) at the School**

As we discussed in Chapter 4, the basics can typically be studied alone, and at home. With the advent of modern computer technology, this has become both easy and convenient to organize. However, some schools may continue to offer more conventional in-house classes. These will usually be made up of large groups, particularly when the purpose is to cover more basic material. The standard teaching approach would be to provide a one-way flow of information, often aided by a large number of overhead illustrations. A textbook might also be assigned. The professor would typically cover more or less the same material in class as would be found in the textbook. These more basic materials would normally lead to a set of relatively clear "answers" when it comes to the various elements being covered. We are thus dealing with clear facts, with absolutes. Thus, understanding these rather basic materials should be straightforward – no deeper "feel" or intuition regarding the topic at hand would be required.

Most subject areas include some elementary principles which readily lend themselves to the internalization of a basic level of understanding. One area which might, however, call for a deeper sense of "feel" for the subject relates to cutting-edge dilemmas, which, in essence, define the state-of-the-art of a particular topic area. Developing a better "feel" for what such cutting-edge dilemmas might entail, typically calls for a different pedagogical approach from that used for learning the more basic materials. Self-study and/or relatively large, conventional classes/ lectures may no longer suffice, even for Generation Y-ers. What is relatively more important is to be able to shed light on such dilemmas from various angles, drawing on a variety of experiences and theories, and smaller class size would be necessary for this kind of discussion. We have advocated at some length for workshops, where each student might be given the opportunity to participate more actively.

Participants in these workshops will typically be at graduate level, i.e., with a thorough understanding of the more basic materials which characterize the undergraduate level. They are typically also somewhat older and come to the workshops with diverse, practical work-related experiences. Significantly, the participants will also learn from one another, and hopefully they will acquire a deeper appreciation and understanding of the central key dilemmas. This, too, will have to be checked, through tests/exams, but perhaps in essays rather than the "tick box" approach that might be used to check a student's understanding of the basics.

5   Small versus Large

This brings us quite naturally to a discussion of the dilemma of whether to opt for smaller workshops or larger classes. We have previously suggested that workshops focusing on key cutting-edge topics would tend to be relatively small. It would therefore be relatively difficult to benefit from economies of scale in these instances. However, achieving economies of scale might not be as critical as it would be when employing permanent faculty: faculty costs are clearly reduced if extensive outsourcing is used. And it is, of course, pedagogically advantageous for the number of workshop participants to be kept low.

As we have seen, such workshops would differ from the typical undergraduate classes, where achieving good economies of scale is essential. Class sizes might be increased considerably, and the duplication of certain classes might also be relatively easily to do, given that a professor's preparation would already have been done. Scalability is definitely possible!

A school's efforts to build brand recognition and to enhance its reputation would definitely not be related to its size, however. Even though advertising costs and market-specific programs might be more affordable when spread over a greater number of students, the unique workshop setting could nevertheless differentiate truly outstanding business schools from the rest. Enthusiastic word-of-mouth promotion would typically become the case, and even though there would be fewer students, alumni, and corporate customers, positive testimonials would be key! As discussed, the relatively lower cost base that results from making extensive use of part-time faculty could be seen as a "precondition" for this.

6   Local and Global

Most business schools recruit their students on a relatively local basis. Their reputation is largely locally based. In the past, most prospective students have tended to be attracted to their local school. Increasingly, however, many business schools aim at being more international. Student exchanges are one way of achieving this. However, there is also a relatively small number of top-rated business schools that are able to recruit students from all over the world. Top US-based schools, such as Harvard, Stanford, Wharton, Sloan, or Chicago, European schools, such as IMD (Lausanne), INSEAD (Fontainebleau), London Business School, IESE (Barcelona), or Asian schools, such as CEIBS (China) or Nanyang (Singapore) come to mind.

With the emergence of more flexible approaches to the sequencing or timing of the various program modules, as well as a relatively greater focus on shorter workshops, one effect might be that the recruitment of participants becomes increasingly rather local, since it might simply take too much time as well as financial resources for a participant to fly in from a great distance merely to attend a relatively short workshop. There would typically also be elements of a school's curriculum that are locally based. For example, local companies and local executives might provide convenient and accessible practical examples of good practice. And many professors, especially those drawn from business practice, might also be recruited from local sources. Even the more academically inclined professors might more readily be sourced locally, both for time-saving and cost-saving reasons.

Let us now briefly consider the delivery of corporate programs, when seen in this local–global context. Most business schools might prefer to deliver such programs at their own campus facilities, even though some might also be prepared to deliver this type of program at other sites, as chosen by a particular corporate client. Typically, most corporate clients would be locally based, however. The corporate delivery dimension would thus be local or, at best, semilocal. Only seldom, if at all, might in-company programs be truly global. Travel costs would be particularly relevant when it comes to delivering a global program.

So, what might global mean in the context of the business school of the future? We have already pointed out that only a very small group of leading business schools recruit students globally. An even smaller number of the leading schools hire professors based on a global pool of availability. For most schools, the most significant global dimension would be embedded in the content of the curriculum itself. Many of the issues now being taught are, in essence, now global. This would apply to more basic disciplinary topics as well as to the cutting-edge workshops.

Finally, schools need to consider the cross-cultural dimension. At the center of this would be workshops covering business activities in different countries. Cultural distance tends to be highly correlated with physical distance. Hence, a focus on improved cultural understanding is essential for enhancing the global focus of a school's offering.

7   Revenue Generation: Degree Programs and In-Company Programs

Effective revenue generation is, of course, critical for most business schools. A significant proportion of most business schools' budgets would typically come from the public sector (national, regional, and/or local) and/or from associations, such as chambers of commerce (largely in France). However, there is a clear trend toward a higher degree of self-financing for most business schools (Thomas, Lorange, and Sheth, 2014).

We have previously discussed the importance of innovations as a "driver" for revenue generation. The basic argument went approximately as follows (Lorange and Rembiszewski, 2014): Step 1, be clear regarding one's customer target group; Step 2, carry out relatively quick, incremental innovations to satisfy the target group; Step 3, communicate these innovations to the target group, ideally by means of social media, i.e., two-way communication. Result: You might increase revenue and also enjoy higher profits and price, i.e., both top-line and bottom-line growth!

There are typically two major types of revenue generation activities. One would be the sale of degree programs slots – this would be analogous to selling a product. The other would be the sale of in-company programs, which might be more analogous to selling a service. These would, therefore, call for different key selling points, and there would be different critical success factors for each activity, which we will now briefly discuss.

Let us first consider degree programs. Different business schools will, of course, have different target groups. At the Lorange Institute, for instance, the key target group was business executives, typically in the age range of thirty-five to forty-five years, who intend to study an EMBA degree in parallel with their full-time jobs. Relevant innovations implemented at the Lorange Institute to meet the demands of this target group include a more flexible curriculum – in terms of when a participant wishes to enroll in particular program module – truly flexible workshop structures, with world-class part-time professors. These innovations were communicated to the participants, including prospective clients, via the website, again inviting two-way interaction. Some students might elect to only take a relatively small set of related workshops. They might then "earn" a Certificate, which in the case of the Lorange Institute could be in shipping, finance, marketing, or human behavior. Others might elect not to write a master's thesis. They would then receive the E-MSci degree instead of the EMBA degree.

Let us now move to in-company programs. Here, you would market what is essentially a service. In this case, it would be particularly important to come up with a particular program design based on careful listening to inputs from the client company in question. While a client corporation might be under the impression that the program was entirely tailor-made to meet their needs, there is, of course, nothing that to prevent a business school from drawing on previously developed content, say, from the school's degree programs. A business school might thus insist on developing several specific modules to be delivered across various programs. The client would believe that this was tailor-made, however! "Handholding" when it comes to in-company program delivery is also key. Specially assigned dedicated program managers might, therefore, be critical.

We will now briefly touch upon some organizational issues. It goes without saying that since we have in essence two different revenue-generating business models, which might be considered more analogous to selling products versus selling services, the staffing and organization of the sales activities of each might have to be different too. For product sales, i.e., degree programs, the target customer would typically be an individual, and following up with them – i.e., product-based selling – without being "pushy" would be key. For service sales, in contrast, i.e., to the in-corporate segment, the emphasis might be more on highlighting potential benefits to the company, given the strategic direction that the company might have staked out. Helping to bring the company's organization in line with its strategy might thus typically be a valuable sales "pitch." Persistence is also key here!

8   Pursuing Innovation

For many business schools, it may not be enough to pursue the many "innovations in the small" which might occur as a result of the "normal" day-to-day activities of the school – typically related to course development, individual faculty research, advances in pedagogy, or administrative advances. Therefore, selective large projects may occasionally also be pursued to not only, hopefully, result in something of value, but also to further underscore a school's innovative profile. Examples of such projects might be large research projects, typically in new areas, such as those with a focus on emerging markets or geographies (e.g., Africa), the application of new methodology (e.g., cloud computing to identify new routes to market), development of new programs (e.g., by applying the latest in ICT), the undertaking of large-scale experimentation (e.g., by establishing a new laboratory for consumer behavior research), and so on. Typically, such projects tend to be expensive and may represent significant resource commitments by a school – in key people as well as money-wise. The dean/president is therefore often centrally involved in the decision-making and will be keenly interested in the execution of the project. If successful, such projects will clearly enhance the school's prestige.

One academic institution which is widely recognized for its successful implementation of many large cutting-edge projects is the Massachusetts Institute of Technology (MIT). I was a member of MIT's faculty for seven years (1973–80) and was able to piece together a blueprint for how large projects are run there. Their approach is as follows:

> At the center of the project, there is a small team of key people who run the project. This group typically consists of two or three people. They "own" the project and are accomplished academicians in the given area of the project. It should be noted that there is rarely one single individual at the core of the project, but rather a small team, with complementary capabilities.
>
> There is a network of disciplinary experts immediately around the core team of, say, ten people in total. These people would provide expert inputs when needed. This group is given detailed information regarding the progress of the project, with a particular focus on how specific bottlenecks might be overcome. It should be noted that the main purpose of this group is to make available the best possible expert support, and in a speedy way.
>
> There is a relatively large third group, of as many as twenty-five to thirty people. This group tends to be only peripherally involved and represents key stakeholders of various sorts, both those who a priori might respond favorably to the given project and those who might be more skeptical. It is important for this group to include stakeholders who might otherwise be inclined to react negatively to the project. Ensuring "smooth sailing" along the way is the key objective.
>
> Finally, there is also often a steering committee, consisting of the dean/president, as well as the CFO of the business school. This group receives detailed reports from the small core team of project "owners" on a regular basis, which are both financial and progress reports on milestones achieved, meeting regularly to review progress, as well as resource use to date. The documentation for these meetings is typically prepared by the "owners."

This approach to running large projects seems to work reasonably well.

It should be noted that there are at least three success factors to this approach:

> Each key strategic project becomes part of the school's organization, rather than being set up as an isolated, external entity. This is crucial. Having the involvement of a diverse group

people from across the school's organization allows integration to be achieved.

Each specific strategic project that is undertaken is supported to the fullest by the diverse set of competences available within the school, meaning that the best possible support can be mobilized to tackle any bottleneck that might emerge.

"Protection" for the project from potentially negative stakeholders who might otherwise raise questions about the project, or even delay it, can be built in.

Clearly, pulling off such strategic projects successfully is never an easy task. Many deans/presidents end up making mistakes, even though they may have followed something close to the blueprint outlined above. Here is some advice on the five types of common mistakes that can be made by even the most experienced deans:

Do not commit the school to a particular strategic project too early time-wise or/and too heavily. Instead, try to test things out on a smaller scale for as long as possible. And take the time that you need. Being in a rush often leads to expensive mistakes.

Be realistic when it comes to follow-on needs for additional resources (key people; funds). If another organizational entity is involved (say, another business school), then be as certain as you can that this other entity has the capacity and resources to realistically participate in the next stage(s). Also, make an assessment of the potential consequences for your own school if you have to stop a project mid-way due to insufficient resources!

Distinguish between a "good idea" and something that may be more solid. Is the basic proposition that his project builds on based on solid knowledge? Are there other analogous situations that might shed more light on the potential outcomes of this project?

What is the reputation of the key promoters of the project, denoted here as the "owners"? What have they delivered previously? Are they known to be prudent with resources? Are they proven leaders? Are they good with people?

Avoid being too "passive." It is important that the dean/president as key stakeholders are being heard! It may be an early warning sign if the "owners" act as if inputs from the top would be seen as "interference." The dean/president's active involvement is legitimate.

Strategic projects are going to play an ever more central role in the leading business school of the future. The capability to effectively run such projects will increasingly become a core competence for success.

Conclusion

We have now looked at eight key dilemmas facing the business school of the future. These were to focus both on research and practice, on research and teaching, on revenue and profits, on learning at home and at the business school, on workshops and class sessions, on local and global, on degree programs and in-company programs, and, the eighth dilemma, to pursue innovation. There are probably other dilemmas too. It may be safe to conclude that there will be no finite solutions to each of these particular design issues. There will be no "correct" path to take. It follows that the business school of the future might be a rather complex animal!

8   Emerging Business Models
Network Organizations for Business Schools

In this chapter, we will discuss in more detail how a networked organizational form might be beneficial for promoting innovations in the business school space. In the first part of the chapter, we will discuss several general characteristics for network-organized business schools. Then, we shall provide some examples of how this might function. The first example, the Lorange Institute of Business Zurich, is a recently developed top-quality business school which is dramatically different from the more conventional schools. The second example, SHARE, is not a business school as such, but rather a network allowing individual students to work together to create ideas across continents, drawing heavily on modern ICT. The third example, the Lorange Network, is a network for business learning, but it does not issue any formal degrees or certificates. Indeed, it is not a business school as we have come to know it today, but it may point toward what we may expect in the future when it comes to executive learning.

We will also look at other recent developments regarding business schools' organizational models, elaborating on networked organizations, and how these might enhance strategy implementation processes. We will see that this type of organization allows for more flexibility and speed, and a broader set of involvements, often with less bureaucracy. A broader set of involvements in network organizations comes about through the more open context in which people can operate, where formal limits to what would be their mandates are not spelled out, as would be the case in more traditional hierarchical organizations (with people's job descriptions being driven by their hierarchical positions). There is also typically less cross-departmental dysfunctionality, compared with more traditional business school organizations. Above all, many deans or presidents – perhaps the more entrepreneurial ones – might find it advantageous to network with external faculty and/or schools without necessarily having to create a large bureaucracy for this. A key advantage, therefore, in addition to speed, is the added flexibility to "develop the school as you go" (Meyer, 2016).

The Networked Business School

The development of networked business school organizations might be particularly useful when a school is attempting to implement specific large free-standing strategic projects. As we saw in Chapter 7, perhaps one of the best examples of networked organizations applied to large strategic projects might be found in MIT's strategic projects model, with its typical three layers of actors.

Some of the most powerful insights when it comes to understanding effective business school organizations come from studying parallels with the armed forces, in particular those that are based on general conscription, such as the Israeli army. In Israel's case, at least two features stand out as relevant (Senor and Siege, 2009):

• Hierarchy does not necessarily seem to suppress creativity. Creativity that leads to positive initiatives is welcomed from lower as well as higher ranks.

• The military force seems to foster a network of friends, which is then typically maintained. This lasting network seems to facilitate social contacts, become a source for support for members in need, and underscores the power of complementarity among diverse talents.

Table 8.1 compares the characteristics of a typical networked organization with those of a more traditional organization.

What then, in more general terms, are some of the key factors that need to be in place to ensure that networked business school organizations perform well? We have identified ten such factors in Table 8.1, but will

Table 8.1 *Two Prototypes of Business School Organizations*

Networked	Traditional
Visionaries, innovators	Managers, administrators
Relatively small core and headcount	Relatively large headcount
Relatively open culture	Relatively closed culture
Relatively fast, more flexible	Relatively slow, "analysis to paralysis"
Cost-effective; slim routines	More expensive; more extensive routines
In-depth, topical understanding	Generalist
Business-specific knowledge	More axiomatic knowledge
Typically found in a relatively new business school	Typically found in more established business schools
More explicit risk-taking profile	Lack of clarity regarding risk, above all due to complexity
Often manageable at the dean's/president's level	Often too complex to effectively manage for the dean/president alone.

now elaborate in more detail on seven, namely the concepts of control, trust, and compatibility of (standard) parts, compete and cooperate, open-mindedness versus closed minds, prestige and reputation, as well as creativity in groups. Let us now briefly discuss each, keeping in mind that some of these factors may, to varying degrees, overlap with the others.

Control. The concept of being in control may suggest a feeling of "not having to be excessively worried." What we are typically aiming for is a degree of comfort when it comes to the functioning of an organization. The word *control*, however, should not be misinterpreted to mean "dominance." Clarity of purpose is particularly key here. For instance, this may particularly be the case when it comes to intellectual property issues, for example when a specific party wishes to obtain patent protection. The aim might be to possess a "black box," a unique technology, a unique market position. And this would ideally be protected. If we transfer this idea to a business school setting, are the intellectual property dimensions of its governance processes sound? The dean or president of a business school must be clear when it comes to this aspect of performance monitoring, satisfying themselves that progress is being achieved to develop intellectual property that can be protected. Achieving effective protection of intellectual property is, of course, not normally a trivial task. Published materials are usually copyrighted, and plagiarism is neither legal nor honest. But published materials are, nevertheless, broadly accessible, and might be hard to fully protect. A more effective way of protecting intellectual property might be achieved through its integration into pedagogical "packages," where the newly developed materials would become elements in larger teaching modules. A professor delivering such cutting-edge modules might be much harder to copy and there might thus be more protection. In particular, individual professors might not so easily "steal with pride"! And this would be true for competing business schools too. Maintaining a dynamic pace of development might, in the end, lead to the most effective form of protection, in the sense that new research insights and new pedagogical approaches might already have been introduced by the time others have been able to, in essence, copy the "old" materials.

Typically, a networked business school would be set up to deliver on certain milestones. Thus, more generally, are such milestones sufficiently explicit? And are the deadlines realistic? Can each key member of an organization "deliver" their part? We might also ask whether it is wise for more well-established schools to become part of a specific network. Given the possible attempts by some schools to dominate a network, this might be in breach of a cooperative agreement. It would simply not be acceptable for this dominance to lead to the "stealing" of intellectual property! Some business schools "resist" working in networks as a result.

Trust. Trust is also vital. A long-established working relationship between members of an organization might contribute to the development of trust. However, a network should also provide incentives that lead to trust building, so that all parties benefit. Ideally, all parties should want to pull in the same direction, with each member respecting the specific intellectual property of other members of the network. Greed, in the sense that "I benefit at the expense of you," should not occur. It is simply not acceptable for some members to infringe the intellectual property rights of others. Trust-building calls for honesty and a moral stance by all members of the network.

Standardized, compatible parts. It would be beneficial for all the various member schools in a network to be committed to providing their functional inputs in such a way that they are relatively standardized, i.e., "off the shelf," and not too highly "tailored." This would make it easier to slot in certain modules and thus come up with more cost-effective solutions. For instance, a particular functional module might cover a set of pedagogical materials in such a way that it is not only relevant in a given context, but also more generally, say, by using a wide array of examples. There would be less dependence on any one participating school as a result. A network might, therefore, be seen to be more robust, particularly when it comes to cases of unforeseen changes. Needless to say, some schools might prefer to strive for the very opposite, i.e., to establish such a unique profile that they are seen as virtually impossible to substitute. Such attempts by some schools to create exclusivity should, of course, be resisted by the other members of the network.

Compete and cooperate. How can a culture be developed within a network context that emphasizes both competition and cooperation between specific business schools? To address this question, let us first consider why competing is so important. To compete implies that one is striving for high levels of performance, i.e., aiming for true excellence. So, why also cooperate? As noted above, cooperation stimulates the cross-fertilization of strong elements of superior but complementary know-how. Truly superior performance relies on bringing such unique and diverse parts together, hence cooperation!

Open-mindedness versus closed mind. What is particularly critical is creating an effective "we, we, we" culture within networks. An ability to listen effectively is crucial. And, a corollary would be that a listening, sparring partner school might be able to provide more effective feedback, to the point, fast! A "me, me, me" culture represents the antithesis of this.

Prestige and reputation. What gives a member school in a network organization the necessary prestige and reputation to function well? Clearly, the formal standing and educational background of faculty and staff may be a factor. Much more important, however, would be the track record of individual faculty members – are they be able to get things done in superior ways? Do they possess a capacity to contribute something that would represent a truly unique quality?

Creativity in groups. It turns out that bringing parties with complementary attributes together can lead to new insights and enhanced creativity. It is important to be explicit about what each member of a networked organization might be expected to contribute. Members of the network should be aware of the track records of the various member schools. If there are historical negatives, these should be brought out explicitly. Well-functioning networked organizations might thus be able to improve the performance of any individual member school. Individual faculty members with good ideas should receive encouragement from others, to stimulate the development of a "can do" culture. This is indeed another hallmark of a typical networked organization, with individual faculty members in various business schools supporting and "helping" each other.

Networked organizations of business schools seem particularly well suited to support the execution of large innovative projects. We discussed this in detail in Chapter 2, and again in Chapter 7. The opportunity to proceed at higher speed, to enjoy greater flexibility, to mobilize more in-depth business-related knowledge linked to a given innovation, and the opportunity to assess risks more clearly would all be strong positive factors for choosing a network approach. The plus side of this would easily outweigh the potential negatives, which might include creating mistrust, a lack of honesty, and poor communication. The commitment to create a "we, we, we" culture should, one hopes, prevail.

What about dysfunctional silo effects in network organizations? Networks would a priori be less stable than the more traditional, hierarchical organization. Thus, the risk of dysfunctional silo developments here might be relatively low. Only when networks become too stable, might we see the emergence of silos. Perhaps, an occasional shift in the composition of a network might be advisable, therefore!

Let us now consider three case examples of attempts to develop networked business school organizations, intended to create new, ambitious, innovative business school models.

The Lorange Institute of Business

In August 2009, I purchased the former Graduate School of Business Administration (GSBA) in Horgen, outside Zurich. This included the business school's campus facilities, including its lakeside campus (on the banks of Lake Zurich). It consisted of two auditoriums, three study/group conference rooms, offices, a restaurant, and three apartments.

Subsequently, considerable restructuring of the school's curricula took place, coinciding with a shift from a primary focus on the undergraduate segment to on which now solely focused on the graduate segment. Many of the school's original professors were also asked to complete their terms. After a few years, the doctoral program, delivered at that time in association with Leiden University in the Netherlands, was also abandoned. In November 2015, the facilities, school, and physical campus were sold to CEIBS, Asia and China's leading business school based in Shanghai. Over the relatively short time period of six and a half years considerable progress had been made.

While the initial aim was to maintain stability in the school's management team to safeguard continuity, there were nevertheless significant changes in the leadership at the top. There were initially two co-CEOs (co-presidents) from August 2009, who later resigned (in late 2010, and from January 2011). Another individual became the president/CEO. In January 2012, another individual took over, until June 2013. Then, a Swiss national, with a background in the tourism industry became the president/COO in 2013 and also CEO from January 2015. This person had a particularly strong understanding of the working of networks. I acted as president in 2011–12 as well as in 2013–15, was the chairman/CEO from 2009 to end 2014, and was chairman from then on. The chief financial officer left in fall 2014. Most of the original staff had gradually left by the time of the sale to CEIBS.

The strategy taken at the Lorange Institute of Business was essentially similar to that discussed in detail in this book. What were the results of this "experiment"? In general, my assessment is that the results were good. I will briefly discuss three aspects of this below. But there were, of course, also disappointments. I will highlight two of these also.

Three Positive Achievements

First, as noted, the Lorange Institute of Business, school and campus, was sold to CEIBS, Shanghai at a profit at the end of 2015. It is significant that CEIBS is considered to be the top business school both in China and in Asia as a whole. Also, it should be noted that CEIBS is 50 percent owned by EFMD, the Brussels-based accreditation organization, considered to be perhaps the best in its field worldwide. Hence, CEIBS might be considered a professional purchaser, fully able to realistically assess the value of the Lorange Institute and to accordingly put on a fair purchase value on it. Thus, the relatively high sales price might be seen as a manifestation of what had been built up to be a solid business school.

Second, the financial results of the Lorange Institute showed a steady improvement. Initially there were losses, but break-even point was achieved toward the end of my ownership period. A relatively modest positive financial result was shown at the time of the sale. This might indeed be seen as quite remarkable, particularly given the fact that no funding contributions had come from any outside source, public or private.

Third, significant progress was also made when it came to securing customers for the Institute's tailored in-company learning programs. Some of Switzerland's (and Germany's) leading companies became customers. The school's in-company business segment was thus particularly successful.

On the negative side, and quite disappointingly, I would mention two factors:

1 First, there is no doubt that I had expected stronger revenue growth, based on a greater acceptance in the market. The relatively slow progress in the degree market (executive MBA) was particularly disappointing. It is true that the demand for these types of programs, in general, seemed to have diminished quite dramatically during this time period. This was also true for traditionally leading schools in the segment, such as IMD and INSEAD. At the same time, however, we did make considerable progress with tailored in-company programs – more than we had anticipated.

2 Second, we had counted on more active support from the relatively large alumni body of GSBA. In general, the bulk of the alumni were relatively more attached to the older GSBA regime than to the new one at the Lorange Institute. Thus, most of the original alumni did not seem to attach much value to what I had introduced as quality-enhancing innovations. The majority of the alumni simply did not see it this way!

Allow me to add a third factor, for which I must take responsibility, namely, the lack of managerial skills and stability in the Lorange Institute's top team during the first few years of my ownership. I had, perhaps, underestimated the need to have someone in charge with a sufficiently strong academic but also nonconventional background. Hence, progress was very slow. Also, the need for key formal accreditation, in particular to ensure the effective marketing of the Institute, was underestimated. The decision of the new Swiss president to join the Lorange Institute team changed all of this. He brought with him at least three key strengths:

- strong academic credentials, from Australia and from St. Gallen (PhD), as well as administrative experience as the academic leader of the Tourism Program at the Regional University of Chur, and a cutting-edge understanding of network-based strategies
- strong links with the Swiss-based business network, being a Swiss citizen
- a superb ability to organize the various operating tasks of the Lorange Institute

Thus, it would be appropriate to ask why we did not enjoy greater success. There are three reasons:

First, the school was probably too small. This meant that customers might not have wanted to take the risk of committing to a relatively small start-up, even though the quality offered might have been seen as OK. The risk of the school potentially being seen as nonsustainable might be considered too high. What would a participant's diploma be worth if the school eventually faltered? And what about the career risk for an executive who might be looking for an in-company program from such a new start-up school? Another aspect relating to the size of the Lorange Institute might be that the school would not have many differentiating capabilities, unlike those it got when it became part of CEIBS, with unique Chinese competencies now being a credible part of its offering. Both individuals and companies might value this – hence, there would be more students.

Second, a lack of financial resources could also have been an issue. I owned 100 percent of and fully financed the enterprise, so there would naturally be limits to the funds available, for example, for building unique competences, for salaries, for structural renovations, and for marketing. A lack of funding might have been a constraint.

Third, there were also several ill-conceived choices of senior leadership at the Lorange Institute, particularly during the initial years. While I was, of course, fully involved, this did not have much of an impact on the marketing of the new school. Perhaps I overestimated any positive spill-over effects from my success as the leader of IMD? I might also have underestimated the disadvantages of being a non-Swiss national.

All in all, the outcome of the experiment at the Lorange Institute of Business seems to have been largely positive, however. A new institution with a high-quality offering was rapidly established. This might provide some indication to the global business and academic community of the potential shape of the business school of the future. There will undoubtedly be several different formulas for success when it comes to the business school of the future. What I have presented in this book is, however, one of these.

Share

An interesting virtual network-based learning approach has been developed by Mr. Sebastian Frendo, who previously worked for the consulting firm BCG. This approach, which came to be called SHARE, involves almost one thousand students from more than thirty top universities from ten continents. It is an international student think-tank, made up of teams of students from well-known universities. While the bulk of these teams are from Asia (above all, China and India), there are also teams from Europe, as well as one from Brazil. The students are trained online, and are coached by young professionals, from leading consulting firms or corporations. The students thus learn through a combination of face-to-face interaction and individual online study.

Enhancing each student's entrepreneurial capabilities is a key objective, which is achieved by the students working on various innovative projects. These projects typically cover important societal dilemmas and complement the traditional curricula that the students follow in their respective universities. The students then exchange their ideas among themselves virtually, first within a team, and then with students from other teams. Thus, there would be a regional or even a global exchange. This might be the typical sequence of steps of the SHARE process:
- First, individual training, where additional skills might be needed, typically carried out online.
- Initial discussions within a team regarding a prospective project, which the team might later wish to embark on.
- A start-up phase for a project within a given team, which would come up with an initial approach to the chosen cutting-edge dilemma it had chosen to work on.
- A global project phase, where teams would exchange views on how to approach the chosen dilemma among themselves, regionally or even globally, so that, in the end, a (one can hope) superior approach to the particular cutting-edge dilemma might be identified.

Several observations should be made at this point:
- This approach is an example of blended learning, incorporating aspects of what one would presumably learn at a university, together with learning from independent studies, from consulting coaches, and from fellow students. The skills acquired are typically entrepreneurial, professional, and international.

- There are partner firms involved. These would typically be leading global corporations. Ideally, most of the student projects would be closely linked with real-life dilemmas found in the various partner firms. The firms might thus get additional insights and effectively assess students' talents, as well. For the participating firms, these types of inputs might otherwise have been hard to get, even from expensive consulting firms.
- The SHARE learning process is part-time, while a student pursues their university studies in parallel. Participation is for free for the students. The coaches donate their time and running costs are covered by various corporations. So, the SHARE approach represents high-quality learning at low cost!
- There is a strong focus on innovation, or "thinking out of the box," which is typically greater than at some of the leading consulting firms or partner corporations, while the price, and thus also the cost, is significantly lower than that found in many consulting firms or in other leading firms.

The Lorange Network

It should be noted at the outset that the Lorange Network is primarily tailored to an experienced audience, rather than to undergraduates or inexperienced graduate students. The initiative was started in January 2017 and is a membership network for investors and family firms. The general premises behind this are threefold:

- Successful investors as well as family business executives are both very busy and typically rather impatient. Rather than reading lengthy books and reports, they are content to read short summaries of key books or articles. Audio-visual versions of these summaries are also available for downloading, say, onto a member's mobile phone.
- Learning from reports of the types mentioned above may be essential for making better investment decisions, and ultimately also for a member's own improved financial performance. Thus, learning would take place when a member reflects on how more general insights can benefit their individual and more specific context. This learning may be further enhanced when members in the network discuss their experiences, offering comments and/or posting questions, which others might then respond to. We might thus see benefits from the typically critical two-way discussions of key dilemmas. Examples provided by specific members, positive as well as negative, might also be posted in the network.
- The network is totally neutral, i.e., there are no commercial tie-ins. This would be in contrast to the kinds of reports issued by banks, ship-brokers, real estate entities, etc., which may offer their own research,

but which will also tend to "push" their own products. Because the network strives for neutrality, consultants, investment specialists, and wealth managers would typically not be welcomed as members, unless they specifically declared that they would not solicit other members for business.

A dedicated computer-based platform has been developed by the Norwegian-Russian firm Polartech, allowing each member to access all the material that is posted on their laptop computer, iPad/tablet or iPhone, as well as when driving in the car (audio only). A small group of dedicated programmers – four in total – are working on a full-time basis to develop the designated software for LN. These programmers are based in Tamara, Russia. This choice of programming support was dictated by these key factors:

- the ability of this group to deliver quickly, i.e., with speed
- the unique software development competence typically found among many Russians
- the considerable cost savings, relative to having this task performed in, say, Norway or Switzerland

Each member is automatically charged US$100 per month, which is debited to their private business card. They must apply to become a member and give written notice if they intend to leave.

There are circa seventy-five independent contributors or experts, who provide the various short reports that are posted, including topical reports and book reviews, highlighting what is particularly relevant for business, and brief article summaries, again highlighting what is relevant. The contributors or experts, all leaders within their fields, are also all independent: academicians, business people, consultants (cum individuals), bankers (also, cum individuals), and others. There is no full-time staff running this network, but four people who are involved on a part-time basis: I am the chairman/CEO and Ms. Karin Mugnaini is president/COO. Mr. Frode Lervik is CFO, and Per F. Lorange is editor in chief. The content typically falls into one of the following four categories:

- relevant inputs for individual investment decisions, including relevant background content for such decision – this also includes relevant inputs for the portfolio of family offices
- managerial insights, particularly relevant for family companies and/or family offices
- materials to support the further education of family members, investors and family members, particularly the younger ones
- social impact investment issues

So far, the Lorange Network seems to have filled a unique need, even before its formal launch on October 6, 2017! After less than a year, the membership count has risen to around 200 practicing executives. As of March 2018, a total of around 100 postings have been made, with around seventy-five comments from members. All in all, a remarkable degree of speed has been ensured in the process of successfully starting and evolving this learning network. Here too, we may be seeing the rudiments of what might become the business school of the future.

Given my lifelong involvement with leading business schools, it was perhaps a logical consequence of this evolutionary experience to create a network approach for learning, which might also be an example of how a business school of the future might be shaped. As well as the short reports mentioned above, the Lorange Network (LN) offers a learning approach which combines self-study of various topics at home, made accessible through a virtual network, and physical workshops, at which various cutting-edge dilemmas are discussed. These dilemmas are extensions of the materials made available via the LN web for self-study, which is a way of preparing for the workshop. This is indeed an example of blended learning.

We will now take a look at the approach being used by LN to make available relevant materials, and then review how complementary workshops might be offered, based on these materials.

The content is available to members only. As of early 2018, there are more than 200 members, paying an annual fee. There is a specific admissions procedure, based on the following criteria:
• that the individual has a minimum level of wealth
• that the individual is either a member of a family firm, runs a family firm, or is an independent investor
Thus, corporate executives would typically not qualify as members, unless perhaps based on their individual wealth, managed separately from their corporate jobs. Only those individuals genuinely committed to ongoing learning as regards key dilemmas would be welcome. The network's aim is to create a collegial atmosphere between peers to promote an exchange of ideas and mutual learning.

As noted, the various postings may not only be useful as stand-alone readings, but also represent valuable preparatory materials for each individual member, so that they might be prepared to participate in specific workshops. These workshops would typically be highly focused on cutting-edge dilemmas, particularly where there might be no right answers. The number of participants in each workshop would be kept intentionally low, thus encouraging participants to be active members of the discussions. Typically, the professor in charge would first review the key background materials and articulate the dilemmas to be focused on. Then, there might be group discussions, finally ending up with a plenary session, where the professor would attempt to synthetize as far as possible. The individual background of each participant would also represent a potentially important input to the workshop discussions. The participants would also benefit from being exposed to the experiences of others in the group.

Examples of workshop topics might be:

- Strategies for Family Firms
- Strategies for Independent Investors
- Shipping Company Strategies
- Innovation and Entrepreneurship
- Marketing/Routes to Markets/Big Data
- Behavioral Finance
- Women in Business

The format of the learning approach at LN is therefore intentionally short and flexible, well suited to individuals who might want to engage in learning while maintaining a full-time job. And, as noted, much of the learning would take place through self-study, which would easily fit into a career-diverse agenda. The workshops are also intentionally short, of one to two days in length, and can be run at weekends to meet the needs of busy executives.

For whom would this type of learning be best suited? There seem to be two major groups of potential learners. One would be executives, whose primary focus will be on their careers, but who also realize that continuous learning is essential to stay up to date and to be more readily employable in their future career roles. The flexibility that learning through LN offers would be key here. The experience-base of active executives would also be critical for the overall effectiveness of this type of learning. Being able to put the content from specific postings in the context of the learner's own experience would be essential. Meaningful workshop discussions rely on participants being able to draw on relevant experiences.

The second target group for this type of learning would be members of family firms who might co-own a particular business, for example. The types of workshops offered through LN could represent a way for family members to bond, to create stronger teams, and to lessen potential conflicts. This might be an effective way for the leadership of a family firm to build loyalty between a larger group of family members, many of whom might be shareholders but not active in the firm.

While LN may have been developed primarily as a vehicle to support family business and independent investors in making better resource allocation decisions, it also offers promising inputs for executive learning. Its combination of individual learning, including preparation at home by accessing premium condensed inputs on the net and participation in cutting-edge discussions that build on self-study materials, may indeed be what we might expect to find in a business school of the future.

Several questions that typically arise with this approach are:

- How might one be confident that the LN provides top-quality information? Answer: The group of world experts contributing to the program would be a guarantee of quality.
- A network member would typically be very busy, with little time to read. How might this challenge be managed? Answer: As noted, all expert briefings, book reviews, and article summaries are short and concise, with a clear focus on content that is relevant for an investor or family business leader. They will also be available on an audio-visual basis. For busy executives, it is key for these postings to be easily accessible, to be available at those times when the participant might be predisposed to learn!
- How will members' confidentiality be protected? Answer: Members will be able to choose whether to remain anonymous or not when making posts.
- Investors are "bombarded" with information from banks, brokers, or from other sources. How will LN differ? Answer: All LN posts on the platform will be short and to the point. Furthermore, all posts will be of a neutral nature.
- Will the LN be relevant for family teams? Answer: This approach can be targeted to specific family groups, members of other executive networks, or simply on an open enrollment basis. Thus, relevant subsets of posts might be made accessible to participants in individual workshops, without them necessary being full members of the LN.

Let us finally draw a few conclusions when it comes to considering the LN as a potential prototype for the emerging business schools of the future:

- Learning would incorporate distance/web-based computer-based network technology, but also short physical seminars to discuss cutting-edge dilemmas, i.e., so-called blended learning.
- There would be a minimum of fixed features, i.e., no physical campus with permanent classrooms, no full-time professors, but rather part-time facilitators and experts. The number of permanent staff employed, for example, for network programming and administration, would be intentionally kept low, and they would be virtually distributed. Thus, the fixed financial break-even point would be relatively low.
- Flexibility would be high, with a capacity to adapt to new topic areas in a speedy fashion.

While the LN is intended for participants who already have relevant work experience to draw on, there is nothing here that would limit this basic approach to this target group alone. Undergraduate students might also be included! For instance, we saw how the discussion of key dilemmas can work at the high school level, with the so-called Harkness Tables, pioneered at the Phillips-Exeter Academy in the US. And we also saw how the so-called tutorial approach adopted by Oxford and Cambridge continues to offer virtual learning some several hundred years on. We will see in Chapter 9, as well as in our case studies, particularly at Singapore Management University and IE University in Spain, how relevant practical experience to support this type of learning might be accomplished.

Conclusion

We are likely to see many new archetypes for organizing learning from various business providers, including business schools. The traditional business school, with its more hierarchical organizational structure, is likely to be complemented by organizational entities that will be much more virtual and organized through networks. These entities will perhaps be in a better position to move fast, and to deliver high-quality learning at a competitive cost.

9 The Future
A New Context and What We Might Expect

We have pointed out a number of innovations that we might expect to find in the modern business school of the future. As noted, many of the approaches that we have discussed have actually been tried out at the Lorange Institute of Business during the time period of 2009–15 and/or at the Lorange Network, from 2016 onward, and generally with good results. Let us now briefly summarize the key issues that we consider will shape the future for leading business schools:

- Over time, we might expect more and more students/participants in our degree programs to come from the so-called Generation Y, and then gradually from Generation Z (Stieger, 2015). This means that we can expect to see even more technologically inspired innovations: better databases, more on-time delivery of exams, reports, etc., and for the web to become even a more integral part of learning, not only from a "single-loop" dimension, such as access to relevant materials via databases and/or the online library, availability of lecture notes/workshop notes, etc., but also through better "double-loop" learning, e.g., through interactive tests, question-and-answer sessions, participants' postings, planned feedback, etc. This would imply that spending time on campus might become increasingly unnecessary. Also, studying may gradually become more "user friendly," allowing participants to be even more effective when they are actually on campus, typically to attend a workshop. And increasingly, participants may "tailor" their own program of studies, to more fully reflect their individual interests.
- Even more powerful technology-based learning support is likely to be required. Thus, schools must be ready to make the necessary investments here. It is quite possible that they will link up with various other business schools and academic learning institutions into "open" networks.
- Professors should become even better catalysts/orchestrators. As noted, it may be difficult for some traditional professors to effectively adapt to these new roles. This might, to some extent, result from the conventional formal training that many prospective faculty candidates receive in the doctoral programs they attend, where the focus might typically be

on research, with little to no emphasis on learning pedagogy. We suggest that a welcome innovation for business schools with leading doctoral programs would be to introduce more formal training on how to apply one's professorial skills in workshop-like contexts: listen, orchestrate, synthesize! Becoming an effective conductor does indeed require training.

- The classroom of the future. We can expect significant changes here too. Building impressive architectural landmarks has till now been a major attraction for many schools – particularly when it comes to satisfying their financial donors, administrators, and architects! The problem with this approach is that many of the world's leading architects do not necessarily have a good understanding of what it takes to design an efficient campus. The issue of a "correct" pitch, of circa twenty degrees, for classroom floors was apparently initially implemented at Harvard Business School (HBS), to facilitate more effective class discussions based on the case study method that HBS pioneered. Many schools adopted this later, including IMD and the Lorange Institute. But not all new schools have done so. The large auditoriums at the recently constructed new building belonging to BI in Oslo, for instance, have a two-stage floor pitch to be effective. Without this type of pitch, the professor might end up with little eye contact with most of the participants! The issue of "flat rooms" represents even more of a design issue. It is key, then, to come up with a relatively simple design, with ample light and good acoustics. Clearly, some business school administrations have opted to develop "monuments" rather than pedagogically effective spaces! It is also important to allow for enough "meeting places" in new business school buildings. There should be plenty of coffee shops, lounges, etc., where participants and faculty members might naturally gather. The world-famous architect Frank Gehry calls these "amorphous" buildings! Regrettably, such "common spaces" are often lacking.

I recently visited Brasenose College at Oxford University. The outside walls of this quadratic structure were austere and dark, with a few, relatively small windows. The external facade might indeed be seen as uninviting! Entering through one of several relatively narrow gates, a totally different appearance emerged, however: beautiful lawns and rooms with multiple windows, stone ornaments and all. One might suggest that many classical university buildings (Brasenose was founded more than 700 years ago) were designed in this way to actually create barriers against the outside world, with a focus on the inward processes of the College being the priority.

In today's world, this type of isolation would probably not be a valid aim. Indeed, a strong link with the rest of society would be essential for the business school of the future. The campus would now be more open, with "meeting places" where everyone might get together (small cafés or coffee shops, for instance). Likewise, the school's physical facilities might be open to all. Lectures/sessions/classes might be free for anyone to attend. Campus eating facilities and cafés would not only be reserved for course participants but would also be accessible to the local community. Ad hoc art exhibitions on campus, for example, would draw visitors to the business school, and so on. In short, the business school of the future would be much more accessible to a wider society.

There would be very few offices, if any, in this new style campus. Faculty members from various disciplines would be located randomly throughout the building to enhance cross-disciplinary dialogue. The old days of exclusive office suites for each disciplinary academic department seem to be more or less gone. Open office spaces would also facilitate more effective face-to-face communication. In short, the physical facilities might be deliberately arranged to stimulate broader interactions/discussions of key, cutting-edge dilemmas.

One of the dilemmas for many business schools when it comes to the emergence of the new style of layout is what does a school do with its existing buildings that might actually not be that old, but that might be hard to retrofit? Some of these facilities might perhaps be rented out, say to small businesses, for corporate or community meetings, or perhaps even become community spaces for theater/cinema/music. But finding significant new usages might, in general, be hard. Are architects, in general, fully cognizant of these emerging requirements when it comes to client business schools' new physical space, as well as the difficulties of finding new modes of usages for the "old" facilities?

- The so-called MOOCs (Bisoux, 2017; Clarke, 2013) represent another area where we might expect to see considerable progress. Indeed, we might have only seen the start of this phenomena. Today, students are able to study at various schools – virtually. This allows for more choice and flexibility, which may, generally, be a good thing! But, the issue of developing a deeper understanding of key dilemmas might not necessarily be met using this method. Thus, traditional MOOCs – to cover the "basics" – might have to be complemented by enrolment at a specific institution to develop a deeper understanding of a set of key dilemmas, through participation in workshops. In this way, participants will be able to gain a better understanding of the key dilemmas when seen in the specific context of a given school in a particular geographic setting. Thus, the MOOC movement is likely to be complemented by the offering of cutting-edge workshops at particular business schools. This topic will be discussed in more detail in the next section.

- Blended learning is simply the blending of online learning with learning at school (Horn and Staker, 2015). Horn and Staker, in their research, reported on a blended learning focus in the primary school system, as do Horn and Staker. But their argument regarding the virtues of blended learning seem to apply much more broadly than this. The essence would be that much learning might take place alone, typically at home, as well as also with others, through class discussions at school. Thus, academic institutions such as business schools might see a growth in the adoption of blended learning.

Why Blended Learning?

One might ask why blended learning might be so attractive for business schools. The main reason is that this might allow students/participants to more easily keep their full-time jobs, with the prospect of undisrupted career progress, while studying part-time through a blended learning approach. Thus, this might imply the prospect of access to stronger students.

The debate surrounding the benefits of learning through customizing programs of individual studies versus a more standardized approach for all students is, of course, not new. As early as 1809, through his then revolutionary reforms at the University of Berlin, Dr. von Humboldt proposed more standardization, with axiomatically focused professors, teaching in relatively large classes, and with a structure of supporting institutes of associate professors, assistants, and doctoral students, with each such entity being built around clear axiomatic differences (von Humboldt, 1970). This is in contrast to the attempts to create more individually tailored learning for each student/participant that took place in many of the earlier European Universities (Rüegg, 2004). Tutors working with smaller groups of students were quite common then, and this tradition of tutorials is still maintained at a few leading universities, including Oxford and Cambridge. This is, in essence, a workshop approach!

However, with a blended learning approach the trade-off between a more individualized approach and standardization may no longer be that necessary. This might also mean that the speed of learning might now become more of variable – after all, we all might prefer to learn as quickly as possible, but still at different speeds! We are thus again seeing the power of student/ participant-centered learning and a relatively individualized, competency-enhancing focus. As we have seen, distance learning might be particularly well suited to cover more basic competence-building, while complementary workshops might consist of somewhat more tailored learning, addressing more cutting-edge dilemmas.

Horn and Staker (2015) recommend a five-step approach toward identifying key learning problems, and have labeled this as the so-called SMART approach:

- Specific: Identify a specific area of improvement – for our setting this might, for instance, be how to come up with more efficient approaches for distance learning, with appropriate tailored materials, better technology, effective test questions, etc.
- Measurable: What would be the relevant indicators of progress? In our business school setting, this might include how to review student/participant feedback over time. Is a student's degree of satisfaction improving?
- Actions: Who is responsible? In our case, a specific program administrator might be responsible for putting core materials together. This would typically come from the particular professor in charge, and include tailored readings, control questions, etc. The necessary technology might be purchased from specific software providers, such as Moodle, for instance.
- Realistic: Can these results be achieved realistically? For us, the key question is whether a particular faculty member might be able to and be willing to develop the necessary materials needed for efficient distance learning. A professor may simply not have the required competences when it comes to this, nor the energy and/or time.
- Time-line: By when? As already indicated, time is often at a premium. It therefore is particularly important for a professor to be given a realistic timeframe in which to develop their distance learning materials over several iterations. This implies a certain degree of stability regarding the topics/workshops assigned to a given professor. They should be reasonably convinced that the time and energy that it might take to develop such learning materials would be worth it in terms of the sessions allocated for a project based on distance learning.

Hence, we can see that blended learning, perhaps analogous to a classroom lecture exercise combined with an off-campus visit to a corporation, also seems to involve a process of improving a given professor's capabilities over time. An appropriate culture for this way of learning would have to be created (Schein, 1988), and this may imply changes in attitudes, particularly among those faculty members involved. As noted, this would typically no longer involve the primary function of "delivering" specific knowledge for students to learn, but rather the development of appropriate course materials that would allow the professor to act as a discussion partner, a catalyst, implying more two-way interaction, with a discussion of key dilemmas at the heart of it all.

Troublesome Knowledge

The business school itself, to be seen as an effective learning institution, will perhaps experience the biggest change of all. Schools might typically become smaller (economies of small scale), faster (less bureaucracy), and less political (shorter meetings!). During its first 400 years, the university was fundamentally virtual (Rüegg, 2004). It was only after von Humboldt's "reform" of the University of Berlin in 1809 (von Humboldt, 1970) that university institutions got shaped the way we see them now. And most business schools of today are shaped along such lines too. We do anticipate that significant changes will take place, however, in order for us to move back to what were the dominant trends before 1809: more virtual, often part-time, nonpermanent faculty, smaller/faster academic institutions, virtual programs of studies and research, and so on!

So, more ambiguity in the way business schools operate will perhaps become a reality once more. We might indeed expect the business school of the future to deal with an abundance of key dilemmas that might be seen as "troublesome knowledge" (Perkins, 2006). For instance, while those of us in the so-called Western world might consider the government sector as an adversary, this might not be the case when it comes to much of the developing world, where the public sector might be seen as an ally, and often as a major customer. Kenya, like many other African countries, has a government sector that tends not to work all that well: a lack of stability is quite normal. However, in Kenya, the church represents stability, and businesses might develop strategies to take advantage of this (Hunderi, 2018). Therefore, while the so-called stakeholder map in the Western world might be relatively narrow, encompassing employees, customers, and shareholders, it might be far broader in the developing world. Let us consider another "troublesome" dilemma, relating to ethics. In the Western world, so-called corruption is seen as unacceptable. But this is an accepted practice in many parts of the world. In general, how should business schools cope with what might be seen as an increasing number of areas with "troublesome" knowledge? Maybe the French author Marcel Proust was correct when he stated that "the world is often seen through the eyes of others" (Proust, 1900).

There are also many uncertainties when it comes to dealing with what might be seen as relevant curricula in the future. What would the market need or want? The economic "health" of the business school of the future might be at risk if inappropriate choices are made. Potential changes in regulation may represent another source of uncertainty. Developing a pedagogy that can cope with this form of uncertainty might indeed be necessary for a business school to survive (Shulman, 2005).

Measuring Progress

How will we measure progress in the business school of the future? Traditionally, academic progress has tended to be measured according to the numbers of citations achieved by faculty member, derived from their research publications and, above all, single-authored articles in so-called A-rated refereed journals. Another way of measuring a school's progress is through how it fares in the *Financial Times* (FT) rankings, which apply to several aspects of a business school's outputs (e.g., quality of its MBA program, executive education), various geographies (e.g., Asia, Europe, US) and/or various types of programs (e.g., Undergraduate, EMBA). The basic direction of the FT rankings, however, tends to be quite similar to traditional rankings based on citation indexes, i.e., reflecting a concept of quality that might fit these traditional business schools, but not "business schools of the future" as such.

How, then, might progress be measured in the future? Let us consider five classes of factors (Lorange and Thomas, 2016):

- Rankings. We have already discussed the FT rankings, but there are a number of other considerations below.
- The measurement of values. How might values be measured when it come to a school's ability to innovate versus copying, their willingness to support the profession with more ethical "citizenship," and pro bono work, for example? This would, of course, not only relate to business schools, but also to individual professors.
- It may also be necessary to take steps to avoid schools "growing" (i.e., claiming superficial levels of growth) to be able to move up the rankings. Schools may attempt to do this by creating special subsets of their MBA programs with particularly "desirable" characteristics (e.g., international participants, women, wealthy); by double-consulting counting research outputs by including the other party in a joint venture; and by measuring internationalization on the basis of different passports rather than in terms of generic nationalities. Many so-called joint ventures with various foreign business schools may be nothing more than on-paper arrangements, rather than reflecting de facto internationalization. Why, therefore, should such arrangements be registered as indicators of internationalization?

- Measuring the quality of the students at the beginning of the course. These test scores have traditionally been important. While the development of test scores over time might be usefully tracked, it is probably even more critical to assess the incoming student body in terms of
  which companies they come from
  their career paths so far
  their previous education, including the name of the institution
  nationality and gender
- Personal interviews might still represent the "best" way of getting answers to these types of questions, despite the fact that his approach is expensive, time-consuming, and that it also assumes a relatively high quality from the interviewers.
- Tracking the progress of the financial performance of a business school is, of course, also essential. A good financial performance might signal that the attendance rate is satisfactory, even improving. But it may also signal that a business school is able to deliver high-quality programs, thus allowing the school to charge a reasonably high level of tuition fees. A good financial performance might also reflect the fact that its costs (including staff/overhead costs) are under control.
- The outputs of its faculty would, of course, also be a good indicator of whether a school is on the right track or not. Traditionally, single-authored, refereed articles in the leading journals have tended to be what has been counted. In the business school of the future, whose key focus will be on exploring cutting-edge, current dilemmas, a broader set of outputs might also be counted, such as books, practitioner-oriented articles, or even cases. The key here would be for these publications to be shedding light on some key dilemmas. Many of the visiting faculty will also, of course, publish their research, as refereed articles, books, cases, and as more practitioner-oriented articles. All of this might count for the purposes of assuring progress.
- The status of the pool of part-time professors might represent another means of assessing whether progress is being made or not. Here, a judgment might be passed about the academic institutions supplying the guest professors, and the same applies to corporations, consulting firms, etc. The general reputation of a part-time professor might also be assessed, particularly when it comes to their competence regarding a given set of cutting-edge dilemmas.
- Finally, the progress of a business school of the future might be measured in terms of its physical spread. The number of campuses it owns might be one such measure. CEIBS (Shanghai), for instance, also has campuses in Beijing, Shenzhen, Accra, and Zurich. Other physical sites

that are being used for educational purposes, including corporate settings for executive education, might also be counted.

Emerging New Contexts

There are several fundamental factors that may dramatically impact business schools' contexts. We will discuss each class of change factors in turn, and we will then use these to argue for a revised business model for a successful business school of the future. We have touched upon these factors elsewhere in this book, but not in a comprehensive way. This is the purpose of this chapter.

Let us now address each of these fundamental shifts in context, as we see them:

1   The Cost Explosion

The costs of higher education have risen steadily over the last decades. This is largely due to the fact that it has become more and more expensive to offer higher education at a certain quality. And, as we have noted, the traditional business model for good business schools is more or less similar to what it has been for a long time:

- Relatively few opportunities for scalability. Class sizes are limited by the size of the classroom so there is little scope for additional value creation.
- Relatively "light" workload for most professors, i.e., with a relatively low productivity per head of each income generator.
- Relatively heavy commitments to research, which tends to be expensive.
- An increase in the ratio of support staff to faculty, reflecting the increasing complexity of school's operating contexts.
- Increased costs of distance learning support, without seeing much (or any) decrease in any of the four factors discussed above.

On top of this, there also is a generally decreasing willingness or ability for the public sector to finance business schools. Increasingly, schools may have to rely on less stable sources of income, which are often both difficult to get and expensive (acquisition costs).

For most students, the financial burden of taking higher education is also becoming more and more of a constraint. Admittedly, there may be student loan facilities available, but such loans need to be paid back – which is often hard for young graduates. Furthermore, the availability of fellowships has always been relatively limited.

Running a high-quality business school is becoming increasingly expensive. There are several cost factors, all of which seem to be

increasing enormously, and some of which are almost out of control! Here
are some of them:

Faculty. Salaries are going up. And the revenue-generating workload (teaching) remains relatively light. When a faculty member is not teaching, they are expected to do independent
research, leading to publications, ideally in the form of single-
authored articles in refereed academic journals. And, on top of
this, a faculty member is typically "allowed" to undertake
a finite amount of consulting, say, one day per week.

Two observations need to be made at this point. First, it does not
seem likely that significant further revenue-enhancing productivity gains might be made. On the contrary, the actual number
of hours spent in the classroom tends to be relatively low – the
so-called teaching load. And most faculty members would
resist any increases in their teaching load. To significantly
increase productivity for full-time faculty members is thus
not realistic.

Second, there tends to be only light control, if any, when it comes
to monitoring performance. Admittedly, there will usually be
student feedback on faculty members' teaching. But a poor
teaching performance generally is of little consequence. And
when it comes to faculty members' research efforts, there is
even less control. There tends to be little monitoring of
whether one's research results in publishable outputs and
reaches a certain standard in terms of quality. Furthermore,
some faculty members may abuse their privileges and place
a higher priority on the time they spend on their research.
Thus, revenue-generating productivity gains are, unsurprisingly, relatively rare!

Support staff. Numbers have typically grown in many business
schools, both in absolute terms and relative to the number of
revenue-generating professional staff. Examples of the roles
found include finance/control, PR/communication/marketing,
recruiting and placement, library, legal, research or teaching,
program support, as well as more secretaries/personal assistants. While there have always been support staff, their numbers seem to have grown disproportionally in many schools.
And, surprisingly, there is not as much outsourcing as one
might expect.

The net effect of all of this is that a school's break-even point
might have become far too high – and, in some instances,
completely unattainable. In many instances, faculty and staff

bonuses might also be included as a fixed cost. Initially, these might have been considered variable costs, only paid out when a school's economic results merited it. However, such bonuses now often seem to have become "entitlements" when it comes to salary increases for faculty and staff, i.e., paid out irrespectively of the school's economic performance. The result, again, is a negative effect on a school's break-even point.

Research. This source of costs also seems to have grown considerably. Being engaged in cutting-edge research is clearly a necessity for a school with ambitions to stay on top. But increasingly it seems as if the bulk of a school's academic staff feel entitled to extensive research funding support, including paid leaves of absence. Research activities have thus become driven by the interests of individual faculty member's preferences, i.e., in essence, bottom up, rather than as the result of a more deliberate top-down policy setting/strategic choice process driven by a business school's leadership. So, while many research activities have in themselves become more expensive, this bottom-up-driven research activity typically adds significantly to research costs.

ICT. Data analysis has become a key component of a typical business schools' activities, both as part of its research activities and as an integral part of its educational efforts, as well as in its administration. And this can be expensive! With the typically rapid rate of obsolescence when it comes to hardware, combined with the increasingly specialized and sophisticated software applications now in use (requiring specially trained staff with these competences), this is another area of rapidly increasing costs.

Educational support. The costs of developing current educational materials seems to have increased rapidly – new cases, the latest video tapes, guest lectures by specialists, simulations, etc. – you have it! This could represent a significant and growing expense. On top of this, we might see a growth in the number of student projects undertaken, away from their school's campus, also implying additional costs for travel, room, and board.

Physical facilities. It goes without saying that keeping physical facilities up to date can be expensive. A school's physical space is increasingly seen as an integral part of its educational effectiveness. As we have noted, new types of educational facilities may be called for, such as relatively smaller, flat-floor auditoriums, rather than the more conventional large lecture halls. New "meeting spaces" may also have to be constructed. And more light may have to be brought into buildings through (costly) refurbishments, given that it seems to have become an emerging insight that effective education is also dependent on light and a feeling of spaciousness and beauty! On top of all of this, the school's grounds must be maintained. Meeting these new standards can be costly!

A final word on costs. All of the above suggests that schools' costs may have increased very rapidly and, in some cases, even have "exploded." This is partly due to emerging needs/requirements, relating to salaries, various support functions, and physical facilities, that will allow a school to remain on top. But the fact that growing costs may have got out of control could also be attributable to a lack of proper management in some cases. Costs need to be controlled from the top via proper priority-setting as well as by treating variable costs as variable! But this might not be all that popular among faculty, students, staff, and/or alumni. No wonder, therefore, that we often witness a growth in costs that has gone out of control!

2   Changing Study Preferences

The demographics as well as the preferences of the student body are changing! Let us review three aspects of this:

Finding meaningful jobs is not easy: there are many more applicants than there are jobs like this! Thus, for a young person who has actually found such a job and set out on a promising career, it may simply not be a realistic option to give it all up to take up a course of study. On top of this, learning on the job, perhaps in combination with learning at a business school, seems to have become increasingly attractive. Many young people realize that these two sources of learning reinforce each other. It follows that many of these individuals will be attracted to part-time study, while keeping their full-time jobs and developing their careers. Weekends and vacations are increasingly set aside for part-time studies by such individuals. And, as we will discuss in a later section, this approach may also yield significant economic benefits, in that a participant would be able to maintain at least part of their income stream.

We should stress here that the nature of work may also have changed to become more open to continuous learning. The workplace is perhaps less hierarchical, allowing more opportunities for meaningful experiences. More routine tasks may increasingly be taken over by automation (ICT or even robots!) and there are typically greater levels of diversity among colleagues, including race and gender. So, the prospect of meaningful learning on the job may realistically have increased.

Also, participants today typically demand content that is relevant and practical, including topics that they consider to be applicable to their workplace setting. Thus, what they learn at school might also change – less theory for its own sake, and more of a focus on content with real-world application potential. Thus, to be able to "bring this back to the workplace, and thereby gain further in-depth understanding" also is very much a reality.

3   *Tailored Curriculum Opportunity and Increased Choice of Study Areas*

The changes in higher education are reflected in the operations of the company Keystone, based in Oslo, Norway, but operating worldwide. Keystone is one of the leaders in the business of offering advice to students searching for a suitable program to enroll in, as well as a good university/school at which to study. Initially named Masterstudies, with a primary focus on the selection of MBA programs, the company has gradually widened its scope to include many different fields of study, including at the undergraduate level. The company's clients are schools or universities, typically represented by the admissions office of such institutions. The company is, however, seeing a gradual shift in the nature of its service. Increasingly, a student might no longer be looking for the best single school offering the optimal program, but rather might wish to put together a diverse set of courses, often offered by different institutions, representing the best fit for their individual interests. So, there is a gradual shift toward tailoring a "package" of diverse courses, often from several disciplines, offered by several schools, with the objective of coming up with an individualized "package" of courses that meet the interests of one particular student. The consequences of this shift are quite formidable when it comes to Keystone's business model. No longer will the paying client be a single admissions office, paying its fee to Keystone when a student actually selects that particular university. Rather, several admissions offices, representing a broader set of universities, will now pay Keystone for certain selected courses to be taken at each individual institution. Keystone's service will now include a much more detailed description of specific courses. The result is that Keystone's business model is becoming far more complex!

This trend is consistent with the broader phenomenon known as Massive Online Open Courses or MOOCs. Here, a student can design their own program of studies through distance learning. A wide variety of courses, covering many disciplines, are given by different institutions. A student will be awarded their diploma by the academic institution which has delivered the majority of the courses that a student has taken. It should be clearly stated on the diploma, however, what the specific list of courses are, and which academic institutions were responsible for each course. A student's individual interests have thereby taken priority over the prestige of a particular academic institution. And the distance learning approach focuses on a participant successfully completing a course, rather than on the traditional process of screening through an elaborate admissions process.

A number of firms have already emerged to provide tailored services to students who might prefer to take courses from several different schools, so-called online program managers (OPMs). Most of these are relatively small operations, representing a fairly narrow subset of schools (typically four to five), and thus are only able to offer a student a limited set of course choices. The revenue model for the typical OPM might be that its fee would be split between the various schools benefiting from a particular student's choices and the student themselves. The actual split of the fees should of course be done in such a way that it would be fair to all (the OPMs, students, schools). While we are only just seeing the fragile beginnings of OPMs, these types of firms do indeed seem to meet what might become more commonplace in the future, i.e., demands by students for more bespoke offerings, including courses taken at several different institutions, all inspired by the choice model of the MOOC.

This trend toward catering more for a student's individual needs is consistent with the call for a more practical curricular focus, with an emphasis on what each individual student might see as relevant. After all, it is each individual student who will face the challenge of getting a meaningful job when their studies are finished! This trend shift, toward courses that students might see as relevant, will also have profound impact on the portfolio of teaching programs offered at a particular academic institution. Emphasizing practical relevance, as well making a particular course "interesting for a young student," will now become even more important. Clear take-home value will be key!

It goes without saying that there are potential dangers here too, in that the preferences of a relatively inexperienced student might be given too strong an emphasis, at the expense of what might be seen as less appealing academic rigor. I recall facing a similar dilemma in 1968, when he entered the doctoral program at Harvard. At that time, the bulk of the university was on strike, led by a group of undergraduate students who were calling for more practical relevance in Harvard's curriculum, in the wake of the Vietnam War and the struggle for racial and gender equality. But did those undergraduates have sufficient insight when it came to deciding what might or might not be relevant? What about disciplinary insight, accumulated over many years? I felt that the latter was relatively much more important, and had been, in fact, a major determinant for me in deciding to study at Harvard in the first place.

There are many other factors that could potentially lead to far-reaching changes in the business school of the future. One such factor would be the area of testing and exams. Traditionally, these have been carried out in "controlled" settings, where a student might not have access to any other information than what might be in their head, as well as, perhaps, their lecture notes and a selected textbook or two. This may all change, however, with the advent of online testing. The new reality might be that quizzes and/or relatively short problems might be set and given out in on a regular basis, perhaps complemented by a more extensive final exam or paper. More resources must thus be given to the development of such tests, and more resources will need to be allocated to work through students' responses. Perhaps dedicated research associates will be allocated to these tasks. So, what we may see is an evolution toward a team of actors offering a given course: the professor and a set of dedicated assistants.

It is possible that we will see the emergence of such teaching teams in other contexts too, for example, when it comes to guiding project-based learning and/or study trips. It goes without saying that the resource requirements for these particular activities may be high. Paradoxically, relatively more teaching staff might be needed to effectively deliver distance learning, not fewer!

While most of the more basic or straightforward material can be efficiently taught via distance learning, some physical gatherings of students and professors in classroom settings will still be necessary, to ensure the best learning results. As we have discussed at some length, the format of these physical classroom gatherings will differ considerably from the traditional approach.

In summary, there is no doubt that the campus context of the business school of the future will be very different from today's experience; it will be smaller and more tailored to distance learning. This may represent a growing dilemma for the more traditional schools, which often have relatively large and conventional campuses. Retrofitting such facilities may be both expensive and difficult. Perhaps this will be one of the main factors contributing to the shakedown that will determine which schools become cutting-edge in the future!

4   The Network Model

Let us for a moment consider the challenges posed by the leading management consulting firms, such as McKinsey & Co or Boston Consulting Group (BCG), or the leading diversified consulting firms that may have initially sprung out of accounting practices: Ernest & Young (now E&Y), Price Waterhouse Coopers (now PWC), etc. These organizations have a worldwide presence, and they typically have good working relationships with leading corporations and other organizations. They also tend to be doing relatively well economically, which also implies that they are able to attract the best tutors to work for them, offering generous pay/benefits packages! And these firms are, of course, in a unique position to generate significant amounts of relevant practical cutting-edge knowledge, largely paid for by their clients! So, it would be only a small step for such firms to expand into executive education – they have the relevant knowledge, the smart/experienced staff to teach others, and they are already linked up with the clients/customers. All in all, these would pose formidable competition to leading business schools, and we are already seeing growth in this direction!

The above is a prime example of a networked organization. Scalability exists: the knowledge base can be drawn on in a new context, the consultants-cum-teachers likewise, and the link with customers can easily be broadened. This contrasts with management consulting of the distant past, where the consultants were essentially "selling" their time, and that was it! The old model was quite similar to that of a taxi driver – you sell billable time! Unfortunately, many of today's business schools fall into the nonscalable category too. But distance learning may provide an opportunity for business schools to become more scalable.

There are four factors typically present in successful network organizations, which we also expect to become central for business schools of the future. To achieve greater scalability, it is key to emphasize:
- Fast expansion/fast growth is key in network organizations, through building on scalability, similar to what we saw in the consulting company examples.
- One must be prepared to invest quite heavily in the network: developing customer contracts, establishing unique content based on an exclusive offering, investing in a proprietary software for one's network, etc.

- Spillovers. It may be relatively easy for others to copy one's network-based strategy. It would therefore be important to create access restrictions. And, it would be essential to take advantage of intangible investments in, say, a customer base which might have been expensive to develop, and hard to copy.
- Synergies. Most of the core know-how, customer links, and/or key people might be made use of in other settings, such as learning combined with education, art, travel, food/restaurants, real estate, etc. (Haskell and Westlake, 2018).

We have already seen how the business school of the future is likely to be a network organization. And we have already discussed to what extent the Lorange Institute was successfully built on this. We may perhaps also argue that the present Lorange Network has the potential to become an example of an effective business school of the future, par excellence! Let's now see how this was put into practice.

A Networked-Based Strategy in Practice

Let us revisit some of the experiences I have been faced with, having been associated with several leading business schools throughout my career, and, as a consequence of this journey, why I have come to the conclusion that a networked-based strategy will be key for the business school of the future.

I spent a total of eighteen years as a professor at MIT's Sloan School of Management, and then at the Wharton School of the University of Pennsylvania. These were both business schools that were rated among the very best, with the best students, world-class faculty, and with a particular emphasis on research. But there was little attempt to build a more networked-based strategy, so as to take more advantage of scalability. Both schools had (and have) excellent relations with their alumni, for instance. But initiatives to utilize this advantage systematically, say, by offering revenue-generating programs for this group, or/and the companies they represented, were largely absent. Revenue was raised through teaching, and the finite classroom capacity was indeed the bottleneck. One might safely conclude that the core strategies of both the Sloan School and Wharton were rather traditional, and typical of the leading research-based business schools.

When I became president at BI (Norwegian School of Business, Oslo), there was already a strong element of a networked-based strategy in place. This took the form of a set of so-called regional campuses, which offered teaching programs developed at BI's central facility, and with teachers largely recruited from the local business elite and trained by BI's central staff. Supplementary teaching was also done by dedicated central staff. Teaching materials, tests, and exams were standardized throughout this network of regional schools, all wholly owned by BI. This network was further strengthened and expanded on during my time as head of BI, and at the end of my tenure, we had a total of thirteen regional campuses.

Then, when I became president of IMD, one of Europe's leading business schools, with a particular focus on executive education, my colleagues and I tried to develop more of a network-based strategy there too. In particular, we were relatively successful in creating a network of partners and business associates, from companies that also bought in-company programs at IMD. These networks became a central focus of the entire marketing of the school's teaching program portfolio. And gradually, also, distance learning materials were added. Audio-visual teaching materials were also developed, so that, say, interviews with various CEOs based on case studies on their companies might be used in a variety of settings. Of critical importance was the development of relatively free-standing teaching modules, with dedicated faculty members (i.e., specialists in offering particular modules, largely based on their own research and teaching materials). These modules were then offered in various combinations to companies. Each company's program design was thus unique, but many of the modules in such programs were standardized. The result was not only considerable cost savings, but an impressive ability to develop new corporate programs at speed!

A one-week program, Orchestrating Winning Performance (OWP) was successfully offered once a year, where all of IMD's faculty were involved, offering their latest research and pedagogical findings. Participants would have an opportunity to choose what would interest them to a certain degree, i.e., an example of a student-tailored curriculum, which is in line with current trends, as we have noted. Since the program took place over a short, six-day period, there was an emphasis on speed. By the end of my tenure as head of IMD, more than 800 participants were enrolling in OWP each year, and the program became a backbone of the school's financial success. However, we did meet with faculty resistance when it came to expanding this network-based offering, for example, by repeating the program several times per year and/or offering it in other geographic locations.

So, when I launched the Lorange Institute of Business in Horgen, a major ambition was to create an effective network-based strategy without being hampered by traditional faculty conventions. No full-time faculty members were hired. Many of the part-time faculty members came from nonconventional sources, being either leading practitioners or consultants. The key was that each faculty member would bring to the table their own specific know-how. This know-how would thus not have had to be financed by the Lorange Institute and developed there. This by itself is not much of a network-focused strategy, however. This is where the learning pedagogy of the Lorange Institute comes in. Extensive banks of teaching materials and background reading were made available to the students via distance learning. And, onsite teaching was carried out in relatively short modules (typically two to three days each), with a strong focus on discussions of key dilemmas. There would thus be a lot of flexibility for a participant to focus on those topics of key interest to them and on a part-time basis, in parallel with their main careers. Testing would be carried out by students writing a short paper after having studied preassignments but before each workshop (to test that the prereading had actually been studied and understood), and then another short paper would be given after each workshop to test that the discussions on key dilemmas had indeed led to deeper insights. All in all, this network-based strategy worked well. It provided the Lorange Institute with a lot of capacity, and at a relatively low cost. It allowed for flexibility, speed, and innovation, and it was largely in line with participants' needs and preferences. On top of this, the Lorange Institute's campus in Horgen was a modern structure, with a lot of light and high ceilings, and was located in a beautiful setting on the shores of Lake Zurich, close to the airport, and with its own restaurant.

But, why have a campus at all when it comes to the business school of the future? Why not post original dedicated learning materials on the web, provided by independent faculty members now labeled "experts" or "contributors"? And why not bring together groups of learners (i.e., subscribers to the expert briefings) in short conferences, fireside chat discussions or/and in short discussion workshops, say, over weekends. This is exactly what we have done at the Lorange Network, which is perhaps a rather radical prototype of a business school of the future. There are no faculty members, but a cadre of about seventy part-time experts/contributors (professors, consultants, leading practitioners), and the students are paying members of this online web-based service. There is no campus, but meetings are held at various convenient places (close to airports). In addition, learning also takes place through dialogue between network members.

A Summary of Network-Based Strategies

We have already referred to Haskell and Westlake's analysis of successful network strategies with their emphasis on the following four key criteria for success:

- More scalable!
- More sunk costs
- Easier for others to copy; sill-overs
- More synergies.

In our opinion, factors one and four may be the relatively most important ones, however. In addition, we shall add another three key factors, out of which the first of these shall in turn also have three subfactors. These are:
- Closeness to the customer/student
  • Subfactor one: faster, more speed!
  • Subfactor two: easier to innovate
  • Subfactor three: a progressive culture; more dynamic
- Cost-effective
- More prone to attract/innovate/motivate the best people; appearance of "smallness," "flat"/less hierarchy; flexible regarding workplace/rules more in line with today's values!

Conclusion

It is clear that the context for successful business schools is changing. We have discussed three such major context changes in this book. First, the students are changing – today's careers patterns are different, and there is a clear shift toward part-time studies; second, today's student requires more relevance – i.e., a more tailored curriculum, with a greater focus on two-way discussions of key dilemmas; and third, the economics of education has changed, both for the students (it is now much more expensive to study) and for the business school itself (it is much more expensive to deliver high-quality education, and therefore much harder for a school to reach break-even). We have also suggested that the paramount strategic change that business schools need to make to be able to successfully cope with the changing context is to adopt a so-called network strategy. The business school of the future will in all likelihood be shaped around these principles. The Lorange Network is one example of a robust concept for a network-based strategy for a business school. This is, in my opinion, a sign of what we might expect when it comes to the business school of the future. We do not yet have the full picture, of course. All that we can surmise is that the business school of the future will be dramatically different from what we find in many of today's business schools.

We will now, in Chapter 10, examine a number of case examples of leading business schools, including the successes and challenges they have experienced in implementing the types of innovations we propose.

10   Eight Case Examples

In this final chapter, we will provide eight case examples from eight different business schools. Each might be seen as representing particular cutting-edge practices that could become part of the business school of the future. Several of these examples, in particular those of IMD in Lausanne, IE International in Madrid, and BI Norwegian School of Business, illustrate how modern technology may be changing the nature of various learning programs. Two of the examples, from Zurich Institute of Business Education, Zurich and Hult International Business School, London, illustrate how an internationally distributed geographical presence can have positive programmatic impacts, as well as revealing some of the key challenges of a multicampus approach. There are also two examples which illustrate how specific courses might evolve as part of this new world, as well as how such a program design might impact the evolution of the entire academic institution. These are WHU – Otto Beisheim School of Management and, again, BI Norwegian School of Business. Introducing an institutional culture that supports such programmatic innovations seems particularly key. The final two examples, Cardiff Social Science Park and Singapore Management University (SMU), Singapore, illustrate above all the importance of cross-functional learning activities, in contrast to the more traditional eclectic or discipline-based approach. Relevant knowledge sets might be developed in this way, in terms of becoming more innovation-minded (Cardiff) or by allowing participants to gain more relevant managerial experience (SMU). In both cases, we see how having a unique architectural building in which to study can impact on the participants' experience, both content-wise, in terms of a greater focus on innovation, and in relation to the creation of relevant new pedagogical approaches.

While the eight examples, grouped in four pairs, are meant to illustrate particular evolutionary features that we might expect to find in the business school of the future, it should be noted that all the examples provided illustrate other important evolutionary aspects. Thus, each of these schools should perhaps be regarded as exemplifying several key factors that may take on increased importance in business schools in the years to come.

At the end of this chapter, there is an Appendix which provides a way for students to undertake self-assessments of their learning experience, developed by Dr. O. Brenninkmeijer. These student self-assessments might be particularly appropriate for assessing the degree to which students might actually benefit from the various innovations discussed in each of the cases in this chapter.

The Executive MBA (EMBA) Program at IMD

IMD is world renowned for its executive programs and has repeatedly been ranked by the Financial Times as having the best EMBA program offering. This case example details just one aspect of the EMBA program, past and present; namely how their programmatic efforts have been particularly important for their success and the development of virtual learning at IMD in general. This case is divided into six parts, the first four of which relate to the EMBA program, as follows:
• The history of the EMBA program
• The present structure of the EMBA program
• Virtual learning
• A distance learning executive program in marketing
• Short transformation programs
• Major innovations: a summary.

The History of the EMBA Program

The EMBA program was first launched at IMD in 1999 as an extension of the school's well-established 10-week PED program (Program for Executive Development). Having completed the PED, participants could take a further four modules of two weeks each, plus a one-week study trip – the so-called discovery event – and would then receive an EMBA degree.

The further evolution of this program required several major steps. The extension of the PED program was dropped and executives would now apply directly to the EMBA program. The largest part of this (i.e., the previous PED) was shortened, and split into two modules, respectively called Foundation of Business Leadership and Advanced Management Concepts. A participant might now prefer to enroll in only one of these modules, and not go through the entire program sequence.

This initial development (four modules of two weeks) was later modified in several ways, including the evolution of study trips. These gradually became fully integrated program elements, not "industrial tourism," nor merely "discovery events." They now involved advance preparation, such as the identification of specific institutions to be visited, themes to be focused on in these companies, participant team assignments, project evaluation procedures, and so on.

More online study activities were also introduced, with complementary shorter modules offered at IMD. Some of these might involve:
• Discussions of key dilemmas
• Written papers
• High-quality feedback

The present format of the EMBA has thus evolved over time and now offers:
• Highly individualized learning offerings to meet the specific needs of each individual participant
• A lot of flexibility regarding how time is spent
• A program designed in such a way that it might be easily be combined with a full-time job
• Hence, an even more efficient program.

Present Structure of the EMBA Program

This brief history of the evolution of the EMBA program brings us up to the present. It should be noted that there have been several significant changes in the environment in which EMBA programs are delivered:
• As we have seen, prospective participants now increasingly demand shorter periods of time away from their jobs. They are typically intent on combining their studies with their full-time jobs, and also expect more or less all aspects of the program to yield immediate insights for them, so that they can apply these in their jobs!
• Candidates are now typically fully computer literate, generally being comfortable with learning via the computer at home. They also see the benefits of face-to-face discussions in school, especially when it comes to discussing cutting-edge dilemmas. Learning from other participants with different educational and work experiences is typically seen as particularly attractive. These modules on campus are expected to be short and intensive. Weekend work is also anticipated.

The profiles of the student participants have also changed. They are typically now even more demanding, more experienced, and they are older and even more highly motivated, given that this way of learning implies a lot of extra effort for most of them, as well as a sacrifice in terms of how their time is spent!

To meet these contextual changes, IMD's EMBA program would evolve to encompass a well-developed online component, with self-study through distance learning and virtual teams, investigative research, and publishable case writing, all in a setting of intense experiential learning (see below). In particular, two additional features were incorporated into the EMBA programs:

- Even more experiential learning, largely achieved through study trips abroad. As noted, each of these lasted for one week. A participant would be expected to choose three out of five offerings. The options for countries that might be visited would typically change from year to year, but in one recent year they were Brazil, South Africa, India, China, Vietnam, or the US. These trips were meant to provide experience of business practices and key issues in various local contexts, but still within a global setting. Typical examples might be understanding local market potentials, labor/productivity issues, and the assessment of business climate and political stability. In-depth contact with successful local actors was sought, in particular. Thus, this was not considered to be "industrial tourism" or "mere discovery."
- A three-day crisis management simulation.

In sum, the EMBA program was now structured around three stages:

Step 1: Foundations for Business Leadership. This was a three-week module, given at IMD, and was in fact the present version of the original five-week PED program! It was offered four times per year, and was meant to provide prospective participants with not only a basic managerial foundation, but also a lot of flexibility regarding scheduling. Many participants elected to enroll in this offering on a free-standing basis.

Step 2: Advanced Management Concepts (AMC). This consisted of a five-week module, in total offered in the form of distance learning, and was given three times per year. The focus here was for the participants to master the various fundamental business concepts provided in Step 1 (strategy, finance, marketing, and decision analysis), and also to allow each participant to experiment with their ability to manage their time (in preparation for Step 3). There would be an exam at the end of these five weeks. A pass grade was required to be allowed to progress to Step 3. This would typically ensure a more "level playing field" at the start of this final stage, and thus also improve the likelihood of an accelerated pace of learning.

Step 3: Mastery Stage. This final stage would last for twelve months. Here a participant might choose between two offerings per year. Each offering would include three study trips, as mentioned, and three one-week modules at IMD, with face-to-face discussions of key dilemmas (including three days of crisis simulation). In addition, there was a lot of distance learning, focusing on company-specific applications, adding up to a full year of learning.

The program's Director, Ms. Terry Akitt, makes the following observation: "Learning is key! But this must be done in such a way that the participants experience a high degree of consistency, not lack of coordination, both when it comes to face-to-face learning in the various sessions at IMD, given by different professors, together with the various distance learning modules. A high degree of planning is thus needed, so that the various inputs from IMD as well as those via distance 'hang together' in a cohesive and integrated manner, to provide an even more enriching, challenging, and unique learning journey."

Virtual Learning

The EMBA program at IMD might be seen as a forerunner when it comes to distance learning. Paul Hunter, Director of Digital Learning at IMD, made the following observations concerning the future of digital learning. For this to be fully effective and yield a strong, positive, measurable impact, there are seven key aspects of digital learning that should be adhered to:

- Start at the end when it comes to the creation of any learning experience, so that the participants' learning objectives are clearly defined. This would, of course, be true for more traditional classrooms settings, but it would be of paramount importance for online learning.
- Treat executives like executives. A more scholastic approach, such as deploying multiple choice questionnaires, may seem expedient but would typically not be appreciated by executives. In many cases, such questionnaires will therefore fail to provide meaningful data, perhaps other than checking for basic knowledge retention. On the other hand, asking executives to test hypotheses, draw their own conclusions, and to submit evidence-based results regarding how they might have used a particular concept in their own professional arena will have a better chance of creating a higher level of commitment.
- "Change the channel." A common error is to assume that online learning would be more or less a virtual version of what works in the classroom. The best online executive programs, however, have a "fresh" learning design, built around the virtual channel. A greater focus on relatively short, self-contained submodules might be particularly useful.

- Respect the "holy trinity" of virtual learning. Successful virtual programs weave together these three distinct elements:
  - design, covering learning objectives and the approach to evaluation
  - production, of videos regarding various types of content and online interaction mechanisms
  - delivery, via a specific platform, with online coaching
- If any of these are undertaken in isolation, there is a risk of being unable to deliver sufficiently significant and stimulating learning experiences.
- Keep the content fresh and easy to digest. Executives who like virtual programs expect (and acknowledge) fresh, cutting-edge content. If the materials are too old or stale, not even an outstanding presentation will save the day. Similarly, even the latest technology will not impress without cutting-edge content.
- Demonstrate impact. A learning assignment that does not have direct relevance to a busy executive's own working life would, in all likelihood, be seen as a waste of their time. The best way to tap into their intrinsic motivation is to pursue learning that is likely to have measurable results and useful applications in their own workplace. Relevant managerial payoff is essential!
- Feedback is key! An executive is usually motivated to take feedback, and will be ready to do so, particularly if the provider of such feedback has their respect. Change might actually then happen! In contrast, unstructured feedback from random sources, with little to no relevant experience, would not be likely to meet the expectations of busy executives.

A Distance Learning Executive Program in Marketing

One of the innovations introduced at IMD was a major distance learning program on marketing. This purely distance learning-based interactive program, known as the Value-Based Marketing Management program, lasted for eight weeks and was developed for Hilti, a multinational company that develops products for the construction and mining industry. This program might be considered a cutting-edge example of a so-called interactive learning journey. For each week-long module, the following four steps apply:

- Probe into a specific aspect of marketing
- Interact with others, at Hilti as well as at IMD, regarding the specific learning issue covered. This is thus an example of two-way interaction!
- Each participant should aim to apply the specific marketing issues raised to their own job setting, i.e., active use of learning!
- Improvement of these specific aspects of marketing, largely based on feedback from the coach.

Distance learning materials were developed, covering each of the eight one-week modules, covering:

- Marketing's value in the firm
- Customer lifetime value
- Competing for value
- Understanding customer value
- Co-creating value
- Capturing value
- Organizing for value-based marketing
- Drawing it all together!

The developmental costs of such a program can be considerable! It is thus advisable to ensure that each module is created in such a way that it might be deployed in a range of different programs. At IMD, this approach to modular program design is known as the "Lego Brick approach"!

Short Transformation Programs

Let us now briefly look at a series of digital business transformation programs. To further build on its capabilities when it came to online executive learning, IMD has launched a series of short programs on digital business transformation. This was based on the premise that advances in digital technologies might now be transforming most industries, thus potentially opening up for new business opportunities. Traditional strategies, leadership approaches, and/or one's organizational structure might have to be changed! Key features covered would be artificial intelligence, machine learning, the block chain concept, and "the Internet of Things." These offerings consisted of a 5-day core course, coupled with seven relatively shorter courses of 2½ days. A participant might earn a diploma in Digital Excellence upon successfully completing the bulk of this course sequence (the longer core + 4 of the shorter offerings). The pedagogy was based on blend of learning, partly virtual, partly at IMD, and with distance learning exams.

Major Innovations: A Conclusion

According to Matthew Simmons (senior advisor on distance learning and R&D; ex senior executive at Sutzer), there were three major innovations coming out of the distance-based virtual learning initiatives at IMD:

- Excursions. Not "industrial tourism" but deep local immersion: (working with local actors, on specific projects)
- Spending a minimum amount of time away from the office. For example, one might drop time-consuming activities that add nothing, such as

the GMAT, a conventional test used to assess managerial proficiency. It should be noted that the GMAT test was dropped because it seemed to add relatively little value to executive learning, in addition to being a very time-consuming (and expensive) activity. This test was replaced by another test that was deemed to be more relevant for proficiency assessment in executive learning (the AMC test).

- Creating more relevant learning activities, above all, by "listening to the participants." This active learning approach involved: "plan; do; observe; reflect." This might, in time, lead to a more effective learning experience, and, in the long term, better results in the participants' companies.

As a result of the above, there would be no nonessential elements in the program. Matthew Simmons was also responsible for a renewed focus on coaching, and for ensuring that there was effective feedback to participants. He was also involved in the organization of the excursions.

IE Business School, Madrid

IE Business School was founded in 1973 by local entrepreneurs, and was organized as an independent, private, not-for-profit foundation. It is located in the center of Madrid, in the city's main business district. The basic philosophy of the school has always been to be entrepreneurial, to focus heavily on its customers' needs, and to be flexible and responsive. Over the years, several other schools were added to IE (law; architecture/design; human sciences/technology; international relations), and the umbrella name for the institution was changed to IE University. This group of schools were highly successful, with strong enrollment growth.

It might perhaps be useful to briefly compare the evolution of IE with what might be typically found within the university sector. An excellent review of what might be considered the main evolutionary stages of higher academic institutions was made by Ritzen. His analysis focuses on the evolution of Dutch universities since 1945, but this was equally applicable for business schools, as well as for other academic institutions. He identified five stages (Ritzen):

- The academic institutions of tradition
- The democratized academic institution
- The bureaucratic academic institution
- The professional academic institution
- The innovative academic institution. (This issue has already been discussed in Chapter 1)

Overall enrollment in IE Business School had grown to more than 3,600 students by 2017.

Its success might be attributed to several factors, including a strong international faculty, a robust pedagogical approach, as well as a strong research focus, an excellent student body, and so on. But two particular features in particular make IE Business School stand out as truly unique, namely its leadership in technological excellence, having integrating IT into its academic value creation, as well as its unique joint venture with the *Financial Times* (FT). In this case example, we will discuss each of these in turn.

Technological Excellence

IE Business School was a pioneer in integrating IT into its value-creating activities. On the teaching side, the school pioneered the development of online learning materials, which, combined with strong class sessions focusing on relevant key dilemmas, helped to make IE a leader in blended learning. The more basic dimensions were usually covered via distance learning, while follow-on class discussions went into more detail regarding key dilemmas on particular themes. Joint activities with other leading academic institutions (Brown University, Singapore Management University, Antai University in Japan) reinforced this, with relevant substantive inputs being provided more generally from partners. Visiting faculty thus came from these academic institutions, and now and then from other academic institutions too, or from practice.

Furthermore, a unique and innovative learning laboratory was developed. Here, the focus was on developing specific innovations that might have potential for commercialization. Students benefited from each other's inputs on these types of projects. A main feature of this laboratory was to bring a diverse group of students together, from the various schools of IE University, to "allow" creativity to take place through extensive and eclectic interaction.

Once a week, a subset of innovative projects was selected to be presented to potential investors. Several projects were commercialized in this way. Feedback from this commercialization stage was also provided to the students. IE was also a leader in and early adopter of so-called MOOCs (Wilson, 2013). The key premise was that students might take different virtual courses at different institutions, providing greater flexibility. Significantly, most of the students who enrolled tended to remain committed and completed their degrees, in contrast to what one might find at many other schools, where one or a several virtual courses would not necessarily be completed. IT-based learning activities definitely gained positive momentum, and the typical relatively high drop-out rates did not seem to be a major issue at IE. This trend may be to do with the fact that there had been a significant evolution when it came to virtual courses offerings, from the typical MOOC-type offerings, given exclusively virtually, to a mixed pedagogical model of virtual and in-class study, i.e., blended learning.

A recent innovation at IE Business School has been the so-called virtual innovation classroom. Here, groups of students, of up to forty at a time, are able to experience some of the latest features of today's virtual reality. These include exposure to expert inputs via screens, including two-way discussions with experts; exposure to background facts about a given area; discussions with senior executives in the company featured in a case study; interaction with student groups from other campuses; exposure to lectures, discussions, interviews, etc., featuring specific professors. In sum, the virtual classroom is yielding promising results.

The school was also a pioneer when it came to applying IT to research. Faculty members typically work virtually with colleagues from other academic institutions, as well as from business. One example of this was the successful development of its Laboratory/Center for Entrepreneurship (WOW), where virtual teams focus on various start-up/entrepreneurial/family business issues. This is closely linked to the innovation and learning laboratory activities discussed above.

The Joint Venture with FT: A Corporate Learning Alliance

The 50/50 alliance between IE and the *Financial Times* (FT) was created in the fall of 2014. The other party was now owned by Nikkei (of Tokyo), after recently having been sold by the Pearson Group. The basic rationale for this strategic alliance was to be able to offer cutting-edge executive programs, particularly to corporations, by combining IE's unique pedagogical capabilities and the FT's cutting-edge substantive knowledge when it came to many current business areas. This joint venture was headquartered in London, at the FT's facilities, with a subsidiary at IE's campus in Madrid. The joint venture had its own autonomous organizational setup. IE's portfolio of corporate programs was transferred to the joint venture.

The venture's success has been formidable. A number of other academic institutions were subsequently invited to join the joint venture, typically for the delivery of specific programs (Yale School of Management, Fundação Getulio Vargas; Monterey Tech; Singapore Management University; Jian Tong and Renmin Business School (China)). It should be noted, however, that its success was related primarily to the design and delivery of executive programs for corporations. Corporate clients might perhaps be best placed to appreciate the combined benefits of the two partners: accessing the latest pedagogical advances and cutting-edge factual business knowledge!

It is interesting to observe that other organizations have also attempted create similar joint ventures, to combine business schools' pedagogical and program delivery capabilities with substantive cutting-edge business knowledge from business news organizations. The joint venture between Cornell and Fortune Magazine is perhaps the best example of this.

Conclusion

It is safe to conclude that IE Business School had made significant advances in its use of IT, and over a relatively short time period. Not only had its enthusiastic adoption of the latest IT-based technology been a key determinant in its success, but also, it had the ability to enter into truly innovative networks for mobilizing know-how. Here, the combination of network capabilities (primarily from IE) and substantive inputs (primarily from FT) seem critical. A business school would typically not be able to come up with such a comprehensive package of new knowledge on its own. Flexibility, speed, and open-mindedness all seem to be key, and IE scores highly on all of these issues. Above all, IE Business School did not seem to be enamored with the preservation of traditions which might have made these strategic moves more difficult.

The International Master's Program at Zurich Institute of Business Education

The campus of this school is located in Horgen, on the shores of Lake Zurich. Legally, the school is owned by a Swiss foundation. De facto, however, it is part of CEIBS, Shanghai, the China-based business school, jointly owned by the Chinese government and the European Union. Formerly the school was the Lorange Institute of Business Zurich. CEIBS is not permitted to own campuses outside of China, as stated in its by-laws, hence the ownership is through a Swiss foundation. From a strategic and promotional point of view, the school is part of CEIBS's global efforts. Similarly, a campus in Accra, Ghana, is managed in this way.

This case example provides an overview of graduate and executive education at the Zurich Institute of Business Education, CEIBS's Zurich campus. First, we will provide a brief historical review of the major developmental trends of the recent past, when the school was the Lorange Institute of Business Zurich. Then, we will take a look at how the Zurich Institute of Business Education's EMBA program has been designed, including an assessment of the major benefits accrued from being part of CEIBS, as well some weaknesses. We will also highlight some of the major innovative challenges for the parent school, CEIBS. The final section, on government regulation and the business school of the future, highlights some of the key innovation-related challenges for Swiss business schools in general if the country is to remain a leading international center for higher business education.

Lorange Institute of Business

The school was called the Lorange Institute of Business Zurich from 2009 to the end of 2015. The focus was mainly on master's-level and executive education. As the Lorange Institute of Business Zurich did not have the legal authority to grant degrees, formal cooperation was initially established with the University of Wales, and later with Ashridge Business School. The Lorange Institute also was accredited by AMBA in London, EPAS (Brussels), as well as by several Swiss accreditation entities.

Sets of educational modules were developed to serve the executive MBA as well as the executive education segments. These were generally offered over relatively short, intensive time periods, most often taught by part-time faculty members who came from all over the world, and who were leading experts in their fields. The so-called Zurich Living Case approach was a crucial element of the executive master's program. This involved student teams analyzing a key real-life problem of a company and reporting their conclusions to the company's senior executives. A live classroom debate would then take place between the students and the executives. Finally, the company would receive a report from the students. This would be quite similar to a consulting project.

The executive education activities were primarily focused on delivering in-company programs to a set of leading companies in Switzerland and in the rest of Europe. These programs were also modularized, but some were delivered at different sites, as chosen by the client company. The majority of the programs were run at the school's Zurich campus, however. There was a high degree of overlap between the core offering of the executive master's program and the executive development programs.

Zurich Institute of Business Education

As noted, CEIBS took over the school at the end of 2015 and it was renamed Zurich Institute of Business Education. The EMBA program at the Zurich Institute of Business Education, a carry-over from the Lorange Institute of Business Zurich, was now modified to resemble the global EMBA structure that was in place at CEIBS's other campuses. This revised program was labeled Global Executive MBA (GEMBA). There would now be yearly class cohorts with students from China, Africa, Europe, and elsewhere. Some of the existing modules were retained, but a lot of new educational content was developed, specifically covering China and Africa. Significantly, the GEMBA program now aimed at developing an even stronger multicultural competence, based on CEIBS's presence on three continents, with approximately one-third of the students coming from Asia, one-third from Africa, and one-third from Europe. This diverse cohort group of students worked together: studying, discussing, undertaking group work, and engaging in projects. This cross-cultural cooperation seemed to work well and to yield good results.

The former Zurich Living Case approach was further evolved. It was now positioned as a capstone project in the GEMBA program, featuring the so-called real situation learning method, which involved the development of a short case on a given company, prepared by a professor, which was analyzed beforehand by each student and followed up in an initial class discussion. Then the student would visit the given company, and there would be a final class discussion. Significant improvements were thus made to the "Living Case" approach with the addition of real-life company visits. A case would be developed beforehand also, highlighting a key cutting-edge strategic issue that this company was currently facing. This case would be developed by a faculty member, who would be working closely with the management team of this given company. There would be more in-depth class discussions on the key issues, one before the field visit to the company, and one after. Thus, the initial case discussion that would take place before the company visit would be based on the facts given in the case only. Then, after the company visit, which would give the students the opportunity to interface with management, a final case discussion would take place. Finally, senior executives would come to the Institute and discuss the case with the students, in a departure from the past when less senior executives would have come, or when there would be no executive presence at all at these debriefings.

There would also be programmatic electives. These might be taken at any of the campuses in the CEIBS group. Each of these electives would cover twenty days of studies. A systematic program of study trips was also organized. These typically involved visits to one or two companies, combined with relevant class sessions at the Zurich Institute.

The Zurich Institute of Business Education would also go on to more actively pursue open enrollment programs. The school attempted to draw on CEIBS's unique position as being the only leading graduate business school in the world with a strong presence in the fastest growing continents of the world: Asia/China and Africa! In theory, the CEIBS group would be able to mobilize a strong presence, with five functioning campuses on three continents, and with a well-established network of key executives in business positions on each continent. In reality, however, Zurich Institute of Business Education was left more or less alone to implement its own executive education programs. There would be relatively little input from the other CEIBS schools, and the client base remained largely Swiss.

The CEIBS alumni organization in Europe constitutes five active chapters. The alumni from the former Lorange Institute of Business Zurich have also become members. An active drive to increase the market's awareness of CEIBS and of the Zurich Institute of Business Education was undertaken. This was not a small task, given the fact that these two school entities were largely unknown in Europe so far. A series of evening sessions were organized, some for the alumni and some for a wider network of contacts. These would typically consist of a relatively short presentation on a current topic, by a well-known expert on this particular topic. Then, there would be a discussion, and it would conclude with cocktails and finger food in the school's lobby. Typically, around fifty people might attend each session. Building brand awareness in this way was, however, seen as both a relatively slow and expensive process.

Clearly, being part of the CEIBS group would significantly strengthen the Zurich Institute of Business Education, not least when it came to the prospects of receiving accreditations. Since the Chinese parent organization had accreditations from AACSB and EFMD, this had also benefited the Zurich Institute of Business Education. However, it was now also attempting to obtain the highest official Swiss accreditation, and the fact that CEIBS had permanent faculty in Shanghai would count when it came to satisfying the faculty requirement. This was significant, given the fact that the tradition of exclusively making use of part-time faculty members was retained after the buyout. But, what about the program side? Since programs were, in theory, delivered as cooperative efforts throughout the entire CEIBS network, how then might the Zurich Institute be recognized as having a minimum of two free-standing programs, developed onsite, which was a requirement for Swiss accreditation? The lack of permanent faculty was indeed a bottleneck!

Dr. Philipp Boksberger was head of the Zurich Institute of Business Education. He had previously led the Lorange Institute of Business Zurich. He felt that there were several significant positive aspects associated with being part of the CEIBS group. Perhaps the most important of these would be to have become part of a truly global leading business school. As for CEIBS, a well-established leading business school in its own right, a strong presence in the Swiss market was now also in the process of becoming a reality. The former Lorange Institute of Business Zurich, in contrast, could never have dreamed of being part of such a strong organization. There would have been considerably larger credibility hurdles to overcome, including an almost total lack of presence in the fast-growing Asian markets as well as in Africa, and when it came to having sufficient economic resources. Incidentally, an expensive school renovation program was initiated by CEIBS. This would not have been feasible in the past.

As noted, the Zurich Institute of Business Education was granted considerable autonomy, especially when it came to its own program design. It was now, for instance, pursuing the development of a new marketing program, with a special focus on "routes to markets." This program would also benefit from research on big data analysis through cloud computing. And a tie-in had been initiated with the world-famous school of Hotel Management in Lausanne, leading to a joint program of management in the tourism sector.

Dr. Boksberger insisted that the Zurich Institute of Business Education was legally and financially autonomous and managed as a profit center within the CEIBS group. While this was basically beneficial, in the sense that it ensured efficient operations, there were also some potential downsides to being part of CEIBS in general. For example, more innovative program design might become problematic. Experimentation (carefully executed, of course) might also now be dropped. And there might be more bureaucracy, compared to when the Institute was independent, in an earlier phase. Also, there might be new constraints on program offerings. In particular, any new program offering would now have to be compatible with what was offered in Shanghai. The tourism education initiative referred to above, had, for instance, been carefully coordinated with the Shanghai headquarters to avoid overlaps. He also noted a relatively strong silo mentality at the main campus in Shanghai, with a potential negative spillover effect from too little dialogue and coordination between the various entities in the group. An example of this was that he felt that some key people in Shanghai might see Zurich as some sort of a competitor. Hence, these factors could combine to make things more difficult at the Zurich Institute!

Governmental Regulation and the Business School of the Future: Examples from Switzerland

Much of the existing governmental regulation in Switzerland is based on models for higher education that no longer represent the reality in today's business schools. For instance, as previously noted, the regulatory requirement for a school of higher education to have at least two programs of its own to receive official Swiss accreditation might not now be entirely realistic, given that several schools will typically cooperate to offer various cutting-edge programs. Ideally, a lot of programmatic cooperation would take place between schools in networks, but this would be difficult to achieve within the Swiss system of accreditation. Paradoxically, the innovations required to enhance programmatic quality might thus be hampered by formal regulations.

Governmental regulations may pose further limitations when it comes to opening new schools for higher education, to pursue a new way of doing things. While it is relatively easy to establish new schools in Switzerland, it might be next to impossible in other countries, such as the UK. Strict regulations might also hamper innovation.

The strong global reputation of the two Swiss federal institutes of technology, ETH and EPFL, therefore represents a true conundrum within the Swiss university/higher education system. How can these institutes be so innovative while operating within a relatively highly regulated Swiss educational system? The large number of entrepreneurial spin-offs at ETH and EPFL might perhaps provide a clue to this. In order for such spin-offs to become successful, they would have needed to incorporate cutting-edge technology and business processes. This, in turn, could put pressure on these two organizations to actually provide for this, and thus be more innovative themselves!

Conclusion

This case example demonstrates how a global presence was able to transform the offerings of a high-quality Swiss-based business school. Being part of a larger, more well-established resource base and an institution with an international profile made it considerably easier to develop innovative new programs as well as to secure important accreditations. Specifically, we saw that being located in major growth markets (China and Africa) as well as in the well-established Swiss market gave CEIBS a strategic advantage, particularly when it came to pursuing a truly global strategy, with an explicit mix of student participants from each of these continents. We also saw, however, that there were real de facto constraints to be faced when attempting to implement such a global presence. Building strong market awareness typically requires significant resources and takes time!

Hult (London)

Hult is an international business school with campuses in several countries, on three continents. The school was founded when Bertil Hult (Swedish) took over the former Arthur D. Little Business School in Cambridge, Massachusetts in 2003. Mr. Hult was the founder and owner of the EF, the world's largest private Language School. EF recruited many MBA and master's students from business schools worldwide, so Mr. Hult has a natural interest in global business education. The ADL school was renamed Hult International Business School and was formally a Massachusetts charitable organization. During the first few years, Bertil Hult's son, Philip, served as president in parallel with running parts of a fast-growing EF. In 2006, Stephen Hodges became president. He was a former McKinsey partner and had led a credit card division of a large bank in Hong Kong. As of 2017, the executive vice presidents of undergraduate and postgraduate education, the head of Ashridge (executive education) and the chief academic officer reported to the president, in addition to support staff. Ashridge Business School in the UK had joined Hult in a strategic alliance in 2014. Dr. Jochen Roos had become chief academic officer in 2015, having previously been dean of Jönköping International Business School (Sweden) and, before that, Copenhagen Business School (Denmark).

This case discusses the evolution of Hult, including its strengths, weaknesses, and core values. In the concluding section, we see how a strategic vision, combined with clear core values, led to Hult becoming a successful multicampus international business school.

Evolution of Hult

The initial decade of Hult Business School's existence might be characterized as having a major focus on gaining revenue growth through attracting more students. Stephen Hodges was a key proponent of the vision to become the world's most global business school and this was followed through in its marketing and sales activities. A basic philosophy at Hult was that the students would gain a greater sensitivity to key cross-cultural issues through a flexible enrollment policy involving all campuses, as well as by being part of a truly international student body.

By 2017, Hult had two undergraduate campuses – in London and in San Francisco – with a third opening in Boston in 2018. At the graduate level, it had four campuses (London, Boston, San Francisco, and Dubai), plus two more so-called rotating campuses (Shanghai, New York). All campuses were located in major business centers, where there presumably might be good job opportunities. All campuses offered more or less similar experiences. Student support was universally high, and faculty and staff were deliberately chosen from among experienced managers or consultants. Thus, Hult put strong emphasis on practical relevance.

After a few years of searching for a partner in executive education, Hult formed a strategic alliance and an operational merger with Ashridge Business School in early 2015. Ashridge is a UK charitable trust, however, and a full merger was not possible. By 2017, the two schools had started to operate under the same strategy and brand, and their governance structure was mirrored. The mission of Hult International Business School is to be the most relevant business school in the world, defined as relevant to employers.

Following the alliance, it became increasingly clear that strengthening the academic side was a priority. This effort became the centerpiece of CAO Jochen Roos's activities, from the time he joined Hult in January 2016. His mandate was threefold:

• Develop, implement, and cultivate a cross-institutional research strategy. He based the strategy on (1) focus, (2) research relevance in line with the mission, (3) outstanding research support to faculty, and (4) total output orientation. Two broad research challenges (Transforming Behavior and Creating Disruptions) were built on the existing strengths of faculty members of both Hult and Ashridge and served as the focus for internally funded research activities. In contrast with traditional business schools, the strategy has a strong focus on the research output's relevance for business, in addition to conventional academic research outputs. A broad incentive system for research was devised to reward output, not effort. To manage this, the school offers a simple yet effective way to initiate, register, approve, and then support research projects.

• To further evolve and strengthen a nonbureaucratic model for academic governance, which had been at the core of Hult since its inception. The CAO chairs an academic board who work through committees with faculty representation, but with minimal bureaucracy.

• To prepare Hult for successful accreditations from leading accreditation agencies: AACSB (Florida), EFMD (Brussels), QAA (UK), and NEASC (Boston). During 2017, QAA and NEASC approved its six- and ten-year review, respectively, of Hult and Ashridge as one school. AACSB awarded Hult initial accreditation and Ashridge sustained accreditation (in the next accreditation round, the schools will be considered as one entity). EFMD planned to assess the schools as a single entity for potential EQUIS accreditation by the end of 2017. This is impressive progress in a very short time period.

Core Values at Hult

As noted, Hult's success was embedded in a set of core values, not dissimilar to what one might find in other organizations developed by leading Swedish entrepreneurs, such as IKEA (strongly influenced by its Swedish founder, Ingvar Kamprad). These seven core values might be summarized as: entrepreneurial spirit; quality; passion; nothing is impossible; attention to detail; innovation; cost-consciousness. These were all elaborated on in a small handbook which was widely distributed among faculty and staff. This handbook concluded with a set of five characteristics which were meant to illustrate what Hult was not: hierarchical; inflexible; insecure; arrogant; perfect.

The impressive momentum of Hult might best be summarized in a statement from the Chairperson of the NEASC review team during spring 2017: "A well-managed institution, already impressive in many ways and diligently working to improve." In the following section, we will consider some of the feedback from the accreditation bodies on Hult's perceived strengths and weaknesses.

Strengths

One of the key strengths of Hult was seen to be the process by which it reduced the large pool of leads and applicants (220,000 in 2017) to the small number of students admitted (2,000 per year). Peer reviewers were impressed by the considerable degree of individualized support provided to each partial and confirmed applicant in the "narrowing down" process. In fact, Hult offers considerable support to its students when it comes to individual advice regarding course choices, including transfer between campuses, which enhances its global outlook. In sum, Hult was proud of the strong support it was able to offer to students before and during their studies.

Hult had developed a no-nonsense way of running the school. This was seen as the "Hult DNA," reflected in its management processes, as well as in the values of students, faculty, and staff – a positive "necessary bureaucracy only" culture.

Research support to faculty was seen as second to none, focusing on clarity of research problems and questions, alignment with the school's focus, high-quality deliverables, and the relevance of these research outputs. In total, Hult stood out as a well-managed and well-integrated institution – agile and highly responsive to emerging market trends. Jochen Roos summed this all up as "attempting to transforming behaviors while creating disruptions to conventional ways."

Challenges

There were also challenges, as highlighted by the accreditors. Above all, there was a need to further clarify core academic policies, and to conform to well-accepted academic norms without weakening Hult's uniqueness. Further development of the research function was seen as central, in particular to encourage increased faculty engagement, and to further develop faculty incentives when it came to practical research.

A new focus on virtual learning was also being implemented. Several so-called nano courses were developed. These were hybrids between online self-study and classroom discussions. The broader aim was to reinforce a stronger digital and future-oriented mind-set in the students. These efforts were further facilitated by building on what had already been developed at Ashridge, including its so-called Virtual Ashridge set of program modules which executives might subscribe to, and which might also be put together in a master of management offering.

Conclusion

The strategic vision of Bertil Hult was to create a leading international business school. He and his colleagues seem to have succeeded with this, in part by articulating and consistently applying a set of core values. What is important here is a conviction that a strong faculty is needed but perhaps with a somewhat different profile and mix than might conventionally be found in traditional business schools. This includes a faculty that is both practical and managerial in focus, as well as more traditional full and part-time faculty members; room for successful practitioners as well as classically trained academics; and a bonus scheme that reward strong performance in the classroom as well as managerially relevant research. There was also a recognition that research, albeit more managerial than traditionally academic, is also part of the school's vision.

This case shows how a truly global, multicampus institution can be established, with a strong "footprint" in the leading commercial centers of the world. The key challenges of managing such a multiplicity of locations as well as its strategic aims have been highlighted, including the positive as well as less positive outcomes. The key to making this work, however, was a strong culture, clearly expressed, to hold it all together, and with a clear top-down managerial focus. Private ownership was, perhaps, also particularly key here. All in all, the case demonstrates the international multicampus nature of this example of a business school of the future.

WHU–Otto Beisheim School of Management

WHU–Otto Beisheim School of Management is a private business school, located in Vallendar near Bonn and Dusseldorf. Founded in 1984, and financed mostly through private means, it was considered to be perhaps Germany's leading business school. As of 2017, it had approximately 1,500 students, of which slightly less than half were undergraduates. At that time, the school had thirty-eight full professors, as well as an additional sixteen faculty members who were assistant professors or adjunct professors.

The school strove for the highest quality, particularly in the eyes of business:

- The teaching had a heavy focus on entrepreneurialism and new business generation. While what was considered to be particularly relevant for business was given primary focus, there was also a strong emphasis on bringing cutting-edge research-based inputs into the classroom, driven by current theories as well as by "best of practice."
- Top-quality research was thus seen as key, as evidenced by a strong research output by the school's professors, which was often published in the leading international journals. Research at WHU, however, also had to be considered relevant for the school's business stakeholders. And, as noted, the research would have to find its way to the classroom. Cutting-edge research and teaching were seen "two sides of the same coin."

In this example, we will first discuss in some detail the role of entrepreneurial and family business teaching, as well as research in this area. We will see that an open-minded, "fast" culture seems key for achieving a successful entrepreneurial/family business-driven innovative focus, and that a relatively small, new, nontraditional academic institution such as WHU can provide a good example of this. We will then draw a few comparisons with what might be found at many more traditional universities.

Entrepreneurship and Family Business at WHU

The creative and innovative environment at WHU is particularly well suited to cater for the development of entrepreneurial abilities among its students. WHU has several internal institutions that support this, including entrepreneurial incubators and new business development accelerators, a network of angel investors in entrepreneurial activities, various venture funds, access to several entrepreneurial start-ups, all of which are a source of guidance on pitfall avoidance. A strong link with Germany's number one entrepreneurial hub, Berlin, had also been developed. A special master's program in entrepreneurship formed a central offering at the school.

The core classes in entrepreneurship at WHU were also firmly grounded in family business, reflecting the belief that the two (i.e., entrepreneurship and family business) typically tended to be go hand in hand in many real-life business situations. Two key features made these classes on family firms and entrepreneurship particularly unique:

- There were many excellent guest speakers, typically from the best of practice! The professor in charge, Dr. Nadine Kammerlander, stated: "for every minute of me, the same amount of time will be allowed for good visiting speakers!"
- There were no formal exams, but each student was required to apply what they had learned to practice. For instance, in one course, students had to apply their knowledge about family firms to two case studies, which were identified by the students themselves. These case examples could be drawn from several sources, including the local community, or from the press.

As noted, there was a significant amount of student support provided to make this type of nontraditional "clinical" approach work, particularly in view of the high degree of freedom that the students, by necessity, would have. For example, questions might be raised by students at any time, either directly to the professor, or/and to a designated PhD student who would be assigned as a coach to the course, either face-to-face or via email. Direct access and rapid response was seen as key. Students were also actively involved in practitioner-oriented events and conferences, such as the "Campus for Family Business" series, in which family business owner-managers would share their challenges and best practices, all in an interactive setting.

This basic approach was more or less the same both at the undergraduate and the graduate levels. But at the latter, more of an in-depth level of interaction was expected, which applied to the guest speakers in particular, as well as to the students. The graduate students were thus expected to be more focused than their undergraduate counterparts when it came to "answering" managerial dilemmas and suggesting solutions, similar to what one might expect from a management consultant. Indeed, they were expected to dedicate a substantial amount of time to solving a real-life problem for a real family firm, and thereby generate sustainable value. Maintaining a family business focus was, of course, a key objective for both the undergraduate and the graduate course modules. All topics and problems that were identified by the students were also "tested" for relevance in a family business context. The ultimate aim when it came to teaching would thus be to strengthen entrepreneurial family business activities!

Welcoming Innovations: A "We, We, We" Culture at WHU

The unconventional approach taken when it came to the family entrepreneurship course at WHU was generally welcomed by the other professors at WHU. There was much collegial support for this type of innovation. Nadine Kammerlander attributed this, above all, to the relatively young average age of the faculty, and to the relatively small size of WHU, as well as the relatively young age of this private institution itself. In general, according to Professor Kammerlander, the type of dysfunctional, time and energy-consuming faculty debates about innovations, often lacking closure, found in many traditional business school settings were relatively rare at WHU.

To emphasize the contrast with typical public university settings, Professor Kammerlander made reference to a professor colleague who had an appointment at a public university. She felt that the following observations might be made:

- High teaching quality might be relatively less important at many such public institutions: good or bad would both pass, without any notable consequences.
- Feedback on performance would be typically relatively slow or/and relatively "light." This would be the norm!
- The main differentiating factor for professors in such public institutions would be the research dimension. Most professors at public universities would be expected to provide high-quality outputs, both to secure their standing at their institution and also in academia in general, as well as to boost their own self-respect.

In sum, it appeared that the generally good standard of academic teaching and research quality achieved at WHU might not easily be matched in most public universities. These institutions would typically be large, and thus often relatively bureaucratic, as well as relatively heavily regulated. They would also typically have larger and older faculty groups. Hence, they would often be strongly influenced by old academic traditions!

Conclusion

In terms of how the WHU experience might offer relevant insights for a business school of the future, we might, in particular, focus on its entrepreneurial and family business teaching and research, putting lead-ing practice much more firmly at the center of things. The unique culture at WHU might be seen as a precursor for a "fast" and open-minded future! Perhaps the relatively young age of WHU, its faculty, and its relatively small size might be the key to providing a realistic context for an open, innovation-oriented culture. The contrast with what can be found in many public universities – larger, older, and more traditional in values – seems dramatic!

Blended Learning at BI (The Norwegian Business School)

As of 2017, BI is one of Europe's largest business schools, with four campuses, and more than 450 faculty members. It has more than 20,000 students, of whom around 65 percent are undergraduates and 35 percent are graduate students, including executives. It has thirteen different under-graduate programs, and around thirty-three master's programs (including three different EMBA programs), eight of which are taught in English. Nine programs incorporate study modules taken outside Norway.

BI is organized as a private foundation and depends on being profitable to stay in business. The vast majority of its competition comes from government-owned institutions. These learning institutions charge sig-nificantly higher tuition fees than BI. Traditionally, BI had been able to compete successfully, because of a strong innovative culture, inspired by the school's close contacts with practice, in the private sector as well as in the public sector. The location of BI's main campus, in Norway's capital, Oslo, is a comparative advantage. Furthermore, its three other campuses are located in the second, third, and fourth largest cities of Norway.

This case example primarily discusses the introduction of a so-called blended learning approach at BI. However, there have been several other related and relevant initiatives that are based on today's emerging digital realities.

We will discuss five such initiatives later in this case example:
- the use of more powerful data analysis
- the BI 2020 Initiative
- various other blended learning innovations
- the Learning Lab(oratory) – to enhance improved student learning
- differ – an app, custom built, for active student learning

Big Data

So-called big data analysis or cloud computing has arrived, and this is also the case at BI (see, e.g., Marmara, 2017). This is, in part, due to the availability of more computing power, so-called quantum computing, as well as recent break-throughs in mathematics, physics, computer science, and other disciplines. The essence of big data is that one might be able to analyze many more paths simultaneously to get better and faster answers.

A key question for BI was how this analytical approach might translate into better program offerings. Did this approach, in essence, represent a new technology that would allow for further growth? The answer seemed to be yes! For instance, advances in curriculum design, as well as in dynamic marketing, seemed now to be possible, including finding better routes to market to promote educational programs, as well as in the optimization of pricing and marketing campaigns. Advances in the school's logistics and its operations management had also been made possible, not the least as a result of big data analysis.

For business schools, many new opportunities were opening up. In particular, it became much easier to come up with more innovative designs for program content, perhaps by blending inputs from several more traditional axiomatic fields and/or by adding entirely unconventional content. While these steps to modernize content could be professionally designed, this also provided schools with an opportunity to become much more objective about why a particular design might have been chosen.

An Approach to Improved Program Quality: Blended Learning

Competition had, however, intensified perhaps especially since around 1990. The biggest competitor had traditionally been the government-owned NHH (The Norwegian School of Economics and Business Administration), but increased competition was also coming from other governmental and private institutions, as well as from foreign schools. As a consequence, the number of students enrolled at BI began to flatten out, and even dropped slightly. Strengthening the quality of BI's program offerings, starting from 2016, would therefore become a top priority, to counteract the erosion in student enrollment, and even to increase market share. One of the key steps taken was a so-called blended learning approach. As previously defined, the concept of blended learning involves a mix of traditional face-to-face learning with online learning at home. The key to the anticipated quality improvement through adopting blended learning on such a scale was a fundamental belief that the students might become active learners, and thus be able to "learn to learn" more and faster.

The head of this project, Mr. Kjell Joergensen, associate dean and professor of finance, believed that there were at least three fundamental aspects to such a blended learning approach:

- For the teachers to understand the critical importance of listening. All issues relating to student's questions or concerns should thus be "on the table."
- A more explicit delineation of the main benefits of blended learning, so that this might become a reality.
- The logic of a blended learning approach would have to be presented in a cohesive way to the students.

Faculty Reactions to a Blended Learning Approach

Naturally, the role of a faculty member would need to change when adopting a blended learning approach, from one-way communication in a traditional teaching setting to more of a two-way communication approach: listen, exchange viewpoints, synthesize, in short, perhaps be more like a conductor of an orchestra! It might not come as a surprise that many faculty members would resist this new approach to providing courses and to their teaching style.

Kjell Joergensen felt that the faculty would be likely to fall into four groups when came to their fundamental beliefs and potential objections to blended learning, and their generally diverse motives:

- The skeptics: They might ask: "What research evidence is there that this approach will be effective? In the end, this may be a hype, and nothing more!"
- The economies of scale proponents: This group would consider it was more cost-efficient to fill up large classrooms to provide lectures in a traditional classroom setting, particularly when their preparation might be done just the once, even though there might be several such classes.
- The star lecturers: They might have developed their "own" course over many years, jokes and all. They would no longer have the gratification of being heralded as a star by their students.
- The dreamers: This group might see this way of delivering learning as a path toward actually having to spend less time on teaching, so that relatively more time might be spent on other things, for example, research. I would venture to suggest that this view would be far from reality!

Further Development and Implementation of Blended Learning

The bulk of the development task of providing teaching materials for blended learning would typically be carried out by cross-disciplinary teams. One member of this team might ultimately become responsible for a particular course offering. They would then continue to draw on the entire development team. There would also be team members with diverse relevant disciplinary knowledge, as well as pedagogical experts and learning designers. The aim for each of these developmental initiatives would be to come up with course materials and other learning activities that might be shared at all of BI's four campuses.

The basic structure of a typical blended learning course offering might be:

- An introductory video for each student group.
- Several face-to-face sessions with the students, with a focus on developing understanding through discussions of key dilemmas.
- Several webinars and live TV modules.
- Several digital learning support modules in the form of videos, podcasts, texts, etc.
- Feedback modules, delivered by professors in classrooms, by assistants, or, from students to students. It was important to avoid the predictability of traditional exams here, which a bright student might cotton on to, and perhaps be tempted to learn to pass rather than engaging in more fundamental learning.
- Course communication from faculty member to faculty member regarding online activities, at a class and group level, as well as direct messaging from peer to peer, to align activities in respect of learning outcomes and course assessments.

Kjell Joergensen felt that there were three difficult questions that might remain unresolved:

- How to better harmonize individual net-based learning activities with what might be going on in the rest of the campus.
- How to strengthen the advisory/coaching dimension (delivered by professors, assistants, doctoral students?).
- How to motivate professors to make them readier to change their teaching practice (time, competence, compensation?). (Owen, 2011)

The BI 2020 Initiative is a project that draws on cutting-edge digital technology to stimulate new ways of teaching and learning at BI and is therefore crucial in positioning the school as a leading provider of business education in the digital age. The project was at the core of BI's strategy and was fully supported by Dr. I. J. Henjesand, BI's president. Dr. Henjesand stresses that the development of the school's faculty was key, in order for them to gradually be able to make use of new digital tools and services in effective ways. This factor would also impact faculty hirings.

The BI 2020 Pilot Program Initiative was led by a program committee, headed by Mr. Jens Petter Tøndel, executive vice president, and six other senior members. Overall coordination of what might otherwise be rather diverse initiatives would hopefully be achieved in this way.

Petter Tøndel remarked that it might be particularly difficult to successfully implement significant pedagogical innovations in large business schools such as BI, which typically had large, well-established faculty groups in place, with well-proven pedagogical approaches, and hence quite "large areas of conservatism" that would potentially be resistant to pedagogical innovations. As previously noted, this can be a particular dilemma for big business schools, often purposely built to achieve large scale by offering large classes. The BI 2020 Initiative was set up to counteract this, notably by stimulating the implementation of various aspects of digital technology in the school's evolving pedagogy.

Prototypes for Blended Learning

BI has developed three concepts, prototypes for blended learning:
- Net-based courses: here the physical get-togethers are kept to a minimum. A clear set of guidelines has been developed for the steps to be gone through before the course begins (6 in total) and there is a yearly seminar/workshop for updating. Particular focus is given to the establishment of virtual discussion groups among students, and on systematic feedback, also carried out virtually.
- Mixed courses: these would involve online modules for self-learning built into courses based around classroom lectures. This mixed model was attractive to students, in the sense that they might be more in control of their own learning. At the same time, there would still be a relatively high degree of faculty "control" over the learning progress. It goes without saying that a considerable number of faculty teaching hours might be "saved" in this way, although there would be additional investment required to develop the virtual modules, including additional faculty preparation time. As an example, one of BI's basic multi-section undergraduate courses would involve faculty members in class for a total of 550 faculty hours rather than the previous 700 faculty hours. The first sections of this case example deal with a blended learning approach which falls into this category.
- Courses based on classroom sessions, but with the integration of various virtual technologies, such as videos, individual testing, chat functions, etc. A large number of BI's courses seem to follow this approach. While there are no evident savings in faculty resource costs, it seems significant that these courses come across as "modern" in the eyes of the students. Fundamentally, more effective pedagogy and learning has been achieved. Needless to say, this approach represents the least dramatic change from what might have worked so well historically.

The Learning Lab

The Learning Lab is a central resource center set up at BI to support virtual teaching and learning. Headed by a senior staff member, the Learning Lab is intended to make the implementation of virtual technology and evolving pedagogy easier and more effective for faculty members. The lab has four main features:

- A faculty "help desk" to offer hands-on support when needed, including in times of "crisis"
- A video-development group, who specialize in developing modular video-based inputs as part of various courses
- A "teaching and learning" group that provides basic pedagogical support to faculty members who might be in the process of modifying their courses
- A project group, which supports special initiatives, such as BI's "flipped classroom" initiative, or the Differ project (see below).

Differ

"Differ" is a messaging app, with a built-in chat function, supported by special teaching assistants, intended to create more active learning. The focus was to create a virtual learning community of students who might or might not have met, in order to

- provide better shared themes for learning
- facilitate group chats, for study groups as well as ad hoc learning groups
- facilitate direct messaging between students and teachers

Differ was set up as an independent entity, with investors from outside of BI, and with users from other learning communities within BI. The experience so far is that Differ has been able to achieve far more innovation and progress than might have been expected, certainly more than would have been the case if Differ were a more integrated part of BI. In this case, outsourcing was chosen to speed up the rate of innovation! A fully in-house project, on the other hand, might have become too "stale," too slow, and too bureaucratic. A start-up such as Differ needs to be allowed to make key business decisions quickly (i.e., outside BI's "normal" decision-making structure).

In addition, at least two further pedagogical further were being developed:

- A chat-function (Differ), allowing pairs of students to directly exchange experiences (see below). This would also allow the professor to provide guidance/support when needed.
- A feedback mode, where fellow students, as well as professors and assistants might offer feedback and raise critiques. This might also

including coaching on specific business issues, as well as on specific techniques and study approaches.

Conclusion

Petter Tøndel reflected on the potential competitive advantages for BI arising from this massive input of resources into virtual technology and new pedagogy. He felt that not only would this enhance the quality of learning at BI, but it would also be more effective in attracting the "new" breed of students that had grown up with virtual technology (Generations Y and Z). He also felt that evolving BI's business model, to remain profitable as a nongovernmental institution, would rely on implementing ways of becoming more efficient in "delivery," i.e., that virtual technology might offer opportunities for "scalability," which would simply not be the case for more conventional relatively cost-inefficient classroom teaching. BI would, in short, become even more competitive!

While BI was at a relatively early stage when it came to implementing blended learning across a broader cross-section of courses, the aim was nevertheless to deliver all of its teaching this way over the next three to four years. Progress had been very good so far. It was recognized that modifications and improvements were likely to be needed on a frequent basis, and that a culture of accepting that "good must always be done even better" would be key. Cooperation with other leading business schools on blended learning might also be necessary. BI was, in fact, working closely with IE (Madrid) on this (see the second case example).

Cardiff: A New Social Science Center Park – Critical Importance of Modern Architecture

Cardiff University is a full range research university and was highly rated (No. 5 for quality and No. 2 for impact) in the 2017 UK Government's assessment of UK universities. Its business school is also one of the leading schools in the UK, ranked No. 6 when it comes to quality of research. Cardiff Business School had developed a comprehensive strategy for research, for teaching and societal engagement, as well as for its internal structures and processes, in line with three key principles, at the core of which were foci on:
• Collaborations across heterogeneous sets of actors
• Cross-disciplinary identification of key problems and problem solving, and approaches on how to incorporate relevant theories
• Cross-disciplinary interactions and dialogue between key actors regarding research.

The Business School saw itself at the interface between economic values and social values from which it might create relevant public values. Its stated aim was to promote economic and social improvements through cross-disciplinary research and teaching activities. A new Social Science Center was at the heart of Cardiff's ambitious strategy.

The Technological Revolution

It might perhaps be appropriate here to restate some of the key implications of what Cardiff was trying to achieve in the light of relatively recent technological developments.

As we have seen, the emergence of the Internet has had a major impact on business education and on global educational communities. This quiet revolution was particularly disruptive during the first two decades of the Internet's existence, from 1994 to 2014. The higher education industry has, of course, been transformed, both directly and indirectly. The availability of market inputs, competitive information, and, in particular, a decreased reliance on axiomatic sources, were just a few of the direct effects. Indirectly, the importance of speed, particularly when it came to interactions with other entities within and outside one's academic organization, also dramatically changed the way in which the higher education industry operated. The increased flow of sociopolitical data, including national economic data, has also created a huge change. Alec Ross discusses these issues in his recent book *Industries of the Future* (Ross, 2016).

The Social Science Center Park (SPARK)

Important research at MIT pointed toward the importance of short distances when it comes to research processes, to increase the likelihood of relevant communication. This had clear implications for how to better organize physical space, so as to enhance innovation (Allen and Hense, 2011). The so-called Allen Curve, which illustrates this, is shown in Figure 10.1.

Several other research projects had corroborated this (Kyungjoon et al., 2010; Catalini, 2012). In line with these findings, modern academic buildings ought to be designed in such a way to easily facilitate physical interactions. We have referred to this trend earlier in the book, especially in relation to the design of the new business school building of the Sydney Institute of Technology, designed by the world-renowned architect Frank Gehry, who states that a key aim when it comes to constructing new academic buildings is to create "amorphous structures."

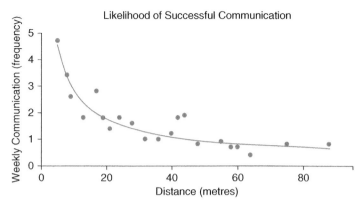

Figure 10.1 Likelihood of successful communication.

The Social Science Park at Cardiff University was designed to be "amorphous," to better facilitate constructive interactions between a wide set of individuals from various social science disciplines (business, sociology, anthropology, economics, geography, etc.), as well as from corporations that have chosen to locate their developmental activities (in part or entirely) at the Social Science Park. In short, the aim was to come up with more impactful innovations. The approach taken was built on the belief that the articulation of basic sociology was a means of producing useful outputs (Buraway, 2004), as well as linking this back to social reform (Brewer, 2013). While "basic sociology" might be seen as a rather broad concept, the core meaning of their focus was mere on "sociology of people," and in particular on the fundamentals of how people interact. One might, for instance, observe how members of various axiomatic disciplines found ways to interact, and how they might also attempt to "integrate" such interactions by, say, coming up with "faster," more readily implementable innovations. This could be seen as socially desirable!

There had been several earlier successful undertakings when it came to so-called science parks. The first was probably developed at MIT (Media Lab), and several others had subsequently been developed, both in academia (Stanford, London, University of Illinois, Jerusalem, among others) and in private settings (Philips Research Experience Lab, SRI, Rand, Bell Labs, Xerox Park, among others). All of these, however, primarily drew on bringing together eclectic science-based disciplines, in contrast to Cardiff's Social Science Park, where social sciences were the key disciplinary drivers. This was arguably becoming more realistic, not least due to the emergence of three parallel evolutionary trends:

- New computational capabilities for cloud computing (cheap and powerful), which might make analysis of large-scale data sets more realistic.
- Big data: large data sets were increasingly becoming available, from business, media, social databases, etc., and were, in general, relatively less constrained by conventional assumptions regarding statistical distributions. Interesting new findings might now be identified, such as "new routes to market," for instance.
- New analytical realities: while many of the underlying algorithms might have been available for some time, the advent of big data analysis has opened up many more realistic applications.

It goes without saying that all imaginable aspects of this computational revolution could now form a prominent part of modern Social Science Park hardware, as well as software. As noted, this would clearly have implications for architectural design, including avoiding "barriers" created by heating/air-conditioning/ventilation due to heat emission from hardware, cabling, choice of building materials (e.g., to allow to better wave transfer). A modern approach to architecture would be much more broadly based than the traditional architectural norms, and would therefore go hand in hand with innovation effectiveness. Several such features, linking extended design issues with effective innovation processes at science and social science centers have been reported (Laure-Fayard and Weeks, 2011; Doorley and Witthoft, 2012; Coulson, Roberts, and Taylor, 2011). These include:

- more open and transparent workplaces, to break down potential isolationism/silo effects
- providing private areas for confidential discussions, undisturbed thinking, and confidential phone calls
- no symbols of differences in rank when it comes to assigning each work station
- availability of recreational facilities, to better combine work and fun, for example, sports facilities (e.g., Barcelona med-tech center's basketball courts)
- an "amorphous" architecture, with as few walls as possible, places for social interaction, say, over a coffee break or lunch, few chairs, i.e., little to no sitting down
- space to grow

So, Why SPARK?

In order for economies to be able to stay competitive, more rapid and more successful innovations will be called for. Coming up with teams of skilled, well-educated workers who can meet such challenges will be increasingly important. Thus, pressures from the global competitive environment were a major factor in the development of SPARK, partly from external drivers such as new social challenges, or the blending of (axiomatic) competences in novel ways, as well as evolving governmental interest in staying competitive relative to other countries and/or regions, for example. Another driver would be the availability of funding from a mix of public and private sources, domestic and international. It would also be increasingly easier to get funding for cross-disciplinary rather than disciplinary research, not least due to the fact that sciences themselves seemed to be moving in this direction. So, the new center, extending to approximately 12,000 square meters, was intended to create facilities for various research groups to co-locate and interact in better ways.

Conclusion

In this case example, we have seen how important a new approach to the physical design of academic workspaces can be in the drive to facilitate innovation. Breaking down conventional barriers is key. These barriers might perhaps stem from academic traditions, such as the existence of axiomatic academic fields, or they may result from traditional building design, including separate offices assigned to different ranks, walls, corridors, etc. All such barriers must be broken down when designing the campus facilities of business schools of the future.

Singapore Management University (SMU)

Singapore Management University (SMU) is a free-standing university with its primary focus on social sciences, funded by the government of Singapore, with 2,000 graduate students and 8,000 undergraduates. SMU is organized into six schools: law, information systems, social sciences, economics, accounting, and business. While many institutions of higher learning had traditionally innovated at the graduate level, with students typically able to draw on their own practical experience (they would typically have worked for some time, and they were usually older), undergraduates tended to lack such real-life experience. Thus, it was a particular challenge for academic institutions to provide relevant pedagogical innovations that would increase the quality of learning in respect of innovation and practical business development at the undergraduate level.

Under the leadership of its president, Arnoud De Meyer, who among other roles had previously been the dean of Cambridge University's Judge

Business School, as well as deputy dean of INSEAD, SMU had attempted to tackle this challenge (i.e., to improve the quality of under-graduate entrepreneurial and business practice learning) by addressing the issue of general lack of practical experience in two ways:

- By developing a system of internships that would involve all under-graduate students
- By developing a context in which students might be given the opportu-nity to work on new, typically unstructured, cross-disciplinary problems. A special learning facility was established for this, the so-called SMU-X laboratory.

This case example covers each of these two initiatives.

As a general background, it should be stressed that SMU is a relatively small academic institution, with small classes of around forty-five stu-dents, with a lot of interaction in the classroom. The types of discussions involved would clearly benefit from some fundamental level of experi-ence on behalf of the students. While the commonly used label flipped classroom tended not to be used at SMU, this was indeed what was attempted.

Basic Learning Philosophy

The basic underlying learning philosophy at SMU is based on having the individual student take greater responsibility for their own learn-ing. How to do this would be up to them, but it would include four elements:

- The course
- An internship
- A professional overseas experience
- Community service

Flexibility was provided to the students so that they might meet these requirements in different ways. SMU also provided a web page for each student to monitor their progress. Should offerings attract too much student demand, there would be a bidding system. Each student was offered an equal amount of "e-dollars" with which they could bid for the preferred sections of the different courses.

Much of what is described in this case example relates directly to undergraduate education at SMU. But was this approach also applic-able to its graduate students? Internships (to be discussed later) were provided for them too, but based more on their existing experience. The SMU-X lab facility (see later) would also be available to graduate students but was actually not used that much. Individual faculty members might also use the SMU-X lab, although this would be rare.

Internships

A total of 3,400 internships were provided per year. These were compulsory for the undergraduate students. An SMU-instituted system of working with institutions to provide internships had led to more than 5,000 being offered per year. About 15–20 percent of the internships were based overseas. SMU's ambition was to increase this percentage, but practical visa problems provided limitations here. The internships tended to be of a high quality, and the students tended to do a good job. Thus, this general sense of benefits being higher than costs had led to a lot of "repeat business" when it came to companies offering internships on an ongoing basis.

While the students tended to be highly motivated in their approach to the internships as well as offering good, relevant skill-bases, they had also been given preparation at SMU on "how to be effective as individuals in real-life business organizations." This internship process thus gave the students important additional experience in "how the business world worked."

A potential shortcoming of the internship process was the fact that SMU would not have much control over what actual learning might take place. Experiences varied considerably when it came to this, in terms of both the different business settings and the quality of the internship experiences in the given organizations.

SMU-X

The SMU-X laboratory was housed in an existing building at the center of the campus, a converted office building that had previously housed a publishing company. A local company specializing in service apartments, The Ascott Ltd., was a coinvestor with SMU to make this feasible. All four floors of the building were occupied by the lab. Various meeting "spaces" had been created, incorporating space to write, computers, cozy corners, special furniture, different colors, etc., all intended to enhance creativity.

The space was deliberately designed to offer a lot of flexibility. It was key to create meeting spaces where students would find it attractive to work together. There were also classrooms with flat floors in the building, set up to pursue action learning, where the students were grouped around tables to facilitate easy interactions and discussions, with a computer screen at each table. Again, there would be a focus on addressing real-life problems, with productive discussions taking place in these "flat rooms."

SMU-X was managed in close cooperation with SMU's library, but with two important differences from the traditional library: group discussions were encouraged, and students were allowed to bring their own food to their workstations, and even to sleep there, if their project called for this! Based on experiences of the present building, the plan was to later construct a permanent new facility for the SMU-X lab. Careful measurements were being collected to aid in the design of this new facility, scheduled to be opened around end 2019. The students provided feedback on the design and functioning of this preliminary SMU-X building, to provide further guidance for the new building.

At SMU-X, the overall ambition was that students would be able to work together to solve real-life business problems. Typically, a faculty member would also be involved in each of the projects pursued, to ensure that a certain minimum amount of structure would be provided. Partners from real life, mostly companies and some NGOs, would be involved too, and would provide specific technical inputs as required. Most projects tended to be interdisciplinary.

It should be pointed out that these projects might be viewed as different from typical consulting projects, in several ways:
• The active involvement of cross-disciplinary groups of students, faculty members, and companies
• Set in the SMU-X learning environment
• With continuous feedback from the business side, i.e., essential inputs to improving a given project as it was evolving, thus acknowledging the typically incremental nature of such projects, but with a logic (Quinn, 1980).

Some Key Dilemmas

Dr. De Meyer saw at least three key dilemmas and challenges relating to this type of learning:
• The physical learning space. Normal classrooms might not be that well suited to this type of learning experience for the following reasons: student groups would generally have to come together in effective ways to be able to work together over longer time periods, which were often intense, and which sometimes included eating and even sleeping there! Features such as flat rooms, tables where people would be able to sit around and speak directly to each other, plenty of computers with screens, boards for writing, etc., might point toward alternative ways to envision the classroom of the future!
• The faculty. Initially a small group of faculty enthusiasts, of five to six members, were involved in the SMU-X experience. However, after its

initial success, the number of faculty involved had increased steadily, and now numbered around thirty to thirty-five. A total of thirty-five experimental course modules were now offered to the students, with around forty-five to fifty participants in each. These were intended to provide learning structure and support for the broad array of problems that were being worked on. But this could imply a lot of work for a faculty member. They would have to develop a good understanding of relevant knowledge to draw on for a given problem in this context. There would be no "safety net" for a faculty member here, in contrast to normal classroom-based courses, where the professor might be able to draw on their research and/or disciplinary insight. To ameliorate this problem, a mature research assistant would be provided by SMU.

• The scale. How might one scale up this experience? Or would this approach always constitute a set of unique, relatively small workshops, each distinctive and difficult to scale up? While SMU-X seemed to present some particularly strong limiting factors when it came to opportunities to scale up, the internship process did lend itself to a somewhat higher degree of scale-up possibilities. For example, SMU was working on developing better links with 200–250 companies, both in Singapore and overseas, to come up with, say, 500 projects per year that might fit into the SMU-X context. Over time, this might lead to some repeat experiences for the faculty, while allowing for greater scaling-up of internship projects and, perhaps, the uniquely creative side of the SMU-X experience.

Some Limitations

Dr. De Meyer saw at least three major challenges ahead. As an initial observation, he reflected on how the SMU way differed from his experience at Cambridge. Much of the pedagogical approach at Cambridge, with its so-called tutorial system, consisted of individual preparation beforehand followed by discussions of key dilemmas in relatively small classes, but he felt that while Cambridge tended to offer deep disciplinary support, SMU would be fundamentally more interdisciplinary.

However, the typical rankings, in particular the one offered by the Financial Times (FT), tended not to provide credit for applied approaches, but put more value on the delivery of more classical disciplinary offerings. Thus, SMU would not necessarily be ranked as highly as might have been justified by its innovative, quality-based approach.

Also, Dr. De Meyer wondered whether such unique programs as those developed at SMU, based on "fresh" projects for each intake of students, might be able to carry on. Could scalability be found to allow their continuation, and would faculty be willing/ready to expend the energy that might be called for? Would new ways of compensating faculty be needed and found? Finally, how might better support systems be found to facilitate the interaction with companies, to help with monitoring student progress, and to lessen the sense of "control"? SMU would have its own reputation as a leading institution at stake when it came to this strong focus on projects. Ensuring that these were carried out in a professional manner would thus be important for SMU's leadership. Hence, there would be some degree of control by SMU faculty over the work done by the students.

Conclusion

A strong focus on developing and learning from practical experience was achieved at SMU through a well-developed system of internship programs and, in part, through creative entrepreneurial projects at the so-called SMU-X laboratory. These objectives – to build stronger student business understanding through practical involvement in internships and/or developing innovative projects in laboratory setting (such as SMU-X) (as we also saw at IE, Madrid) – may also become key elements of the business school of the future.

The unique learning approach developed at SMU over the last few years seems to have been highly successful. SMU's Board of Trustees had been highly supportive of this new approach to learning. But would this innovative approach to academic value creation be continued given that President De Meyer announced that he would step down by the end of 2018? A continued high level of inputs from an incoming new president would surely be required. We will watch developments with interest.

Concluding Remarks on the Eight Examples

We have seen in these eight case examples how critically important various aspects of digital technology can be, in terms of both pedagogy and research. And it will be interesting to observe how emerging technologies will drive business schools of the future to become more innovative and probably also more effective. Program design, for example, might become radically different from that of today, with profound impacts on business schools.

Aside from technological advances, perhaps the most critical issues raised by these case examples are:

• That it is essential to put the modern practitioner cum learner at the heart of the learning process. Topics covered must be seen as relevant, and a sufficiently flexible, pragmatic structure must be offered by the business school. Learners must be able to pursue a dual-track career: on the job and at school.

- Virtual learning will be key, in the sense that modern technology now allows for distance-based learning at home, with cutting-edge seminars at school, which are shorter and focused on key dilemmas. This should be seen as effective blended learning!
- The importance of special-purpose learning laboratories or incubators to facilitate the further development of entrepreneurial capabilities and effective business skills, i.e., "good practitioners' points of views."
- That there is an open culture within higher education that would welcome innovation, including increased speed, smaller organizational entities, and one that acknowledged the virtue of private initiatives. In particular, the message needs to be put across that quality is relatively more important than scale for the business school of the future!
- How critical modern architecture seems to have become, as an integral part of what we might expect when it comes to physical facilities in the future.

Finally, the eight examples, in their own way, seem to lend credence to the general picture we have portrayed throughout this book about the opportunities and challenges for the business school of the future.

Appendix: Students' Self-Assessment of Learning Experiences

In order to find a better way to assess the capabilities of students, as well as the capabilities of individual faculty members, Dr. O. Brenninkmeijer, Dean of the European University's Munich campus, has developed a useful self-assessment instrument that might be self-administered by an individual student or faculty member. This is based on six criteria for assuring "best practice," according to how the respondent sees this, as well as another six criteria for measuring one's own personal learning experience in a given setting. Thus, a total of thirty-six measurements can be made by an individual respondent. They may write short answers in each of the three cells or rank these from, say, 1 to 5, with 1 being "best" and 5 being "worst." By comparing sets of respondents for a given class, it should be possible to detect how the perceptions of various students differ, and this, in turn, might be compared with the feedback provided by the professor(s). Alternatively, at the department level, six similar sets of comparisons might be made between professors within a department, between the students, and between the two groups. Such comparisons might also be drawn for an entire school.

Appendix A *Students' Self-Assessment of Learning Experiences*

The "best practice"	I	II	III	IV	V	VI
	Design: The desired learning outcomes (Los) flow from the module's objectives, and are clear for the facilitators and for the participants	Preparation: The Los and key messages (objectives) are the guide for the session, the supporting materials and the facilitation	Staying on course: Keeping to the key message (the red line or golden thread) using the supporting materials	Methods match need: Adopting the appropriate facilitation style and technique	Content flexibility and adaptability: Ensuring that the contents of the program/course remain relevant to the needs expressed by the participants; may require including feedback from previous courses, as in VI	Meeting expectations: considering postcourse feedback from the participant regarding evaluation of their own transfer of learning
The personal experience ↓						
Observing/ Learning/ Reflecting	(1) Your personal preparation (incl. prep. together with cofacilitators) (What did I experience in this part of the work?) (2) Your online facilitation (incl. onboarding) during the first phase (What did I experience in this part of the work?)					

Appendix A (cont.)

	The "best practice"	I	II	III	IV	V	VI
	(3) Your facilitation in the seminar/ workshop (if relevant; also collaboration with cofacilitators) (What did I experience in this part of this work?)						
Double-loop Learning	(4) Your reception of and reaction to the participants' feedback (What did I experience in this part of the work?)						
	(5) What sense can you make of your experience, and which will you add for the next time (So what?)						
	(6) What do you consider that you need to focus on or improve (What next?)						

Source: Dr. O. Brenninkmeijer.

References

Aaronson, S. (2013), *Quantum Computing since Democritus*, Cambridge University Press.

Allen, T., and Hense, G. (2011), *The Organization and Architecture of Innovation*, Routledge.

Allison, G. (2017), *Destined for War*, Scribe.

Anand, N., and Barsoux, J.-L. (2014), *Quest: Leading Global Transformation*, IMD, Lausanne.

Argyris, C., and Schön, D. A. (1978), *Organizational Learning*, Addison-Wesley.

Arthur, M. B. (1994), "The Boundaryless Career," *Journal of Organizational Behavior*, 15, No. 4, pp. 295–306.

Ashton, T. S., and Hudson, P. (1998), *The Industrial Revolution 1760–1830*, 2nd ed., Oxford University Press.

Atkavala, M., Davis, R., and Mying, M. (2008), "The Integrated Business Curriculum," *Journal of Education for Business*, 85, No. 3, pp. 295–301.

Bennis, W., and O'Toole, J. (2005), "How Business Schools Lost Their Way," *Harvard Business Review*, 83, No. 5, pp. 96–104.

Berg, E. (2015), *Hold Munn Eller Gå*, Emilia.

Bisoux, T. (2017), "What Makes a MOOC?," *BizEd*, June 1.

Bostrom, N. (2014), *Superintelligence*, Oxford University Press.

Bowen, J. A. (2012), *Teaching Naked: How Moving Technology out of Your College Classroom Will Improve Student Learning*, Jossey-Bass.

Bower, M. (1966), *The Will to Manage: Corporate Success through Programmed Management*, McGraw-Hill.

Brenninkmeijer, O. A. S. (2017), "Generic Model for Self- or Personal-Evaluation, Based on Best-Practice Criteria in Light of Actual Performance" (unpublished note).

Brewer, J. (2013), *The Public Value of the Social Sciences*, Bloomsburg.

Brooks, D. (2012), "The Campus Tsunami," *New York Times*, March 5.

Buraway, M. (2004), "Public Sociologies: Contradictions, Dilemmas and Possibilities," *Social Forces*, 82, pp. 1603–18.

Campbell, N. D., Heriot, K. C., and Finnay, Z. R. (2006), "The Defense of Silos," *Journal of Management Education*, 30, No. 2, pp. 316–32.

Canals, J., ed. (2011), The Future of Leadership Development, Palgrave Macmillan.

Canals, J. (2012a), "Rethinking Global Leadership Development," in Canals, J., ed., *Leadership in a Global World: The Role of Companies and Business Schools*, Palgrave Macmillan, pp. 29–61.

Canals, J. (2012b), *Leadership in a Global World: The Role of Companies and Business Schools*, Palgrave Macmillan.

Carton, G., McMillan, C., and Overall, J. (2018), "Strategic Capacities in US Universities – The Role of Business Schools as Institutional Builders," *Problems and Perspectives in Management*, 16, No. 1.

Castells, M. (1996), *The Rise of the Network Society*, Blackwell.

Catalini, C. (2012), "Microgeography and Direction of Inventive Activity," Working Paper, Rothman e Business School, University of Toronto.

Christensen, C. M. (1997), *The Innovator's Dilemma*, Harvard Business Review Press.

Christensen, C. M., and Horn, M. (2008), *Disrupting Class: How Disruptive Innovation Will Change the Way the World Learns*, McGraw-Hill.

Christensen, C. M., Dillon, K., and Allworth, J. (2012), *How Will You Measure Your Life?*, HarperCollins.

Chua, A. (2018), *Political Tribes: Group Instinct and the Fate of Nations*, Penguin.

Clarke, T. (2013), "The Advance of the MOOKs (massive open online courses)," *Education and Training*, 55, No. 4/5, pp. 403–13.

Coulson, J., Roberts, P., and Taylor, I. (2011), *University Architecture and Planning: The Search for Perfection*, Routledge.

Davidson, C. N. (2017), *The New Education: How to Revolutionize the University to Prepare Students for a World in Flux*, Basic Books.

Dabas, R. S. (2014), *Success and Beyond*, New Age International.

Delbridge, R. (2007), "AIM," Research Report RES-331-25-0014, ESRC, Sweden.

Delbridge, R. (2014), "Promising Futures," *Journal of Management Studies*, 51, No. 1, pp. 95–115.

Doorley, S., and Witthoft, S. (2012), *Make Space*, Wiley.

Economist (2018), "Going to University Is More Important than Ever, but the Financial Returns Are Falling," February 3.

Eriksen, H. T. (2001), *Tyranny of the Moment: Fast and Slow Times in the Information Age*, Pluto Press.

Eyring, H. J., and Christensen, C. M. (2011), *The Innovative University*, Jossey-Bass.

Foldnes, N. (2016), "The Flipped Class-room and Cooperation Learning," *Higher Education*, 17, No. 1, pp. 39–49.

Forssell, A., Fälting, L., and Kvarnhöhe, E. (2017), "Using Collegial Discussions for Better Management Teaching and Teachers," NFF Conference, Bodo.

Fragueiro, F., and Thomas, H. (2011), *Strategic Leadership in the Business School*, Cambridge University Press.

Freedman, L. (2015), *Strategy: A History*, Oxford University Press.

Frendo, S. (2016), "SHARE – Global Student Think Tank," brochure.

Gilbert, X., and Lorange, P. (2001), "The Difference between Teaching and Learning," *European Business Forum*, 7, No. 8.

Gilder, G. (2016), *The Scandal of Money*, Regnery.

Gingell, J. (2015), "Economics Jargon Promotes a Deficit in Understanding," Guardian, August 14, https://www.theguardian.com/media/mind-your-language/2015/aug/14/economics-jargon-promotes-a-deficit-in-understanding.

Gordon, R. J. (2016), *The Rise and Fall of American Growth*, Princeton University Press.

Haanaes, K. (2018), *Agility and Smart Simplicity*, IMD, Lausanne.

Haskel, J., and Westlake, S. (2018), *Capitalism without Capital: The Rise of the Intangible*, Princeton University Press.

HBS Alumni Bulletin (2016), 93, No. 2, p. 48.

Holstein, W. (2013), "The Multipolar MBA," *Strategy + Business*, January 21.

Horn, M. B., and Staker, H. (2015), *Blended: Using Disruptive Innovation to Improve Schools*, Jossey-Bass.

Humboldt, W., von (1970), *University Reform in Germany*, Minerva.

Hunderi, J. M. (2018), "Doing Business in Kenya," Lorange Network.

Ignatius, A. (2015), "They Burned the House Down," *Harvard Business Review*, 93, No. 7/8, pp. 106–13.

Iniquez, S. (2011), *The Learning Curve: How Business Schools are Re-Inventing Education*, Palgrave Macmillan.

Isaccson, W. (2011), *Steve Jobs*, Simon and Schuster.

Kahneman, D. (2011), *Thinking Fast and Slow*, Farrar, Strauss, and Giroux.

Kammerlander, N. (2016), *Familienunernehmen im 21 Jahrhundert*, WHU.

Kanter, R. M. (1995), *World Class: Thinking Locally in the Global Economy*, Simon & Schuster.

Kellan, L. (2012), *Rising Stars*, Palgrave Macmillan.

Kennedy, P. (1987), *The Rise and Fall of the Great Power: Economic Change and Military Conflict from 1500 to 2000*, Random House.

Kets de Vries, M. F. R., and Rook, C. (2018), Coaching and Challenging Executives, INSEAD Working Paper 2018/01/EFE.

Khurana, R. (2007), From Higher Aims to Hired Hands, Princeton University Press.

Killing, P. (2002), "Globe (A) and (B)," IMD Case Studies, Lausanne.

King, M. (2016), *The End of Alchemy: Money, Banking, and the Future of the Global Economy*, Little, Brown.

Kuhn, T. (1962), The Structure of Scientific Revolutions, University of Chicago Press.

Kyungjoon, L., Brownstein, J., Mills, R., and Kohane, I. (2010), "Does Co-Location Inform the Impact of Collaboration?," *PLoS One*, December 15.

Laure-Fayard, A., and Weeks, J. (2011), "Who Moved My Cube?," *Harvard Business Review*, July.

Lepore, J. (2014), "The Disruptive Machine – What the Gospel of Innovation Gets Wrong," *New Yorker*, June 23.

Libert, B., Beck, M., and Wind, J. (2016), *The Network Imperative*, Harvard Business Review Press.

Lorange, P. (2002), *New Vision for Management Education*, Pergamon.

Lorange, P. (2008), *Thought Leadership Meets Business*, Cambridge University Press.

Lorange, P. (2017), "My Biggest Mistakes Regarding Investing," Lorange Network.

Lorange, P. (2019a), *Adaptability and Flexibility in the Family Firm: A Brief History of S. Ugelstad Invest*, Skyr.

Lorange, P. (2019b), "Entrepreneurship Anno 2020," submitted to *European Management Journal*.

Lorange, P. (2020), *Innovations in Shipping*, Cambridge University Press.

Lorange, P., and Häberli, A. (2016), *Innovations – Elaborating on Christensen's Framework*, Zurich.

Lorange, P., and Rembiszewski, J. (2014), *From Great to Gone*, Gower.

Lorange P., and Thomas, H. (2016), "Why Rankings Can Be Mis-interpreted," *Journal of Management Development*.

Maerki, H. U. (2008), "The Future of Leadership Development," IESE Conference, Barcelona.

Marmara, P. (2017), *Cloud Computing and Route to Market*, Globalpraxis.

McMillan, C., and Overall, J. (2016), "Wicked Problems: Turning Strategic Management Upside-Down," *Journal of Business Strategy*, 37, pp. 34–43.

Meyer, M. (2016), "Das Ende der Hierarchien," *Bilanz*, 22, pp. 64–68.

Minzberg, H. (2004), *Managers, Not MBAs*, Berret-Koehler.

Montgomery, B. L. (1958), *The Memoirs of Field-Marshall Montgomery*, Collins.

Morieux, Y., and Tollman, P. (2014), *Six Simple Rules: How to Manage Complexity without Getting Complicated*, Harvard Business Review Press.

Nadella, S. (2017), *Hit Refresh*, HarperCollins.

North, D. C. (1961), *The Economic Growth of the United States: 1790–1860*, Prentice Hall.

Nueno, P. (2012), "What Role Management Development Has to Play in Growing International Companies," in Canals, J., ed., *Leadership Development in a Global World*, Palgrave Macmillan, pp. 129–44.

O'Sullivan, P. (2015), "The Nadir of 2008 and Its Aftermath," in O'Sullivan, P., Allington, N. F. B., and Esposito, M., eds., *Philosophy, Politics, and Economics of Finance in the 21st Century*, Routledge, pp. 3–20.

Owen, M. G. (2011), *Gratitude: A Way of Teaching*, Rowman and Littlefield.

Perkins, D. (2006), "Constructivism and Troublesome Knowledge," in Meyer, J. H. F., and Land, R. (eds.), *Overcoming Barriers to Student Understanding: Threshold Concepts and Troublesome Knowledge*, Routledge, pp. 83–96.

Peters, K., Smith, R. R., and Thomas, H. (2018), *Rethinking the Business Models of Business Schools: A Critical Review and Change Agenda for the Future*, Emerald.

Porter, M. (1986), *Competitive Advantage*, Free Press.

Price, A., and Delbridge, R. (2015), *Social Science Parks: Society's New Super-Lab*, Nestan.

Proust, M. (1900/1987), "On Reading Ruskin," in Aubret, J., Burford, W., and Wolfe, P. J. (eds.), *La Bible d'Amiens, and Sésame et les Lys*, Yale University Press, pp. 82–98.

Quinn, J. B. (1980), *Strategies for Change: Logical Incrementalism*, R. D. Irwin.

Ritzen, J. (2010), *A Chance for European Universities*, Amsterdam University Press.

Ross, A. (2016), *Industries of the Future*, Simon & Schuster.

Rousseau, D. M. (2015), *I-deals: Idiosyncratic Deals Employees Bargain for Themselves*, Routledge.

Rüegg, W. (2004), *The History of the European University*, Vol. III, Cambridge University Press.

Sahlin, K., and Eriksson-Zetterquist, U. (2016), *Kollegialiet*, Studentlitteratur.

Schein, E. (1988), *Organizational Culture and Leadership*, Jossey-Bass.

Schumacher, E. F. (2010), *Small Is Beautiful*, HarperCollins.

Schwab, K. (2017), *The Fourth Industrial Revolution*, Crown.

Senor, D., and Siege, P. (2009), *Start-Up Nation*, Hackette.

Shulman, L. S. (2005), "Pedagogies of Uncertainty," *Liberal Education*, 91, No. 2, pp. 18–25.

Simon, Herbert A. (1967), "The Business School – A Problem in Organizational Design," *Journal of Management Studies*, February.

Sked, A. (2011), *Metternich: Imperial Victor and Military Genius*, I. B. Tauris.

Snyder, E. (2012), "Five Easy Questions," in Canals, J., ed., *Leadership Development in a Global World*, Palgrave Macmillan, pp. 145–62.

Spender, J. C. (2016), "A Brief and Non-Academic History of Management Education," and "How Management Education's Past Shapes Its Present," BisEd., January/February.

Steen-Utheim, A., and Foldnes, N. (forthcoming), "A Qualitative Investigation of Student Engagement in a Flipped Classroom," *Active Learning in Higher Education*.

Stieger, R. (2015), "Bridging the Digital Divide," EMBA Thesis, Lorange Institute of Business Zurich.

Susskind, D., and Susskind, R. (2015), *The Future of The Professions: How Technology Will Transform the Work of Human Experts*, Oxford University Press.

Tett, G. (2015), *The Silo Effect*, Little, Brown.

Thomas, H., Lorange, P., and Sheth, J. (2014), *The Business School in the 21st Century*, Cambridge University Press.

Tinbergen, J. (1934), "Tonnage and Freight," De Nederlandsche Conjunctuur.

Van der Zwaan, B. (2017), *Higher Education in 2040: A Global Approach*, University of Amsterdam Press.

Watson, D., Hollister, R. M., Stroud, S. E., and Babcock, E. (2011), *The Engaged University*, Routledge.

Weber, L. (2019), *L'Université au XXI Siècle*, Economica.

Weightman, G. (2010), *The Industrial Revolutionaries: The Making of the Modern World 1776–1914*. Grove Press.

Wells, H. G. (1923), *A Short History of the World*, Waterlow and Sons.

Wilag, D. C., and Thomas, H. (2012), "The Legitimacy of the Business of Business Schools," *Journal of Management Development*, 31, No. 4, pp. 318–76.

Williamsson, J. (2017), "Putting the 'Business' Back in Business School," NFF Conference, Bodo.

Wilson, D. (2013), Presentation at EFMD's Annual Conference, Brussels.

Wingfield, N. (2014), "Satya Nadella Says Changes Are Coming to Microsoft," *New York Times*, July 10.

Index

Tesla, 20–21
Tett, Gillian, 43–44, 46
Thomas, Howard, 27
Thucydides, 21
Toffer, Alvin, 1
Tollman, Peter, 10–11, 12, 14
Tøndel, Petter, 186–87, 189
Top-down management, 62–63, 66–67
Top-line versus bottom-line growth,
    115–16
Toshiba, 63
"Trading table," 95
Training of researchers, 85–86
Trend analytics, 13–14
"Troublesome knowledge," 145–46
Trust in network organizations, 128
Tutors, 42, 143
2008–2009 economic crisis, 9–10

Uber, 20–21
United States
    economic growth in, 4
    evolution of business school in, 28
    MOOCs in, 4
Universities
    business schools attached to, 31
    in China, 3
    dilemmas in, 1
    in India, 3
    reputation of, 82–83
    research at, 82–83
University of Chicago, 118
University of Pennsylvania, 31, 104–5, 156
University of Phoenix, 3
University of Wales, 171
U.S. business school model, 24

Value measurement, 146
Van der Zwaan, Bert, 3
Venturing
    analysis in, 16
    disruptive forces and, 16
    organizational structure and, 16
    people driving, 17
Virilio, Paul, 49
Virtual learning, 164–65, 166–67, 179

Visiting faculty, 50, 51–52, 113–14
von Humboldt, Alexander, 24, 80, 83,
    143, 145

Wang, Gerry, 98–99
Watson, David, 43
"We, we, we" culture, 32, 35, 66, 96, 111,
    129, 182
Websites
    culture change and, 100
    marketing on, 88–89
Wells, H.G., 1
Westlake, Stian, 21
Wharton School, 28, 31, 41, 118, 156
WHU—Otto Beisheim School of
    Management, 180–83
    generally, 180, 182–83
    entrepreneurship at, 180–82
    family-owned firms and, 180–82
    innovation at, 182
    "we, we, we" culture at, 182
Wind, Jerry, 21
Wirtschaftshochschulen, 28
Workshops
    Dean/President, role of, 67–68
    dilemmas in, 117
    innovation in, 40
    instructional process in, 74–75
    large classes versus, 118
    at Lorange Network, 136–37
    physical setting, 73–74
    tutors compared, 143

Yale University, 82

Zürich Institute of Business Education,
    170–76
    generally, 170–71, 175–76
    accreditation of, 173
    alumni organizations, 173
    autonomy of, 174
    electives at, 172
    EMBA program at, 171–72
    global focus of, 174
    open enrollment at, 173
    regulation and, 175